THE POLITICS
OF INDIVIDUALISM

THE POLITICS OF INDIVIDUALISM

Parties and the
American Character
in the Jacksonian Era

Lawrence Frederick Kohl

OXFORD UNIVERSITY PRESS
New York   Oxford

Oxford University Press

Oxford   New York   Toronto
Delhi   Bombay   Calcutta   Madras   Karachi
Petaling Jaya   Singapore   Hong Kong   Tokyo
Nairobi   Dar es Salaam   Cape Town
Melbourne   Auckland

and associated companies in
Berlin   Ibadan

First published in 1989 by Oxford University Press, Inc.,
200 Madison Avenue, New York, New York 10016

First issued as an Oxford University Press paperback, 1991

Oxford is a registered trademark of Oxford University Press

Library of Congress Cataloging-in-Publication Data
Kohl, Lawrence Frederick.
The politics of individualism: parties and the American character
in the Jacksonian era / by Lawrence F. Kohl.
p.   cm.   Bibliography: p   Includes index.
ISBN 0-19-505374-5
1. Political parties—United States—History—19th century.
2. Political oratory—United States—History—19th century.
3. United States—Politics and government—1829–1837.   I. Title.
JK2260.K64 1989
324.273'09—dc19   88-4224
ISBN 0-19-506781-9 (pbk)

2 4 6 8 10 9 7 5 3

Printed in the United States of America
on acid-free paper

To my mother and father,
Rose Marie and John Kohl,
with love and gratitude

Preface

The politics of the Jacksonian era has seldom received its due from historians. Of course there have been some superb books written on the subject over the years, but there has also been a persistent tendency to underestimate the significance of the party battles of the 1830s and '40s. Historians have been particularly prone to belittle the political ideas expressed in the rhetoric of the era's great party spokesmen. This fact was impressed upon me toward the end of my years in graduate school when, while crossing the campus one day, I ran into a professor whom I had not seen in some time. In response to his queries about my current activities, I told him that I had begun a study of the political thought of the Jacksonian era. He seemed genuinely dismayed at this development. As a student of the Revolutionary period, he simply could not believe that the age of Jackson had any political thought worthy of study. His view was, and is, a common one. Scholars gazing down at the second quarter of the nineteenth century from the lofty intellectual heights of the late eighteenth century often find little to interest them. John Murrin and Rowland Berthoff, for example, in an important article on the Revolution, have commented disparagingly on the "banality of Jacksonian thought," and have asserted that the era's political and constitutional rhetoric "seldom bore any meaningful relation to social realities."[1]

Many scholars of the Civil War have scarcely been more complimentary. They typically charge that there was something artificial about the second party system, since the issue they take to be the most important of the nineteenth century, slavery, did not occupy center stage during the era. From their perspective, the national parties constructed by the Democrats and Whigs appeared to be fragile coalitions that could hold together only so long as more fundamental and divisive sectional issues could be avoided. This view once again implies that there was something shallow about the party conflict of the era, and something irrelevant about a political discourse that ignored the most important issue of the time.

Even some of those historians who have taken seriously the politics of the Jacksonian era have not always considered both parties equally worthy of their attention. Too many otherwise excellent books have dealt with only one party, while too many others, books that ostensibly treat both parties, have really only extended a sympathetic understanding to one of them. Arthur Schlesinger, Jr., whose Pulitzer Prize-winning *Age of Jackson* did more for the era than any other book, summarily dismissed Whig thought with the assertion that it was founded on "subterfuges and sentimentalities." And Bray Hammond, in his own Pulitzer Prize-winning work *Banks and Politics in America,* had even sharper words for the rhetoric of Schlesinger's Democrats. He declared that Jacksonian thought was merely "ignorant but popular clap-trap," filled with hypocrisy and cant.[2]

More recently, the ethnocultural interpretation of Jacksonian politics, first introduced by Lee Benson in 1961, has suggested that the rhetoric of neither party was very important to understanding the politics of the era. In this view, Jacksonian party battles were merely the continuation in the political arena of social conflicts based on the hatreds, habits, and beliefs of religious and ethnic groups. These groups and their conflicts predated the issues and the parties with which they later became affiliated. Ethnocultural historians imply that, however interesting the political rhetoric of the era, it had little to do with creating party loyalties, determining stands on issues, or winning elections.[3]

If I have seen something new and important in the politics of the Jacksonian era, it is because I began my study highly skeptical of the common notion that this whole generation of Americans was ignorant or confused about what the real issues of its day were, and because I refused to believe that the rhetoric of either party was banal, hypocritical, or irrelevant. I resolved to listen carefully to what the spokesmen of this era had to say, and I took their words seriously, though not always at face value. I was rewarded for my pains, for these Americans were confronting one of the most important social transformations of the modern era. They were struggling to build an entirely new social order, and their political parties were intimately involved in this struggle. There was nothing irrelevant or insipid about the politics of the Jacksonian era. The Jacksonian generation was confronting fundamental issues that the Founding Fathers, with all their prescience, never even anticipated, and they were dealing with problems that the Civil War generation, with all its awareness of the problem of slavery, ignored and left to future generations to solve.

What I found in my study of the Jacksonian era confirmed my belief that this was indeed a seminal period in American history. One might even argue that, in some ways, the rest of our history has been but prologue and epilogue—a gradual building up to this civilization and a belated attempt to recapture its essence under changed and more difficult conditions. If I have done nothing else in *The Politics of Individualism*, I hope I have restored some sense of the integrity of the Jacksonian era and of its significance for our understanding of the American past.

Emerson once said that "good criticism is very rare and always precious." If that is so, then I am indeed fortunate, for this work has profited from perceptive critics in every stage of its development. Early on, Gerald F. Linderman gave most of the manuscript a painstaking reading and shared with me his superb knowledge of the English language. If my prose is still deficient, it is only because I did not always take his suggestions on how to improve it. At a later stage, Raymond J. Cunningham devoted a great deal of time and energy to helping me clarify my argument and prepare the manuscript for publication. His willingness to put aside his own work to assist me at a critical moment in my career will always leave me in his debt. At Oxford University Press, Stephanie Sakson-Ford found many ways to improve what I thought was already a perfect manuscript.

J. Mills Thornton III saved me from many egregious and horrendous errors in both my argument and my prose. I know the mistakes were "egregious" and "horrendous" because these were the words I found scrawled in the margins of my returned chapters. Most of all, however, I want to thank him for being the most dedicated champion the manuscript had as it traveled that tortuous road from idea to dissertation to book. My greatest intellectual debt is to Shaw Livermore, Jr., who directed the dissertation on which this book is based. It could be said of Shaw Livermore, as was said of Emerson, that his greatest gift was that of "imparting a ferment." His profound speculations on the meaning of American history have had a powerful and stimulating effect on my own thinking. After countless hours of conversation over many years, it is no longer possible for me to separate the ideas in this work that are original with me from those that are but the pale reflection of a brighter star which was their source.

During the writing of this book my wife Maureen has been my research assistant, my editor, my typist, my companion, my friend, my joy, my love. It would take a lifetime to try to repay her for her sustaining faith in my eventual success—but I look forward to making the attempt. My sons, Jonathan and Christopher, were not even born when I began this book, but their presence now helps give its completion added meaning.

Tuscaloosa, Alabama   L.F.K.
April 1988

Contents

THE POLITICS
OF INDIVIDUALISM

In that land the great experiment of the attempt to construct society upon a new basis was to be made by civilized man; and it was there, for the first time, that theories hitherto unknown, or deemed impracticable, were to exhibit a spectacle for which the world had not been prepared by the history of the past.

ALEXIS DE TOCQUEVILLE

Introduction:
Politics, Society, and the
Individual in the
Jacksonian Era

*[Democracy] has destroyed or modified the old relations of men to
one another and has established new ones.*
                                        ALEXIS DE TOCQUEVILLE[1]

What then is the American, this new man?
                              J. HECTOR ST. JOHN DE CRÈVECOEUR[2]

When Rip Van Winkle returned home after his long sleep in the
mountains he found his world transformed. The drowsy village
he remembered had about it a "busy, bustling, disputatious
tone." It seemed to Rip that the very character of the people had
changed. He found himself lost and alone in this new world:
"Strange names were over the doors—strange faces at the
windows—every thing was strange." Cut off from the familiar
ties of family and friends he began to doubt his own identity.
When a villager demanded to know who he was, the bewildered
Rip exclaimed, "Every thing's changed, and I'm changed, and I
can't tell what's my name, or who I am!"[3]

Irving's tale of a man who slept for twenty years had an
allegorical quality for the Jacksonian generation, a generation

which had seen change come so rapidly that it seemed its world had been transformed overnight. In the half-century since the Revolution the population of the country had nearly quadrupled. The nation's boundaries had been pushed southward to the Gulf of Mexico and westward to the foothills of the Rockies. Industrialism took root in the Northeast, while America's burgeoning population poured over the Appalachians in search of fertile land. These pioneers, however, did not remain isolated in the west for long. A transportation revolution linked them by way of roads, canals, and, later, railraods to the east and ultimately to markets abroad. Economic enterprise throughout the nation was stimulated by legal changes which enhanced the opportunities of the risk-taker in the economy. State banks proliferated, offering easy credit to those willing to expand their operations. Storekeepers became merchants, craftsmen became capitalists. Even simple farmers were caught up in the restless pursuit of wealth. Enticed by new opportunities, they increasingly turned from a household economy of self-sufficiency and barter to production for the market and the cash nexus. High geographic mobility became inextricably linked with the desire for social mobility. The idea of the self-made man emerged as individuals scrambled to improve their station in life.

In many ways this was an old story. Almost since the settlement of Jamestown, competition had been driving out consensus. America had been moving from a world of community, hierarchy, and deference to a world of individualism, equality, and self-reliance. But since the Revolution, these changes had been rapidly accelerating. Individuals could not help but be transformed in the process.

The public world of nineteenth-century Americans became much more than in the past a far-flung net of limited, impersonal, and temporary ties. Men found themselves, like Rip Van Winkle, lost in a bustling world of strangers. Many of them, again like Rip, began to doubt themselves when cut adrift from their familiar social moorings. Others navigated this new world with greater confidence because they had become less dependent on others for direction and support. They had learned to plot their course in life by a kind of gyroscope carried within.

This study is concerned with exploring the political manifestations of the social changes summarized above. It is a study of society seen from a political perspective and a study of politics viewed through the prism of political rhetoric. Americans in the Jacksonian era were consumed by politics and their party loyalties were fierce. Political reforms since the Revolution had given Americans increased power over their governmental institutions and, in nearly every state, adult, white, male suffrage had been adopted.[4] By 1840, when a vigorous two-party system had been organized throughout the nation, voting turnouts reached unprecedented levels.[5] Jacksonian America was a place where, as John S. Wise of Virginia said, "everybody talks politics everywhere."[6] It was appropriate that upon his return to civilization, Rip Van Winkle was plunged into the vortex of a local election and that the first words spoken to him were those of a political orator who drew him aside to inquire on which side he voted. It was an important question to the Jacksonian generation, and historians ever since have sought to understand what it meant to vote on one side or the other.[7]

The key to such an understanding is to be found in the changes experienced by society and the individual in the preceding half-century. It is the thesis of this work that the era's great political division between Democrats and Whigs largely reflected the division between those Americans who were deeply unsettled by the emergence of an individualistic social order and those whose character structure allowed them to strive more confidently within it.

This examination of popular political thought under the second party system is based on my reading of the political rhetoric which appeared in contemporary speeches, newspapers, and periodicals. A fundamental proposition here is that political rhetoric is important to people. The words with which politicians explain and justify their actions form an indispensable link between the people's interests and the actions of their government.

All politicians reflect the concerns of the electorate, but some do more: they anticipate and even precipitate concern for the issues which come to dominate their age. Much can be learned of the historically inarticulate by listening to the oratory to which they listened, evaluating the arguments they evaluated, and drawing once again into the spotlight the politicians and publicists whose words struck a responsive chord in Americans of the Jacksonian era.

Although these sources yield firm evidence only of the thought of the time, my reading of them has been sensitive to the re-markable social transformation which the Jacksonian generation witnessed as well as to related changes in the American character which are reflected in the documents. In a nutshell, my work argues: (1) that the central concern of the Jacksonian generation was the transition from a society based on tradition to a society based on an ethic of individualism; (2) that the party battles of the period were over the kind of human relationships which would obtain in such a society; (3) that whatever the coalitional character of American political parties, the Whigs and Democrats each had a relatively clear, coherent, and consistent view of human rela-tions; (4) that the party affiliation of most individuals was de-termined by what David Riesman would call their "social character";[8] (5) that those whose social character was more "inner-directed,"[9] that is, comfortable with the impersonal, self-interested relationships which characterize an individualistic society, became Whigs; and (6) that those whose social character retained more remnants of "tradition-direction,"[10] those who still felt bound to others in more personal ways, became Jacksonians. The essence of my argument, then, is that politics in the Jack-sonian era was fundamentally concerned with sweeping social changes that were altering the character of the American people.

The Emergence of Individualism

The nature of man has been the single constant in human history, but as historians well know, man has not been everywhere and always the same. Within some indefinable limits his culture will mold and shape him. Every society seeks to inhibit the expression of some individual traits while it liberates and encourages the expression of others. This "more or less permanent socially and historically conditioned organization of an individual's drives and satisfactions" gives to individuals of a given society a "kind of 'set' with which [they] approach the world and people."[11]

Society, of course, is never static and thus social character may change. As Alex Inkeles puts it: "Men change their societies. But the new social structures they have devised may in turn shape the men who live within the new social order."[12] In fact, there have been times in history when social change has been so rapid and so sweeping, producing individuals so markedly different from those who preceded them, that social scientists have been induced to speak of a new type of man. In this sense I am persuaded that between the Revolution and the 1830s a new type of man emerged in America. The emergence of this new man was not confined to America. He was the product of a larger transformation which had been occurring throughout the entire Western world since the Middle Ages, but his outlines were clearer and his presence more widespread in the United States than in any other country in the early nineteenth century.

Of course the social changes transforming America affected women as well as men. But in the nineteenth century, at least, the effect on women of these changes was not the same as that on men. And since law and custom made the political world of this era largely a male preserve, this study will concern itself primarily with men.[13]

The larger transformation in Western society to which I refer roughly corresponds to the transition from "traditional" to "modern" society described by sociologists and cultural anthropologists, and the simultaneous transformation in man corresponds to the transition from traditional to modern man which they have delineated. In general, I have avoided these broad concepts because I wish to focus attention only on certain aspects of these sweeping changes. In my opinion the central thrust of this process has been the extrication of the individual from the tight web of human relationships which characterized traditional societies.

It is obvious that human interaction did not cease. Many of the individual's relations with others, however, were of a very different nature from what they had been under a more traditional social order. The changed nature of the ties which connected a man to a wider world gave him a heightened sense of individuality. He felt more deeply his separateness from other people. As this inward detachment grew, it was accompanied by a new social ethic. In nineteenth-century America, the resulting image of the ideal social order—a Jeffersonian vision based on what Alexis de Tocqueville called "individualism"— constituted a fundamental departure from Western tradition.[14] To understand this transformation, one must briefly consider the individual in the context of traditional society.

Traditional man was so closely bound to others that he had difficulty considering himself as a distinct individual. He lived amid a seamless web of intensely personal relationships. Such relations were the natural and spontaneous products of everyday contact where the scale of life was limited. They were the result of tradition and necessity; they rarely involved a conscious choice to seek out new relations or to question old ones. They were simply the givens of the life into which one was born. Authority in such a world was similarly lodged by custom in certain people to whom the rest were expected to defer. It was a nurturing authority, bound to its dependents by reciprocal obligations and emotional commitments. In a larger sense, however, all were bound, rulers and ruled alike, by the force of tradition. Ingrained patterns of thought and behavior which were passed down through the generations guided the lives of everyone in the community. Hence, the social character in such societies has been called tradition-directed.[15]

The social ties of the early settlers of America approximated this traditional form of human relations. Only a step removed from the life of medieval Europe, the first settlers lived in small, isolated communities where government and the economy were as personal as the rest of life. But over many generations this society was gradually transformed.[16]

Consciously or unwittingly, freely or forcibly, Americans came to be part of new networks of relations which extended far beyond the old boundaries of their communities. Through the political system an individual was tied to men of whom he had little knowledge, deliberating at a distant capital. Through trade he might be related to men residing in foreign ports whom he had never seen. Even ties to relatives and friends underwent changes as mobility and population growth separated kin and multiplied neighbors.

These wider networks forged bonds unlike those of traditional communities. They were not simply extensions of traditional society over a wider area with greater numbers involved. When an individual's social relationships expanded and multiplied they necessarily lost much of their personal character. Rarely were they the kind of enduring emotional ties which grew from constant intimacy. Men could relate to their fellows in large aggregates and at a distance only in abstract and partial ways.

If the new relationships could not be like the old, neither could the old ones remain the same. The unity and harmony of many communities gave way to divisiveness and discord, splintering the relationships of those within its boundaries. At the same time new sources of authority and interest outside the community divested local relationships of some of their significance. Americans still knew their neighbors intimately, but their neighbors were less likely to be their rulers, the purchasers of their crops, or even fellow worshippers in their parish.

As society underwent this sweeping transformation, the individuals within it could not remain unaltered. Communal custom could no longer guide their lives, since in a mobile and heterogeneous society the messages one receives are too mutable and diverse. Individuals needed to develop a new, more flexible type

of character structure, one not so dependent on the perpetuation of shared values, enduring personal relationships, and
traditional patterns of economic activity and political authority.
The inner-directed character type was the response to this need.

The source of direction for such people was "inner" in the
sense that early in life their elders implanted generalized goals
in them which would direct them thereafter. Of course all
people are shaped by parental guidance in their formative years.
For the inner-directed individual, however, such guidance is less
detailed and prolonged. He may carry into adulthood a sustaining sense of purpose, but he remains relatively free of continu-
ing direction and exhibits a greater degree of flexibility in
adapting to the shifting requirements of his society. He is able to
break old social bonds and establish new ones with relative
psychological ease in order to pursue his own self-interest.[17]

No society was ever perfectly tradition-directed or perfectly
inner-directed, nor was any individual. These character types
are the abstract creations of the social scientist, devised to
provide a clear picture of an indistinct but nonetheless real shift
in the character of society and its members. The process did not
proceed at any fixed rate, nor was it altogether irreversible. It
may be that resettlement in America had the effect of slowing or
even reversing the process in some seventeenth-century Europeans. It appears, however, that the shift from tradition-
direction to inner-direction eventually progressed more rapidly
in America than in Europe, and that between the Revolution
and the 1830s it decisively transformed Americans and American life.[18]

It was this new inner-directed individual, a man whose
"feelings were turned toward himself alone," that Tocqueville
observed when he came to America in 1831–32. Tocqueville's
Americans were strangely indifferent toward society at large.
This attitude he attributed to democracy's destruction of what
he called "aristocratic society." In that more traditional regime,
Tocqueville observed, men were closely bound to their fellows.
These were not merely bonds of material interest, but the kind

of personal ties which arose where relations of interest and cooperation were necessary and enduring. Americans, on the contrary, related more widely but not as intensely: "The bond of human affection is extended, but it is relaxed." With their feelings turned inward, they became "indifferent and as strangers to one another."[19]

This phenomenon, which Tocqueville called "individualism" and Riesman "inner-direction," others have called "privatism" or the emergence of "modern man."[20] All these terms have their difficulties, but, since I will follow Tocqueville on this matter, it is important to clear up some common misconceptions about the term he used.

The earliest misconception was the confusion of individualism with selfishness. Tocqueville himself feared that his readers would make this error and attempted to forestall it. Selfishness, he explained, was an "exaggerated love of self, which leads a man to connect everything with himself and to prefer himself to everything in the world." In traditional society, where, it was thought, no one could live a moral and satisfying life apart from the community, selfishness was a wicked desire to enjoy the benefits of society without fulfilling one's reciprocal obligations to it. Individualism, on the other hand, was an entirely different attitude; it was a product of modern life which could not exist to any great extent in traditional society. Individualism, as Tocqueville defined it, was "a mature and calm feeling" that one's fate was of one's own making; it had nothing to do with a malicious love of self which disposed a person to live at the expense of others. The word was a neologism coined by Tocqueville for the purpose of characterizing a society in which people seemed to abandon the centuries-old notion of corporate life and to be seeking meaning instead in private spheres of their own creation.[21]

Other confusions have arisen over the term individualism. One of the most common is that the individualistic American was the frontiersman who pushed westward whenever he could see the smoke from his neighbor's cabin. But Tocqueville was speaking metaphorically when he described the individualist as one who "draws apart" and "willingly leaves society to itself." This withdrawal was psychological, not physical. Tocqueville expressed the idea more clearly when he wrote that Americans "owe nothing to any man, they expect nothing from any man; they acquire the habit of always considering themselves as standing alone, and they are apt to imagine that their whole destiny is in their own hands."[22]

Another frequent misconception is that individualism involves "self-sufficiency," the ability to live without interacting, even in commercial relationships, with others. In an individualistic world the personal element in human interaction is lost, but interaction itself will not cease. Relations of an impersonal nature, consciously manipulated on the basis of self-interest, flourished in nineteenth-century America. Tocqueville's Americans were not compelled to act alone. In fact, as he observed, cooperation and association with others to accomplish ends both great and small were characteristic of a society based on individualism. Thus, corporation stockholders might be more representative of individualism than the self-sufficient yeoman farmer who is too often taken to embody the concept.[23]

Finally, there is the impression that the complete individualist abandons even the most intimate of human ties. This notion too is an error. When Tocqueville's American psychologically severs himself from the mass of his fellows, he does so "with his family and his friends." His social indifference, his impersonal, coldly rational calculations concern only the wider world—the world of economic exchange and public affairs. Within his private circle his relationships remain personal and significant.[24]

The central problem of the Jacksonian era was to work out how these individualistic Americans should relate to each other. The Jacksonian era today appears so modern to us—it is the first period in our history which really seems so—because it was the first attempt of any society in the world to come fully to terms with the implications of the inner-directed or individualistic man. The earlier triumph of the Jeffersonians had assured that

American society would be built on a foundation of individualism, but it was not until the age of Jackson that divisive political conflict erupted over the precise nature of the society being erected on this foundation. This political conflict may well be called the "politics of individualism."

The Politics of Individualism

It is my contention that the fundamental explanation for the ferocity of political combat in the second party system is to be found in the fact that the Democrats and Whigs took different and distinctive stands on the question of how Americans ought to relate to each other. For that reason, each party drew a different and distinctive following based primarily on the social character of individual voters. This interpretation gives new meaning to the political rhetoric[25] and public policy[26] of the era, while it also suggests new explanations of the different social composition of the parties.[27] Of course the concept of social character cannot account for the political behavior of all voters, but I am not so much interested in exceptional motives as I am in general ones. I am less interested in the narrow margins of electoral victories than in the source of the two vast well-balanced parties that made most victories narrow. The significance of Jacksonian era politics is to be found in the nature of the struggle, not in its resolution in electoral triumphs.

The problems posed by the emergence of individualism lay at the bottom of the political rhetoric by which the parties' differences were explained to voters. Throughout the country, whether the audience was local or national, rural or urban, northern or southern, this rhetoric displayed a remarkable uniformity.[28] Banks, currency, corporations, tariffs, and internal improvements were all discussed in language which revealed underlying anxieties over how each affected wider concerns about human relations. These concerns gave shape, force, and appeal to political discourse. Economic issues were of great significance to the Jacksonian generation because, as Tocqueville noted, in an individualistic society the uses of money are infinitely multiplied. It becomes the chief means not only to bind people together but also to allow them to stand above or apart from one another. Thus, the means for obtaining wealth, the tenure of its possession, and the uses to which it is put become intimately involved with questions concerning how individuals are to relate to each other.[29]

The Democratic and the Whig views of human relations I take to be characteristic not only of the writers and orators who revealed them but—and this assumption is a critical one—of their audiences as well. Two considerations underlie this assumption. First, to the degree that the language was *unconscious,* it emerged from the same needs which were felt by those who found it appealing. That is to say that party leaders and partisan editors were the same types of men as party followers. They might have been better educated or wealthier, but they shared with their followers the desires and frustrations which their common social character engendered. Second, to the degree that particular language was a *conscious* choice of partisan leaders, it was shaped to appeal to those who heard or read it. Over time, this rhetoric took on standardized forms that had wide appeal within the partisan ranks to which it was addressed. Once the message and style had been formalized, it could be wielded by leaders who neither felt the same needs nor shared the same aspirations as their followers.

The rhetoric of political persuasions was designed more to reassure the faithful than to convert the infidel. Jacksonian era voters rarely split their tickets and seldom changed their parties.[30] Partisan loyalty, like the character structure on which it was based, was enduring. The politicans of both parties joined carefully chosen words to the more tangible policies they pursued to help their supporters make the necessary adjustments to a new society and cope with the psychological anxieties they experienced in doing so.

Though the age of Jackson was an age of inner-direction, not all Americans adapted equally well to the demands of the age. They were strung along a continuum ranging from strongly tradition-directed to strongly inner-directed. Those toward the tradition-directed end of the continuum were more likely to join the Democratic ranks, while the more inner-directed were likely to be found among the Whigs. Of course one cannot expect absolute consistency in party membership or party rhetoric. Since the character of every American involved some compromise between the extremes of tradition and modernity, one can speak only of the general tendencies of individuals and of the party persuasions with which they identified. Moreover, this ambivalence meant that each voter, in the recesses of his mind, could find *some* appeal in the rhetoric of both parties. Hence, all but those at the most extreme ends of the Democratic-Whig continuum were fair game for the clever politician who, with certain rhetorical formulations, could draw a Whig vote out of a Democrat and vice versa.

The Democratic party appealed chiefly to those still living in the web of traditional social relationships. There was a security in such ties that was difficult to relinquish, though a new social order demanded that they abandon this personal world. Because their character structure was not well suited to modernity, modern institutions and modern human relations seemed constricting and degrading, rather than liberating and beneficial. They condemned the cold and heartless nature of Whiggish institutions and denounced those who would speed their development. Their accommodation to an impersonal world was reluctant and grudging. The fruits of individualistic striving were too attractive to resist entirely, but they longed for the sponteneity and personal warmth they were leaving behind. They shared in the benefits of the new order, but they criticized its moral foundations and blamed it for the anxieties they experienced.

Parodoxically, the Jacksonians' persistent demands for freedom and equality could sound quite modern. And they were sincere in their rejection of hierarchy and deference. Yet, their liberation rhetoric was particularly intense precisely because their traditional social character inhibited their accommodation to society's demands. The bristly independence of their writings and speeches revealed a certain desire to respond to these demands, but it also disclosed their frustration in the attempt. Even more telling is the fact that Jacksonians frequently used the concepts of freedom and equality to liberate them *from* the impersonal social ties which frustrated and exploited them. Their political policies which embodied these ideals were often defensive reactions to the emergence of individualistic institutions, attempts to protect more traditional relationships from the transforming effects of modernity.

Whigs, on the other hand, were generally Americans who had moved further along the continuum toward inner-direction. They were more comfortable with impersonal social relationships. They were able to deal more creatively with the problems inherent in shaping a society based on individualism. Theirs was the world of contracts and constitutions, corporations and voluntary associations. Even though their material success was not strikingly greater than that of the Jacksonians, their striving was more successful psychologically. Whigs felt a sense of mastery over their lives that Jacksonians did not share.

One also finds a paradox, however, at the heart of Whig rhetoric. These inner-directed men continually made traditional-sounding appeals for social order and unity. In fact, a closer examination of their language reveals that Whigs were not trying to reweave the traditional social fabric, but were rather attempting to reorganize and reconnect individuals on the basis of their own self-interest. The abandonment of the customary basis of social life made profound the perennial problems of order and unity among men. What was to restrain and what was to link individuals who were bound by nothing save their own whims? Whigs, because they felt this rootlessness first, felt the more powerful need to confront these problems. And Whigs, because their social character was better adapted to the modern world, pioneered the more modern solutions to them.

Still, there was some Whig rhetoric that actually did reflect remnants of a communal past, some behavior that demonstrated that they had not completely broken free from tradition. The special concern for the welfare of others, expressed in their rhetoric and embodied in countless voluntary organizations, revealed that they could not fully sanction the ends of an individualistic society. The centrifugal force of individualism induced anxiety in those whose internal gyroscopes had been set in an earlier age. This first inner-directed generation experienced a sense of guilt at the extent to which customary social claims had been forgotten. Though comfortable with large, impersonal organizations, Whigs, particularly those with New England backgrounds, felt the need to direct them toward more communal purposes, to humanitarian and religious ends. Yet the very means which the Whigs employed to reach out to others betrayed how much their world and their own character had been transformed.

Partisan conflict was fierce not simply because Democrats and Whigs saw things differently, but because their deepest needs ran counter to one another's. While Democrats struggled to break free of artificial social bonds which plagued them, Whigs worked to re-establish ties between Americans who seemed already too free. Moreover, their public dialogue echoed the internal dialogue carried on within individuals. Each voter saw the opposing party encourage traits he was trying to subdue in himself. To hear an opponent praise what one considered his own worst qualities only increased a man's fears and anxieties. He therefore struck at the outward political foe with a force meant not only to crush this external corrupting influence but to silence the siren voices singing within him. This ability of political discourse to touch and intensify basic psychological conflicts within individuals did much to stimulate political interest and inflame partisan passions.[31]

Each political party, then, had a world view which expressed its distinctive outlook on human relations. To understand the social character of the individuals in each party is to understand the root of each world view, and to comprehend these world views is to comprehend how and why the parties ultimately interpreted the issues of the day in the light of the individual's relations to society, to the rule of law, and to the social hierarchy.

PART ONE

Two World Views

If we cannot fully understand the acts of other people, until we know what they think they know, then in order to do justice we have to appraise not only the information which has been at their disposal, but the minds through which they have filtered it.

WALTER LIPPMANN

Most individuals exhibit characteristic patterns of interpreting their experience. Such patterns, born of the intangibles of human differences and tempered by life, are not the articulate and comprehensive public philosophies which we call ideologies. Rather they are products of everyday experience which give coherence and meaning to the common occurrences of private life.

Yet the understanding which such patterns supply in private life is needed even more urgently when the individual confronts the wider world of which he has no direct experience. For that reason, voters have a tendency to impose the meaning of their private worlds on the world of public events; patterns of interpreting intimate experience are projected onto this less familiar, less tangible environment. This projection is inevitable, for, as Walter Lippmann observed, "We are concerned in public affairs, but immersed in our private ones." Public concerns, then, are viewed in the light of private concerns, and they engage the electorate to the degree that they echo faithfully the hopes and fears of everyday experience.

By the second quarter of the nineteenth century, individualism had made sufficient progress in America that private relations and, hence, public discussions were shaped by one's response to the problems it raised. The Jacksonian and Whig parties tapped the sources of two distinct orientations toward the course of individualism, and their programs were political responses to these orientations. Thus one may properly speak of these orientations themselves as the Jacksonian and Whig world views.

❦ 1 ❧

The Jacksonian World

When I meet a man forward to profess his independence, I am
apt to suspect that he can easier tell what it is than exemplify it.
Boston *Weekly Reformer*[1]

The Jacksonian Democrat was a man torn between the conflicting demands of his character and his society. While, as an
individual, he still relied heavily on the secure relations of a
personal world, his society increasingly bestowed its benefits on
those who were more comfortable with an ethic of individualism. Most Jacksonians found that they could adapt their behavior more easily than their feelings. Democrats were often
induced to take up the new ways, but the political policies they
enacted and the language they used to describe them reveal an
anxiety born of inner conflict.

The standard form of Jacksonian rhetoric was accusatory. It
was critical, unhappy with the world, looking for an evil to
attack, always pointing to a malefactor. This attitude was not
simply envy, as the Whigs often believed, nor was it the resentful
jealousy of ne'er-do-wells, for many Jacksonians were men of
wealth and position. Rather it was the collective cry of men who
felt the world was not treating them fairly.

The Jacksonian looked out on a world organized to thwart his
ambitions. Often frustrated and insecure in his dealings with
others, he was quickly convinced that he had been intentionally
misused. The Jacksonian was prone to the belief that he was

21

always investing more in the world than he was deriving from it. If he did poorly, his fate was undeserved. If he progressed, it was despite obstacles which had been thrown in his way. If he did well, he should have done better. Some reward was always withheld from him. His path in life was a rocky road, traveled with difficulty. Any progress he made was individual and solitary; associations and institutions tended to retard, not facilitate his purposes. The Jacksonian world was made up of victims and victimizers, the fettered and the free, outsiders and insiders. In each case, the Jacksonian felt himself to be the former.

The Democratic party of the Jacksonian era drew together the disparate individuals who shared such feelings and gave them hope. It praised the virtues of those who had not been seduced by the temptations of Whig ways, and it sought to convince them that the lives of those who had succumbed were not to be envied. It also helped Democrats to understand their plight by explaining how the corruptions of their day had come about. This interpretation saw the Jacksonian's difficulties as the work of designing men bent on the destruction of America's democratic experiment. However the Jacksonian suffered, it was not his fault. Others—selfish, grasping, power-hungry others—were to blame. Finally, the Democratic party devised political policies to combat these evil men and their corrupt schemes. This legislative program had its roots in the traditional social character of the Jacksonian constituency. It was designed to thwart the rapid change, the new institutions, and the new type of human relations which modernity had brought. Its great appeal lay in its promise to limit the advance of an impersonal and aggressive world in which the Jacksonian felt powerless and forgotten.

Victims and Victimizers

When Jackson's hopes for the White House were dashed by the House of Representatives in 1824, he suspected wrongdoing.

On his way back to Tennessee, he came to believe that he had been the victim of a "corrupt bargain," a conspiracy on the part of Adams and Clay to cheat him of his rightful reward. This feeling grew as he traveled, and his speeches along the way became louder and more accusatory. By the time he reached Frankfort, Kentucky, it was no longer he who had been wronged; the people themselves had been defrauded. "The people [have] been cheated," he roared. "Corruption and intrigues at Washington . . . defeated the will of the people." Over the next four years no message was more persistent in Jacksonian rhetoric than that Jackson's deserts had been denied him by corruption and that his fate was the people's fate.[2]

Throughout the country this message touched a responsive chord in those who felt the world had unfairly frustrated their own hopes. They rallied to Jackson out of a feeling of kinship with a fellow sufferer. In the years ahead, the Democratic message would never abandon this theme. The source of corruption might shift, the manner of fraud might change, but the sense of injustice would remain a constant. And the Jacksonian was fated to be its victim.

Jackson himself created the continuity between the fraud perpetrated on his political hopes in 1824 and the frauds of later years. His attack on the Bank of the United States convinced many that the BUS was a fountainhead of corruption, and it launched a generation-long Democractic war on banks and corporations. According to the *Democratic Review,* Jackson's first election was a rebuke to the attempt of "corrupt combinations of individuals to cheat the people of their choice of a President." Jackson's second term was meant to preserve the country "against those mammoth monied monopolies and corrupt corporations which were already encircling the liberties of the people, restraining their free action, thwarting their intentions, and cheating them of their hopes."[3]

Henry Clay too became for Democrats a link between the corruption of the 1820s and that which followed. It had been Clay's alleged deal with John Quincy Adams in 1824 which had given him the office of Secretary of State in return for the votes which assured Adams's victory. For this he was known in Jacksonian circles as the "prime *filcher of the people's highest gift*" and "a trickster who defrauded the people of their choice." Clay and the National Republicans were said to have as their object "to monopolize public offices, filch money from the Treasury and the people." They wanted, according to the Jacksonian *Argus of Western America,* to "convert our government into a heartless aristocracy, in which the people are to be transferred, cheated, taxed, and oppressed, that a few may revel on the spoils of the many." After 1834, Clay was the recognized leader of the Whig party, which, the *Hampshire Republican* observed, was the "same in all places. It cheats the people out of their rights everywhere."[4]

Jacksonians believed that nearly every Whig policy was designed to exploit them. The great Whig hallmark of the era, the support of banks and paper money, was, to the *Democratic Review,* nothing but a "stupendous modern fraud upon the industry of the mass of society." The protective tariff, another Whig measure, was, according to the New York *Evening Post for the Country,* but a way for the manufacturer to grow rich at the expense of the farmer. "Between the knaves of the mills on the one hand and the knaves of the Halls of Congress on the other, we are fleeced and peeled . . . mercilessly," it declared. "It is no wonder that the farmers at last suspect that they are cheated." The Boston *Weekly Reformer* went a step further, maintaining that "all most [*sic*] every act of government has been to robb [*sic*]—swindle—defraud honest industry." With the aid of lawyers, it seemed that national legislation could be turned to almost any nefarious purpose. The "art of cheating by law," was "*a trick of the trade,*" handled in Congress "by the adepts in chicanery and machinery."[5]

The Jacksonian was deeply suspicious of the intentions of others. The "leading principle of democracy," announced a correspondent of the Boston *Morning Post,* is that "*No one is to be trusted.*" When the Democrat looked into the nature of man, he found "that he is a selfish being, seeking his own ease and comfort, without much regard to that of his fellow-man; especially when their happiness interferes with his own." For that reason, he concluded that "man is not to be trusted with the happiness of man; for he will surely seek his own, at the expense of the other."[6] Tocqueville's America, where the aggressive pursuit of self-interest ruled the day, was a disturbing environment for the Jacksonian, for he anticipated exploitation at every turn.

The sense of being wronged and the fear of future victimization were pervasive in Jacksonian literature. These fears could verge on paranoia, as when Pennsylvania Democrats reacted strongly against the introduction of the paper ballot. The *Globe* explained their opposition: "Innumerable frauds are concealed under the ballot system of voting; and, as it is impossible to detect them, the innocent and the guilty are alike involved in suspicion." The only pupose that the *Globe* could see for a secret ballot was as a "screen" for "hypocrites" who "want such a cover that they may have it in their power to say that they voted one way when they voted another."[7]

The suspicious nature of the Jacksonian led him to fear wrongdoing wherever men worked in secret. The "money power" worked in secret, he believed, to defraud those "who have neither the time nor the inclination to unravel the mysteries of Banking, or to fathom the iniquities of what Whigs call the 'credit system.'" These iniquities went undiscovered, William Allen of Ohio told the Senate, because banks were permitted to transact their business "not in the wholesome presence of the people, not in the light of day, but in darkness and in secret, between the walls of subterraneous caverns."[8]

There was also a tendency among Jacksonians to believe that complexity in human affairs, like secrecy, was merely a camouflage for injustice. One reason the Bank of the United States was dangerous, the Winchester *Virginian* argued, was because "its operations are so extended and so much detailed that the eyes of Argus could not reach them." The intricacies of the tariff were also seen as a conscious effort to defraud, as indeed were any laws that could not be readily understood by the common man. All indirect taxes were attempts to disguise the weight and distribution of unequal and unnecessary taxation. As the *Bay State Democrat* succinctly put it: "Indirect taxation is a cheat. Unequal taxation is injustice. Unnecessary taxation is robbery." In the same vein the *Globe* bemoaned, "So many miserable drains are devised by the cunning and invention of modern private purloiners, through Government means, that it requires vast intelligence and application to detect the devices by which wealth is abstracted by those who do not work, out of those who do."[9]

Democrats believed the chief victims of such a society were farmers and laborers, men whose livings were earned by the sweat of their brows. These groups were proclaimed to be variously the victims of aristocrats, speculators, machines, factories, banks, currency, government, and lawyers. The list is far from exhaustive. It is true that the lives of farmers and laborers were transformed by modern economic practices, and that to them modernity often meant the corruption of old ways and the degeneration of the Jeffersonian ideal. But modernity was two-edged; it brought benefits as well as injury. Some farmers were achieving a prosperity unknown to their fathers, while some laborers would live the rags-to-riches myth. What bedeviled Jacksonians, however, was the sense that *they* would not be the ones to benefit.

No concept was more important to the Democrat than equality. One of the most frequently quoted portions of Jackson's Bank Veto Message was that in which he expressed his desire that government "confine itself to equal protection, and, as Heaven does its rains, shower its favors alike on the high and the low, the rich and the poor." The peculiar appeal of this hope to Jacksonian minds was that mere equal treatment suggested to them an improvement in their lot. The perception which they had of themselves as victims led them to agree readily with Jackson's observation that "the rich and the powerful too often bend the acts of government to their selfish purposes."[10] Since Jacksonians believed any departure from absolute evenhandedness would work to their disadvantage, they condemned with particular fervor the sins of favoritism, partiality, and privilege. The very word "privilege" had great symbolic power in Jacksonian circles. In its most literal sense it was used to refer to those special powers granted by the state to corporations, which gave these bodies, the *Globe* charged, "increased facilities for the acquisition of gain, and freedom from those responsibilities to which all other classes are subjected by the operation of the general laws."[11] Such violations of equal rights could and did elicit strong objections from Democrats on purely rational grounds. But the concept of privilege also came to represent to the Jacksonian all those ways in which others outdid him and did him in. It had deep resonance in the Jacksonian psyche as an explanation for his abiding sense that the deck was stacked against him and that others did not suffer the same disadvantage.

The Jacksonian attack on privilege should not be taken as evidence of the social position of the Democratic voter. No matter how secure they become, some individuals never lose a fundamental sense of vulnerability; no matter how lucrative the bargain, some persist in doubting its equity. What was crucial to the Jacksonian appeal was not so much the objective circumstances of the individual, but his feelings about his place in the world. If he felt he were vulnerable to the wealth, power, and talents of others, the Jacksonian message would be attractive.

The more distant and impersonal the relationships, the more insecurity and frustration they induced in the Jacksonian. It was chiefly the new institutions—the banks, the corporations, the energized state and national governments—that the Jacksonian mistrusted. He had not yet become Tocqueville's individualist whose "feelings are turned towards himself alone." He invested more emotion, more of himself, in his relations with his fellows than did many men with whom he dealt. Yet, his return never seemed commensurate with his investment. Others seemed to be profiting through their very indifference at his expense.

The Jacksonian naturally sought escape from the relationships which threatened him. The fewer contacts he had with the modern world, the better he liked it. To withdraw from it, however, was not easy. The rewards it held out to those who would enter blinded many to its evils. Moreover, modern institutions were pervasive and powerful; those whom modernity could not seduce it had the power to coerce. It is no wonder that the Jacksonian felt his freedom was in constant peril.

The Fettered and the Free

Jacksonian America demanded, and the values of the age extolled, personal independence. Among Democrats, however, because they felt freedom was always just beyond their reach, the desire for it was intense. To be separated enough from traditional bonds to lose one's security but not to be sufficiently confident to move easily in an impersonal world was bound to leave such people feeling vulnerable and restricted—vulnerable because they lacked the security of old ties and restricted because the remnant of these ties psychologically hindered their ability to function in modern society.

In an age that celebrated individualism, the Jacksonian feared enslavement to the will of others. References to chains, bonds, and manacles were abundant in the editorials of Democratic newspapers. Americans, they argued, were bound by a great variety of restrictions. Many of these originated in the coercive actions of government. Bank legislation, the *Democratic Review* asserted, placed "unnatural and oppressive fetters" on private financial transactions. Corporate privileges, said William Leggett, "are fetters which restrain the action of the body politick." A protective tariff, according to James K. Polk, "placed fetters and burdens on trade and trammelled the productive industry of the mass of the nation." "The American System," concluded the *Argus of Western America*, "runs the whole round of the British devices to enslave a people."[12]

The financial system created its own form of bondage. Credit and debt also robbed men of their freedom. As the *Globe* remarked, "No man who owes more than he can immediately pay feels that his soul is free; and every hour of weary labor bows him with the consciousness that he labors for another." "The debtor," said the *Globe* on another occasion, "is not his own master, and a nation of debtors, though it may boast of its freedom, is a nation of slaves."[13] Modern methods of credit and new means to create money, which Whigs considered agents of liberation, seemed quite the opposite to the Jacksonian—they were attempts to rob him of his freedom.

Even the moral reform societies of the era were considered a threat to the Jacksonian's personal independence. The *Democratic Review* praised William Ellery Channing's declaration that the societies recently created "for the ostensible purpose of improving the condition of mankind" actually threatened "greater danger to the freedom of our political institutions than standing armies." These voluntary associations were dangerous to "independence of thought and action" and were in fact "so many seminaries for systematically teaching multitudes to submit themselves to the implicit management of designing leaders."[14] Orestes Brownson, in his *Boston Quarterly Review,* pictured the land as being overrun by would-be reformers:

> A peaceable man can hardly venture to eat or drink, to go to bed or to get up, to correct his children or kiss his wife, without obtaining the permission and the direction of some moral or other reform society. The individual is bound hand and foot, and delivered up to the sage Doctors and sager Doctresses, who have volunteered their services in the management of his affairs. He has nothing he can call his own, not even his will.[15]

Jacksonians seem to have been particularly intimidated by the opinions of society's elite. Jacksonians had not yet liberated themselves from a sense of deference toward those they considered their social superiors. Their principles, of course, condemned this deferential attitude. It was one of the objects of the Democracy, said the *Democratic Review*, "to emancipate the mind of the mass of men from the degrading and disheartening fetters of social distinctions and advantages." But the party's emphasis on the problem is adequate evidence that this emancipation had not yet been achieved. "To be great men," a correspondent of the Boston *Morning Post* admonished, "we must cease to be slaves; and what slavery is there worse than the slavery of the mind—a slavery to the opinions of others?" He lamented the fact that too many Americans were still too apt to look up to those "whom the world . . . has seen fit to call great, and trust not enough to their own selves, their own resources, for action."[16]

The power their "betters" exercised over Democrats is tellingly revealed in the way the "tyranny of fashion" provoked an impassioned outburst on the part of one Jacksonian. In an 1838 lecture, Charles Warren Brewster objected to attempts to keep up with the fashions of Europe. This imitation was "a kind of bondage [with] which the free citizens of a free republic should do away." Asking "Is there no power to withstand this mighty force of fashion"? Brewster begged Americans to unite to "defy the insidious enemy." Otherwise, they would remain slaves to the fashion world, since, "by simple, individual strength, it is useless to make resistance."[17]

The easy transference of feeling from one issue to another can be seen in this characteristic piece of Jacksonian writing. With few changes, one could transform Brewster's words into a typical Democratic attack on banks or corporations. Horace Greeley, a Whig partisan, perceptively observed the striking similarity of the arguments made by Jacksonians, whether speaking of economic, political, or cultural issues. If any newcomer to the party wished "to immortalize himself as a lover of the dear People," said Greeley, he could merely adapt one of the old speeches of Democratic worthies on the Sub-Treasury and "blaze forth an oratorical champion of the People's Rights with a very small outlay of intellectual capital."[18]

Just as the word "privilege" was the chief symbol of Jacksonian inability to deal on an equal footing with impersonal institutions, the word "monopoly" was the chief symbol of his sense of powerlessness vis-à-vis such institutions. Privilege limited personal freedom, monopoly ended it altogether. "Monopoly" came to represent to the Jacksonian all those forces seeking to rob him of his freedom. It seemed to the *Hampshire Republican* that nearly every field of enterprise was "monopolized by mammouth chartered associations." The *Republican* averred that it used the word "monopolized" advisedly, "for when these associations come in competition with individual effort, the weaker party must either be crushed, or become humiliatingly subservient to the stronger power." Individuals could, of course, band together to oppose these monopolies and attempt to preserve their freedom and dignity, but it appeared that the monopolies were also combining in order to enslave the people. William Allen believed that the great contest of the age was between the people on the one hand and "an organized league of monopolies" on the other. The people were "prompted to [their] defense by the love of liberty," while the monopolies were "fired in the assault by the hope of conquest and the prospect of plunder." A league of monopolies was a fearsome enemy, and to many Jacksonians the prospects for liberty appeared dim.[19]

Though Democrats felt their liberty was vulnerable to many different threats, their greatest enemy was the Whig party. The competition between Whiggery and the Democracy, they were constantly reminded, was nothing less than a mortal struggle between slavery and freedom. The aim of the Whigs, the *Michigan Argus* warned, "is to *force* us into submission and make us wear the yoke of political bondage." Theirs was a comprehensive system designed to subjugate and degrade the Democrat. "They would usurp power," the *Argus* told its readers, "and exercise that power to humble your pride, crush your ambition, . . . oppress you with an incubus of monarchy and aristocracy, and reign over you a body of hereditary nobles."[20]

Democrats were also warned that their opponents were not above using craft and cunning to achieve this end. The Whigs had on their side, the *Globe* charged, "men who can fathom all the mysteries of the human heart; who have studied all the direct and indirect ways of approaching the citadel of integrity, and all the means for undermining or sapping its foundation; men who can seduce with a wink of the eye." Virginia Democrats saw in their Whig adversaries a "suppleness, crooked insincerity and revolting insensibility to shame." The typical Whig, said the Little Rock *Arkansas Gazette,* was like a spider, "because the spider is a wiley enemy, and conquers by stratagem, not by a bold attack. It weaves its web, and the fly, buzzing about, conscious of freedom, suspecting no danger, is entangled in the snare, and falls a victim of art." The *Gazette* cautioned all Democrats to "beware of Whigs, and watch the web they are weaving."[21]

Worse yet, the Whig program admittedly had its attractions. The glamorous opportunities afforded by the credit system particularly blinded men to its power to enslave. Its promise to produce wealth suddenly, without labor, made it "one of the most fascinating, though dangerous schemes that was ever invented." Jacksonian papers constantly warned their readers not to be taken in by "the temptations consequent on the increased facility of borrowing." "Temptation" and "seduction" were the words most frequently used to describe the effect this system had on the Jacksonian. He was tantalized by its possibilities, but he also felt he must reject its sinister allure. The power of gold, however, made this rejection difficult. One Boston Democrat told his readers that "gold will close, as well as open our eyes—it will make fools wise, and wise men fools." He warned them to "remember the power of gold, and not trust too much to your own strength of penetration, or resistance to its arguments."[22]

To be taken in by the Whig financial system was to lose one's liberty. Bank loans were lures which, if seized, became "golden chains, which are stronger than iron." Jacksonians were encouraged to resist the temptation to seize these lures and preserve their independence. But sometimes it seemed that the battle was being lost. To William Leggett it appeared that the liberties of the people had already been encircled: "How completely we are hemmed in on every side, how we are cabined, cribb'd, confined, by exclusive privileges!" he bemoaned. The people, he said, were "led about by the unseen but strong bands of chartered companies. They are fastened down by the minute but effectual fetters of banking institutions." Leggett expressed frustration over the unwillingness of the people to deliver a death-blow to these institutions. "Are the people to be deceived forever," he asked, "and prevailed upon to hug the chains that deprive them of liberty? Will they consent to be saddled and bridled and ridden to death by the beings of their own creation?" If they would be free they must rally around the Democracy. Otherwise, he admonished, they would "be chained to the car of ambition and avarice, they and their posterity forever."[23]

Since the Jacksonian rank and file felt constricted in their own lives, the heroes of the party were those who appeared to be breakers of bonds. They glorified Jefferson, whose Declaration of Independence was a document that clearly burst old bonds, separated men from outworn institutions, and liberated them as individuals. Later, when the Federalists began to betray the spirit of '76, Jefferson created his own political party to break their hold on the national government. The party of Jefferson, said Martin Van Buren many years later, was a "Samson" which "burst the cords" of Federalism "which were already bound around its limbs." But Jefferson's victory over the Federalists did not end the struggle for liberty. "A web more artfully contrived, composed of a high protective tariff, a system of internal improvements, and a National Bank, was then twined around the sleeping giant," Van Buren charged, "in the vain hope of subjecting him forever to the dominion and will of the ambitious and grasping few." Only Andrew Jackson, who at New Orleans had liberated Americans from English influence, could have burst this new web of influence and interest. Jackson willingly accepted his role as "the second Jefferson," and three of the

greatest Democratic measures of the period—the destruction of
the Bank of the United States, the creation of the Independent
Treasury, and the passage of the Walker Tariff—were each
hailed by Jackson's followers as a Second Declaration of
Independence.[24]

Despite the heroic efforts of such men as Jefferson and
Jackson, freedom was a goal not often realized in Jacksonian
ranks. "It would, indeed, appear," the *Globe* admitted sadly, "as
if mankind were destined to be always slaves, in some form or
other."[25] The essence of the Jacksonian was his vulnerability to
the forces which limited and threatened to destroy his liberty.
Much of this vulnerability was internal, a result of the anxiety
which beset him when he was forced to relate in new ways to the
world outside himself. The same institutions which Whigs found
liberating, Jacksonians found restricting. The new ties of self-
interest which the Whig program of economic development
created may have been made of gold, but to the Jacksonian, they
were fetters stronger than iron. Personal independence, he
believed, could be preserved only by those who kept their
distance from the world of banks and corporations.

Nevertheless, Jacksonians often felt drawn against their will
into an artificial and impersonal system. The pull of economic
opportunity was too strong to be resisted in mid-nineteenth-
century America. Material success, however, required an indifference toward others that came hard to individuals still attached emotionally to each other. Hence the system seemed
designed to profit others, not themselves. Their relations with it
seemed one-sided and exploitative. Their inner concerns restricted their maneuverability and they felt hindered and
bound. Yet the system, spider-like, drew them into its web where
their freedom and even their dignity would be lost.

Outsiders and Insiders

One of the strongest bonds uniting the disparate elements
forming the Democratic party was the common perception of

living outside society's dominant sources of power and acceptance. Other men seemed, in a multitude of ways, to be "insiders," while the Jacksonian felt himself to be on the outside looking in. Even many Democratic leaders, including Jackson himself, felt themselves on the defensive against more powerful men who controlled affairs.

In the second quarter of the nineteenth century the Democrat felt like a misfit, an alien forced to fight against what he saw as the spurious values and artificial systems which ruled the age. A scrip nobility was eroding the old Jeffersonian egalitarianism. Government was corrupt. The artificial was superseding the natural, and the false the true. The worthy were attacked by the contemptible. The extravagant got richer while the frugal became poorer. The wrong people got ahead; the wrong people got power; the wrong people were considered worthy, while the truly virtuous man, the Jacksonian, suffered. Without passing judgment on the age one can see that the Jacksonians felt threatened by its demands. They condemned its values and its institutions to escape the moral judgments of others and, more important, the harsh judgments they often made of themselves.

No criticism of oneself is more telling than that in which one concurs. The oft-repeated Whig allegation of Jacksonian inferiority was particularly galling because the Jacksonians themselves suspected its truth. Democrats were prone to represent themselves as something less than they should be: they saw themselves as poor, weak, downtrodden, oppressed, injured, and outcasts. The Whigs, on the other hand, they frequently represented as something more than they should be: swelled, inflated, fat, fortunate, privileged. No evidence of the outsider mentality is more telling than the willingness of Jacksonians to concede Whig superiority—in wealth, in power, in the ability of their leaders.

Whigs, the Jacksonians maintained, controlled most of the wealth of the country. Based in the cities, which were also under their control, they ranged the corporations, the professions, the merchants, and the press in an awesome phalanx against their opponents. Whig power was further enhanced by the allegiance to their cause of most of the great men of the day. "The influence of such men," the *Democratic Review* admitted, "commanding by their intellectual power, misleading by their eloquence, and fascinating by the natural sympathy which attaches itself to greatness . . . produces certainly a powerful effect in our party contests." With so many forces working against them, it seemed to the *Review* "astonishing that the democratic party should be able to bear up against them all so successfully."[26]

The Democrat felt particularly threatened because he believed that this power was aggressive and that he was especially vulnerable to its dynamics. As the *Hampshire Republican* observed, "The encroaching interest sides with the aristocracy: the injured interest, desiring only redress, flies for protection to the democracy, which is always ready to protect the weak and sustain the injured." Jacksonians felt innocent, passive, and weak in the face of the evil in society. Life for them was a constant defensive battle against an "attacking cause" that was "ardent, restless, [and] ingenious." "The lines of fortification to be maintained against the never relaxing onsets from every direction, are so extensive and exposed, that a perpetual vigilance and devotion to duty barely suffice to keep the enemy at bay."[27]

Even the self-esteem of the Democrat was under attack. The aggressive world of Whiggery seemed to devalue physical labor and to enhance the standing of those who lived off the labor of others. "The honest farmer is become nobody," wrote one Democrat, "beside the empty favourite of banks, who sits down in his neighborhood, and puts his rustic simplicity out of countenance." The humble mechanic also felt the scorn of society. According to a long poem in the New York *New Era,* his was a "despised vocation." The "minions of wealth" pronounced the working man to be "ignorant, sordid and base." He was forced to endure the sneers and derision of the society whose wealth he produced. Of course there were many farmers and laborers who did not feel this way, and the appeal of the

Jacksonian message was lost on such men. The Democrat was the individual, whatever his actual social position, who felt scorned by a community organized against him.[28]

The hard-working Jacksonian was told not to anticipate any respect from his opponent. "Contempt for the people," the Milledgeville (Ga.) *Federal Union* explained, "is deep inrooted in the very soul of Whigery." Whigs were men who openly "sneer at democracy" and who love to "talk of the ignorance, vulgarity, and servility of the *people*." The individual who tried to stand against them would be stigmatized and lose whatever social standing he had previously enjoyed. "Touch not, taste not, handle not the things which belong to the democrats, was their rule of action," the New York *Times* complained.[29] One Jacksonian envisioned Whigs snarling and gnashing their teeth when they saw him on the street. According to him, there was a veritable *"reign of terror"* against Democrats.

> No talent, no reputation, no services, have been safe. All has been forgotten; every thing has been trampled under foot. The sanctities of life have been ruthlessly violated. The victim has been made to feel in his honor, his peace, his heart, his affections, his fortune, the resentment which he has so nobly incurred. Social excommunication has been pronounced upon him. Even the lips of "ladies fair" have been curled at him with cruel disdain; . . . he has been shunned as though the plague spot were upon him; he has been thrust forth from the gates of the city like a blasted leper.[30]

Probably few Jacksonians felt rejection this intensely, but the tendency to feel rejected was a significant part of the Democratic mind.

Almost more painful than the community's scorn was its indifference. Jacksonians often complained that others, far from despising them, actually took no notice of them at all. Modern institutions were vilified in the Democratic press not only for cheating and enslaving Democrats but for ignoring them. Such indifference told the Jacksonian that he was not simply unacceptable, but insignificant, not worth even the effort of rejection.

Complaints about impersonality appeared most frequently in Democratic attacks on corporations, particularly banking corporations. The banker's world was an impersonal one in which there was no compassion for those involved in its transactions. Bankers were "arrogant" and "cold." Corporations were "soulless" entities that refused to assume personal responsibility. The system as a whole was a "monster," huge, shapeless, difficult to control, and impossible to conceive in personal terms. Though Whigs pressed banks upon the country in the name of the public good, Democrats found in these institutions little disposition to aid the people. "Are they not so far above the people," asked one Jacksonian editor, "that they hear not their cries of distress, and stand aloof?"[31]

The new relationship between capital and labor also called forth denunciations from those who remembered a more personal world. An "Address to the Journeymen Cordwainers of . . . the United States," published in the Boston *Weekly Reformer* in 1837, lamented the end of the old days when "good feelings were reciprocated between the employer and the Journeyman." Now, however, large manufacturing establishments and "Clockwork" were replacing the human scale and personal relations of the household shops of yesteryear. A ruthless spirit of competition had introduced a "cold, calculating, heartless system" that left workers at the mercy of a band of "purse-proud swindlers." The new manufacturers had no concern for their employees. These selfish men, workers were told, "would leave you as soon as they have accomplished their own designs, to poverty, degradation and ruin."[32]

The Whig party, political arm of the bankers and manufacturers, was also viewed as being destitute of human feeling. "It has no sympathies with the busy world of man," said the Fall River *Patriot*. "Talk to it of freedom, of independence, of human rights, of the good of the many, it has no ears, no tongue, no heart." Democrats, on the contrary, still cared about people.

Theirs was a creed of "universal love," the *Democratic Review* asserted. A toast at a Democratic party dinner in 1840 summed up the difference between the two parties: "The spirit of Democracy—Universal Philanthropy—The spirit of Federalism [Whiggery]—Cold Hearted Selfishness."[33]

Adjusting to a cold and indifferent world must have troubled all Americans, but the Jacksonian outsider knew that society's indifference could be as cruel as any effort to oppress him. He longed for a past in which individuals were connected in more personal ways, in relationships built on a mutuality of caring. He resented those who were destroying this world with their callous selfishness and their impersonal institutions, and who seemed confident and secure in a setting that caused others so much heartache. He felt himself to be in a war for self-preservation and self-respect. Those without the ability to fight would be lost.

One reason why Democrats felt such strong emotional attachment to their leader was that Andrew Jackson was an outsider himself. Jackson's parents were poor Scotch-Irish immigrants who settled in the Carolina backcountry before the American Revolution. His father died suddenly just two months before he was born in 1767. When his mother and his two brothers died during the Revolution, Jackson was left with no family and few friends. He had a wild, undisciplined nature and little formal education, yet he became a lawyer and a Tennessee planter. Later, Jackson's martial prowess against the British at New Orleans and against the Creek and Seminole Indians brought him national fame and the highest office in the land. As Gansvoort Melville put it at a Democratic meeting on Jackson's birthday many years later: "Poor, unfriended, solitary, uneducated; despite all obstacles, he worked his upward way." But he never ceased being an outsider.[34]

At every stage of his career he was opposed by some of the most influential men in the country. He became a candidate for the presidency in 1824 against the wishes of the political insiders who controlled the Republican caucus. He was defeated for the office in that year by the maneuvers of more experienced politicians in the House of Representatives. When he finally attained the presidency, his administration was opposed by all the forces which the Bank of the United States and its friends could muster. Throughout his career the attacks on him were personal as well as political. "There is no man living or dead," the *Evening Post for the Country* observed, who "ever passed through a more fiery ordeal of detraction, misrepresentation, and calumny, than Andrew Jackson." His marriage, his military career, and his public service all drew the fire of his opponents. He was sneered at for being ignorant and uneducated, and condemned for his passionate nature, just as all Democrats were. Yet, as the *Globe* reported, "every attempt to blast his reputation with the People, has only riveted him more strongly in their confidence and affections."[35]

Such slander endeared him to his followers because they identified with his suffering. To be a Democrat was to be an outsider; this was a situation which dated back to Jefferson's time:

> This *putting down* is but a repetition of the *old story* of 1798. It is not Jackson that is personally meant,—it is *democracy*, and the Constitution, *personified* and slandered in him, as they were personified and slandered in JEFFERSON thirty years ago, and as every man who holds the same opinions will be slandered—*though they cannot be put down*.[36]

To be attacked by the opposition was the best evidence of correct men and measures. According to the *United States Telegraph*, "Slander . . . however noxious, abuse however foul and indiscriminate, from the coalition, must be considered . . . positive and unequivocal approvals of the practical reform which the President has commenced." When it became apparent that Jackson would pass on the mantle of Democracy to Van Buren, the Jackson *Mississippian* believed that the New Yorker was a good choice: "The mere fact that he is the object at which all the envenomed arrows of Whig editors are directed, is sufficient proof the he is entirely worthy of the confidence of the democracy."[37]

The traits for which Andrew Jackson was revered were the traits to which his followers aspired, those which they felt they needed to withstand the onslaughts of a powerful and aggressive world. First, there was combativeness. Jackson never backed away from a fight. And his combats were not brought on by himself; he was the *defender* of New Orleans. Additionally, in the course of his public career, he took on the Indians, the Coalition, the National Republicans, the Bank, the Whigs, and the French, not to mention assorted personal rivals and impugners of his wife's honor. Courage was required in a society organized to injure and insult. Jackson's life had demonstrated to his supporters that he had "the heart to protect the humble, and the hand to resist tyranny."[38]

Second, Jackson was fiercely independent. He could not be intimidated by power or seduced by temptation. "Firm, sir, must be the heart of that man, and strong must be his nerve, who dares to complain of the oppression of the banks," said William Allen, and "stern must be his soul, and indomitable his fortitude, before he presumes to rebuke the power of the banks." Jackson was that kind of man. But the ideal Democrat was not only "superior to fear," he was also superior to "selfish interest and corruption." Jackson fit this ideal too. He was known for his "iron will," an inner strength that helped him resist the seductions of the money power and persist in his war against Whig corruptions. This inner strength was terribly important to the outsider, for while he fought an external battle against the aggressions of the Whig world, he also had to fight internally against the temptation to become part of it.[39]

By playing on the natural allure of ambition and the corrupting ties of interest, Whiggery held out opportunities to those insecure in their Democratic faith. Those whose circumstances or psyches would not allow them the pleasures of living on more than they earned became heroic defenders of the old virtues. Jackson's "iron will" was a prized characteristic because only a rigid stance on paper money could resist the seduction of a system which, as the Jacksonians believed, promised to make something out of nothing. He won undying fame because he "renounced the support of the Bank of the United States, the grand resevoir of the monied influence in America, and with it the whole mercenary system" which Henry Clay and his supporters were trying to create.[40] Jackson's will inspired those still fighting the battle. And acclaiming his simple republican virtues enhanced the reputation of those who had won the fight only by forgoing those worldly pleasures which the corrupt enjoyed.

The third trait for which Jackson was esteemed was his immunity to criticism and slander. Democratic publicists delighted in stories of Whig attacks on the President and his undaunted demeanor as he rose above them. "Never man was more grossly calumniated, and never man has triumphed over it more gloriously," boasted the *Globe.* His persecutors found "that virtue's shield is invulnerable," said the *United States Telegraph.* "The acts of General Jackson spoke louder than the calumnies of his enemies," the *Evening Post for the Country* asserted. When Old Hickory stood firm against the winds of Whig persecution and even returned the favor, he was fighting every Jacksonian's battle for dignity and self-determination against similar bands of Harpies. No amount of abuse could shake Jackson's confidence or sway his firm stance in defense of "the people."[41]

His championing of Peggy Eaton early in his first administration demonstrated to Democrats his staunch support for the underdog, the slandered, and the ostracized. When John Eaton, Jackson's new Secretary of War, married the much younger and notorious daughter of a tavernkeeper, Washington society was scandalized. But Jackson, hearing in the gossip about Peggy Eaton the same kind of foul slander that had dogged his own marriage and sent his wife Rachel to an early grave, rushed to her defense. Those members of Washington society, like the Calhouns, who snubbed the Eatons, became *persona non grata* to Jackson, and those who were willing to receive them won Jackson's personal loyalty. His immediate identification with the outsider and his strong attachment to Van Buren when the New Yorker joined his leader in protecting Peggy Eaton demonstrates on a personal scale how Jacksonians battled their enemies and clung to their friends.[42]

The source of this sense of being an underdog was, for most Jacksonians, their character. They were not markedly less successful than Whigs; they just felt more troubled by their progress, less certain of their abilities, less hopeful about their future. Life in Jacksonian America could be profoundly unsettling for those uncertain about their freedom and dignity in an aggressive and uncaring world. The men who followed Jackson respected an outsider with the courage to fight, with an iron will, with an imperviousness to abuse, for he was everything they felt they needed to be.

The Need for Reassurance

When the Democratic party sought the support of those who felt victimized, enslaved, and degraded, it had to respond to their internal as well as their external needs. It had to provide reassurance for the doubters, understanding for those confused about their position in the world, and a plan of action which might give hope and a sense of purpose to its followers. The most important need of the Jacksonian was the need for reassurance. The inner doubts which Jacksonians experienced had to be silenced. In the first instance, party leaders tried to dispel worries about competence, freedom, and self-respect merely by proclaiming their faith that Democrats already possessed them.

Flattery of the electorate has always been a staple of American politics, but it served a special purpose for Jacksonians. Their virtues were proclaimed over and over again. "A democrat," said the Boston *Morning Post*, "is not only the protector of national independence, but he wears the stamp of personal independence on his brow; and he shows it in his actions." To the New York *Evening Post*, he was an "honest incorruptible freeman" who was "invincible to threats or bribes, deception or coercion." The Jackson *Mississippian* described Democrats as those "who rely for their support on their own honest industry, who love their independence better than money, who ask favors from no man, but demand justice from all, who have ever been foremost in defending their country and the last to disturb its peace." Jacksonians were reminded often of these qualities because they needed to be reminded. They were only too prone to slip back into feelings of powerlessness and insignificance.[43]

The party of Andrew Jackson declared that its members were men as good as any other. Any unusual suffering which they had experienced was not their fault, but the result of injustice. Party demands for freedom were interpreted as proof of its confidence in its followers to achieve happiness in any system in which none was privileged. Democrats welcomed immigrants more readily than their Whig counterparts; inclusion of all was evidence of confidence in all. Political offices—even at the highest levels—were to be open to everyone, since all men were equally capable of shouldering their duties. Even free trade was represented as a repudiation of the "degrading idea" that Americans had not "the intellectual capacity sufficient to compete with Europeans." These gestures were meant to reassure voters that the party believed in the capacities of all men, even in those of the most humble.[44]

To encourage those prone to doubt themselves, the party emphasized that human rights and human dignity were inherent in the nature of man. They were not contingent on personal achievement or acceptance by others, but belonged to everyone:

> The rights of man belong to him as man . . . They are the primary, absolute, imprescriptable rights of his nature, derived through the laws of his being, as an immediate gift from him that is over all. They belong to man as an individual, and are higher than human constitutions or human laws.[45]

Whigs, of course, might accept this view in theory, but they were likely to stress the fact that human rights are useless unless practical laws and governments support them. The more idealistic Jacksonian pronouncements were most popular among those who felt vulnerable to the critical opinion of and the exploitation by the rest of the community. To declare human rights and dignity inherent is to reduce the anxiety which occurs in a society where such basic needs seemed prey to the whims of the numerous or the powerful. Shrewdly enough, Democratic spokesmen appealed to those groups which had special needs for reassurance. At the very time that its importance and status appeared to be giving way before new economic interests, the life of the farmer was celebrated in Jacksonian rhetoric. The *Democratic Review* declared that the farmer was "a more natural, a more healthy, a more independent, a more genuine *man*" than his urban counterpart. The *Hampshire Republican* added, "Both philosophy and common sense have assented to the fact of the superior virtue of the independent cultivator of the earth." Country life was similarly extolled to combat the growing attraction of city life for the young and restless. In the country, declared the Columbus *Ohio Statesman,* "among the pure air of the golden fields of harvest—among the robust population of hardy industry . . . health and plenty inspire the very children with independence and virtue in their cradles." In the cities, on the contrary, "you will find impure air—a debilitated population—sinks of vice and immorality." Consequently, it was cause for grave concern that "this heaven-appointed employment should be so often abandoned for the anxious and uncertain pursuits of the city."[46]

Among urban dwellers, laborers came in for their share of praise once it became clear that with the rise of new kinds of employer-worker relationships and new modes of production, labor was less appreciated by society. The party of Jackson believed that, along with the farmers, these men were the true producers of the country's wealth. Unfortunately, they were too prone to underestimate their own value and suffer from a lack of self-respect. The Boston *Weekly Reformer,* however, declared that "the pursuit of the mechanic's calling is highly honorable, because the happiness and advancement of the human race, is

closely associated with it." Moreover, the mechanic was the kind
of virtuous citizen who belonged in the Democratic fold. "For
moral worth and integrity no class of citizens stands above the
mechanics," said the *Reformer,* "and all that is necessary for them
to do in order to place them in possession of their just and
unalienable rights is to respect themselves." One poetic burst
from a New York City paper captured Jacksonian attitudes
toward the urban laborers' plight:

> Mechanic! whose toil is the wealth of a nation
>> Whose hearts are its bulwarks when danger is nigh:
> Though humble your lot, and despised your vocation,
>> You have honor and worth that the world cannot buy.[47]

At the same time the Democratic party reassured farmers and
laborers, it sought to convince them that such reassurance could
be obtained nowhere else. Certainly the Whig party had no use
for common men. Whigs, they maintained, were Federalists in
disguise, men who entertained "a sincere distrust of the competency of the people for self-government." The *Globe* asserted
that Whigs treated the mass of mankind "like beasts of the field,"
while the *Democratic Review* said that they stigmatized the multitudes as "the wild, ferocious herd," to be "passed by with the
rude jest or the scornful look, or at times crushed in the dust like
crawling, loathsome earthworms." Whigs had no respect for the
true producers of the country's wealth. To them they were
simply the "huge paws," men fit only to be "hewers of wood and
drawers of water" for the rest of society.[48]

Nevertheless, too many Jacksonians were apt to question their
own freedom and to envy that of wealthy Whigs. In order to
counter this tendency, Jacksonian rhetoric customarily defined
freedom as independence from Whiggish financial institutions.
Credit was temptation and debt was slavery. The truly independent man was the one who stood apart from the world of
banks and corporations. The only free man was, by definition, the

outsider. To be condemned by Whigs, by bankers, by lawyers, by the leaders of society was evidence of an unwillingness to let others control one's life. For the Democrats, to define freedom as rebellion was to reassure those who felt unfree, and to define freedom as rejection was to reassure those who felt uncared for.

This attitude was reinforced by descriptions of Whigs as men who lacked personal freedom. Jacksonians maintained that the Whig ranks were filled by hirelings and tools, those corrupted by interest and overawed by the rich and powerful. Among the Whigs one could find "purchased editors, bribed declaimers at public meetings, and corrupt electioneers." Whig numbers were swelled by thousands of clerks "who think as their employers think, vote as they vote, and dare not call their souls their own, without they do it in a whisper, or first ask permission." Their party was composed only of "those whose hands are tied with the silken chains of banks—whose heads are bowed down in obedience to the will of the aristocracy."[49]

The pressures to conform to a Whig world caused Jacksonians to envy Whigs and doubt themselves, but the strain could be reduced if the Whig life style were found wanting. By careful comparisons with their Whig opponents, Democrats were made to feel better about themselves. By questioning the value of Whig lives, Jacksonians could reduce their own self-doubts and dispel their own envy of others' success.

The Jacksonian press endeavored to demonstrate that Whig lives were artificial, unwholesome, and of questionable social value. The privileged were said to be sunk in idleness and depravity. "A hair-brained, worthless, unprincipled cohort of dandies upon credit," the *Ohio Statesman* called them. And the lives of the business classes were harassed and unhappy. Each night merchants, "tired and worn out, perplexed and weary," returned to their houses, "not to partake of recreation, and the comforts of social intercourse with their families, but to a feverish, sleepless night's rest." Their exploitation of others brought them only emptiness and anxiety. According to Democratic spokesmen, the troubled life of the Whig contrasted sharply with that of the hard-working Jacksonian who enjoyed a clear conscience and an honest self-respect. But however comforting, such contrasts were more wishful thinking and pleasant nostalgia than pictures of reality. For better or worse, the peace of America's pastoral paradise had been permanently shattered by the modern world, and whatever its undesirable aspects, this new world had the power to draw men toward it and cause even those who resisted its temptations to feel threatened.[50]

The Jacksonian message, then, was aimed at those who felt mistreated or ignored in a changing society. The Democratic doctrines were of the "inherent dignity, the natural equality, the spiritual rights, the glorious hopes, of man." These doctrines, as the *Democratic Review* said,

> speak to oppressed, down-trodden man. They speak to him in a voice of infinite power; they touch the chords of sensibility, and expand his soul to free, generous action; they awaken hope; they administer consolation; they cherish the sense of personal worth; they strengthen faith in truth; they reveal the highest excellence; they demand unceasing progress; they worship the soul as of higher importance than all outward worlds.[51]

Jacksonians sometimes compared their message to that of Christianity, and in a sense the analogy is apt.[52] Like Christianity, the Jacksonian message aimed to "awaken hope" and to "administer consolation" to such as felt themselves in need of this reassurance. It was of the heart as much as of the head and strove to "touch the chords of sensibility." It glorified the down-trodden and had grave misgivings about the wealthy and powerful. The path which it pointed out was said to be difficult to follow, often running counter to the world as it is; only strength of conviction could secure travelers against the temptations which beset them.

Andrew Jackson himself could be portrayed from a pseudo-Christian perspective. Slandered and abused by evil men, he was not only an example to envy and emulate (as a Whig leader might be), he was also to be loved, even as he loved his followers.

Yet had Jackson's image been simply that of the maligned outsider, it would have had no power to reassure the faithful or to confirm them in the cause. Equally important were his mighty public achievements—from the providential victory at New Orleans to his eight years in the presidency. His patriotism could not be questioned; his abilities were proven in peace and war. Here was a man whose message could be spoken "in a voice of infinite power" and who had the ability to "strengthen faith in truth." Had he been solely an "insider," he would have had the power only to inflict further wounds. Had he been only an "outsider," he would have lost much of his power to heal. But he was both, and his importance in shaping and symbolizing the Democracy of the antebellum period cannot be overestimated.

With its two-edged sword of reassurance—lauding the outsider and declaiming against those in the vanguard of modernity—the Democratic party exhorted doubters to action. Democratic orators constantly encouraged independent action and resistance to the frustrations and aggressions of modern life. They begged their followers to assert themselves. "Arouse in your strength," the *Bay State Democrat* urged its readers in a characteristic exhortation, "burst asunder the bonds of your oppressor—assert your rights." But party spokesmen often experienced frustration when these calls for action went unheeded. "Will nothing arouse you to a sense of your own power, dignity and outraged rights?" the editor of the Gallatin (Miss.) *Democrat* demanded in a typical outburst. "*Must the earth quake before you will arise?*" The constant necessity for such exhortation revealed the depth of the problem. Assertive individuals do not need encouragement to bestir themselves. Those who are confident of their abilities do not need to be told that they are capable, valuable members of society.[53]

The Search for Understanding

Human beings have a fundamental need to rationalize their experience. They have to see a pattern in events and comprehend their position in what they take to be an orderly universe. They need to understand why things happen as they do. One of the important functions of Jacksonian rhetoric was to help individuals order their world. It made the unseen visible; the complex, simple; the confused, orderly; and the impersonal, personal.

The Jacksonian search for understanding was particularly important since the central issue of their era, the Whig financial system, was so complex. The Milledgeville *Federal Union* confessed to its readers that the subject of the currency "is very abstruse and the causes of events too widely spread and deeply laid for common observation." To those less informed than partisan newspaper editors it was even more of a mystery. When currency fluctuations caused economic distress in the 1830s, few Americans knew the cause of the problem: "The blow is struck by an invisible hand. It comes like a pestilence, in darkness. We feel the effect, but we see not the cause. We agree in the result, but every man has a different explanation as to the origin."[54]

Democratic leaders told their followers that however invisible the hand that smote them, there was indeed a hand behind the blow, and a human hand at that. Neither God nor nature was punishing them for their sins. Rather the economic problems of their day had arisen because corrupt human beings had upset the natural order which God had created. Designing men had sought to turn America's natural advantages to their own selfish purpose, and the result had been oppression for some and would be ruin for all. Jacksonians had neither seen nor understood their plight because it had been planned by men whose purposes included secrecy and confusion.

The Whig promotion of banks and paper money was only a part of their "American System," a system devised, Democrats charged, solely with an eye to extracting wealth from the producing classes and to giving it to those who did not work. Money, like power, was always passing from the many to the few. Such evil purposes had to be hidden from the vigilant democracy; that is why Whigs worked in secret, why they traded with deception, and why they governed by intrigue. If they could not altogether hide their purposes, they must disguise them with useless complexities to confuse the masses. The Whigs operated "through a machinery as intricate as the differential calculus." They constructed "an engine of adjustments and relations so multiplied and abstruse, that the most practised wisdom is alone adequate to their comprehension."[55]

In his "Fourth Annual Message," President James K. Polk attempted a detailed explanation of how this corrupt system came to be fastened on America. It all began, Polk maintained, after 1815, when some Americans had begun to doubt the viability of republican government. Not trusting the capacity of a free people to govern themselves, these men began to look longingly to the Old World, especially to Britain, for examples of more powerful governments. They looked admiringly at governments "based upon different orders of society, and so constituted as to throw the whole power of nations into the hands of a few, who taxed and controlled the many without responsibility or restraint." They were fascinated by "the ease, luxury, and display of the higher orders, who drew their wealth from the toil of the laboring millions." But because the Constitution of the United States did not tolerate orders and titles, a system of measures was devised "to withdraw power gradually and silently from the States and the mass of the people, and by *construction* to approximate our Government to the European models, substituting an aristocracy of wealth for that of orders and titles."[56]

The "American System," said Polk, was the vehicle by which this alien, Old World system was to be fastened on the United States. A national bank controlled the monetary and financial power of the nation, bringing "many of the active political and commercial men in different sections of the country into the relation of debtors to it and dependents upon it for pecuniary favors." A great public debt "furnished aliment to the national bank and rendered increased taxation necessary." A high protective tariff was instituted "to interpose artificial restrictions upon the natural course of the business and trade of the country, and to advance the interests of the large capitalists and monopolists at the expense of the great mass of the people." To ensure the continuance of the public debt despite the enormous increase in taxation, a scheme of internal improvements, capable of indefinite enlargement, was devised, and any surplus income from the sales of public lands were to be distributed among the states.[57]

The system was designed, Polk argued, to "encourage large and extravagant expenditures, and thereby to increase the public patronage, and maintain a rich and splendid government at the expense of a taxed and impoverished people." It would transform the government from the "plain, cheap, and simple confederation of States" envisaged by the Founders into "a consolidated empire, depriving the States of their reserved rights and the people of their just power and control in the administration of their Government." America would be ruled by and for the favored few who would benefit from the privileges and monopolies created by this new system. It was the ultimate design of the Whigs, said Polk, "to build up an aristocracy of wealth, to control the masses of society, and monopolize the power of the country."[58]

To the individual uncomfortable with the increasing complexity of nineteenth-century society and unable to grasp the massive forces shaping his life, such an interpretation provided security. It made more personal and comprehensible the source of society's dislocations and the inequities from which he felt himself to be suffering. There was not only form in this explanation but intent. In nineteenth-century America, there were few who could not understand selfish materialism and a lust for power and status as the motives behind men's actions. Just as important, the Jacksonian interpretation saw the increasing size, complexity, and centralization of society as unnecessary. Jacksonians pictured an America in which urbanization would be limited, government and institutions small, wealth widely and relatively evenly distributed, and men's relations simple and natural. The whole corpus of Whig policy seemed bent on the destruction of such a society, but Democrats believed the chief agent of Whiggery's dangerous schemes was the "money power."

The money power was the ultimate symbol of the forces which threatened the Jacksonian. It combined all his fears of the commercial economy and its ties of self-interest with his sense that his freedom was menaced by sinister forces with immense, uncontrollable power. By its very nature the concept of the money power did not lend itself to precise definition. It was a vaguely imagined but tightly organized combination of those who controlled the wealth of the country through their privileged access to the banking system. The head of this monster was, of course, the Bank of the United States. But even after Jackson severed the head from the body, and seemingly left the country's banks without the means to coordinate their control over the economy, the money power remained. "It acts in concert," warned J. H. Prince of Salem, Massachusetts, "it is an organized system—it has the advantage of private interest combined with the organization and discipline of party."[59]

The banks controlled the country's money, and money appeared to Jacksonians as the great integrating factor in society. It was tying the disparate elements of society together in an interdependent chain of pecuniary interest, threatening the liberty of the individual and denying him the ability to control his own life. According to the *Globe,* experience showed that "the city merchants have absolute control over the city banks; the town merchants over the banks in towns; the wholesale man controlling the retailer; the great banks over the smaller; and in this way the whole credit system to be based on the point on which trade concentrates." "None can escape it," J. H. Prince concluded, "it reaches the splendid mansion and the humble cottage."[60] If corruption or mismanagement brought ruin to a part of the system, the whole structure would fall and bring down the small with the great, the frugal with the extravagant, and the innocent with the guilty. As long as the money power had the ability to regulate the currency of the country, no man was safe from its periodic devastations, no man could delude himself with the thought that he held his destiny in his own hands.

The government itself was not safe from a monster that drew its power from the influence exerted by wealth. Money, even when divorced from special privilege, exerted "a secret and invisible influence over the actions of man," argued John W. Gildart of Mississippi. Its power was so great, said Gildart, that "we may look upon it as the ruler, the master, the disposer of his temporal destinies." But when that natural power was concentrated and augmented by legislative enactments, it became a threat to all that Americans held dear. The money power, asserted the Montgomery (Alabama) *Advertiser,* "is at war with every interest," and it "governs despite laws and constitutions." Holding everyone and everything within its grasp, it stood "independent of the Government; ready to thwart its purposes and defy its power—to corrupt its counsels and to destroy its energies." The question was, according to Senator Robert J. Walker of Mississippi, "whether this shall be a Government of the Banks or of the people."[61]

There was much truth in these observations. Wealth did exercise extraordinary power in nineteenth-century America. The financial system did bind together individuals and institutions in long chains of credit and debt. The interdependence of Americans engaged in financial markets did compel the many to sometimes share in the folly of the few. What was distinctive about the Jacksonian understanding of these processes was the sense of impending doom they experienced as they watched the spread of the Whig financial system. While Whigs saw in it only the opening of new doors of opportunity, Democrats felt overwhelmed by the awesome power of a wicked force which would subjugate and demean them. They predicted disaster if its development were not restrained. To have to live in a Whiggish world would be a terrible catastrophe.

In an age of boundless expectations, when the idea of progress was a dominant theme, it was important to think of oneself as moving forward. Thus party spokesmen had to reassure Jacksonians that their attack on the Whig program was not a reactionary stance, but a necessary step in the upward march of civilization. While Whigs proclaimed that their policies were the means by which Americans could enter a golden age, Jacksonians maintained that progress was dependent on the destruction of these very policies. Progress to the Jacksonian was purely a process of liberation. The new ties of self-interest, by which Whigs sought to reconnect individuals in an atomized society, seemed far more constricting and threatening to him than the more human ties of his personal world. True progress, then, required the destruction of the corrupt linkages between Americans and the recovery of the "ties of kindred affection" which they imagined had been the natural relations of men before Whiggery had subverted them.[62]

The residual emotional bonds which were felt by tradition-directed Jacksonians were no doubt the basis for their sustaining faith in the natural order of things. From Newtonian physics, to Adam Smith's "invisible hand," to human relations themselves, Democrats believed in an unseen order that would harmonize all discordances if men did not interfere with its workings. In their view there was "a primitive appetite, an original aggregative principle, an inward intuition, ever propelling man to an association of some sort with his kind." The *Democratic Review* declared its belief that men were bound "by countless ties of sympathy and dependence." One had only to throw off the artificial restraints of the man-made order to realize these more perfect and natural relations.[63]

By arguing that the Whigs and the money power had destroyed the harmony of this natural world, party leaders absolved the Democrat of any responsibility for the conflict and confusion of his age. And by arguing that the forces of Whiggery were responsible for the hardships he experienced, they absolved him of responsibility for his own failures. If he suffered it was because the system was false or because those who held power were corrupt. Democratic rhetoric always located the source of life's difficulties outside the Democrat himself. Jacksonians needed to believe that they were in fact being cheated or abused.

The rhetoric of oppression projected outward the inner turmoil of the Jacksonian. A man who doubted himself could find guilt and anxiety unbearable. To believe that it was not his fault, that his sense of failure or degradation was unfairly caused by the outer world, allowed him to release this tension against an external foe. He reassured himself by foisting the burden of his failure onto society at large. Of course, in many cases society *was* implicated in the individual's failure. But what is important here is that the individual's anxiety was such that he felt a special need to share it, to make society shoulder his difficulties. This need may also be viewed as further evidence of the Jacksonian's sense of being controlled by forces outside himself. The individual who does not feel that he is master of his own life feels justified in blaming others for his difficulties.

The appeal of the Jacksonian message was determined by the needs of those who listened to it. Only those who felt cheated, bound, and degraded by the new impersonal relations among men could find this view of the world useful. Only those who still felt the emotional tug of traditional social linkages could have confidence that ties of "kindred affection" would result if these new relationships were abandoned. But merely to comprehend one's plight is not enough. Jacksonians also needed legislative policies which would embody their understanding of the world, policies which would speak to the needs of tradition-directed men in an inner-directed world.

The Roots of Policy

The policies advocated by the Democratic party in the age of Jackson flowed from the social character of the Americans who formed the party. They reflect a profound ambivalence about the growth of modern institutions. Though the Jacksonian was attracted by modernity, he was reluctant to abandon the simpler world it was supplanting. He was uncomfortable with the restless, aggressive, impersonal ways which his contemporaries were adopting. Nevertheless, many Jacksonians found the influence of such behavior too powerful or the rewards of it too attractive to resist. But these Jacksonians did not so much embrace modernity as submit to it.

Democratic legislators distinguished themselves from their rivals most sharply in their opposition to Whig programs for economic development and to Whig attempts to expand the scope of government. Democrats stood firmly against a national bank. At the state level, they were far less likely than Whigs to vote for the incorporation of banks and more likely to try to restrict the use of paper money. They were generally more reluctant to grant corporate privileges, whether these privileges were to be granted to private businesses or non-profit associations. Democrats advocated a tariff for revenue only, and resisted the demand for an element of protection which would stimulate the rise of American manufactures. They generally opposed support for internal improvements by the federal government, though there was less difference between the parties on this question.[64]

Believing that government tended to restrict rather than enlarge the sphere of human freedom, Jacksonians sought to limit its domain. Unlike their Whig opponents, they strictly interpreted the constitutional powers of the national government and used the concept of states' rights to head off any attempts to expand its jurisdiction. They opposed high prices for public lands for fear that it might make the central government rich, and they opposed distributing these proceeds to the states because these funds would enable state governments to expand their operations. They were less likely than Whigs to allow government to build schools, asylums, and poorhouses, to provide depression relief, or to engage in humanitarian reforms. Underlying Jacksonian opposition to the expansion of modern economic and governmental institutions lay a series of principles which held a natural attraction for the Democratic constituency.[65]

The first of these principles was freedom. Policies which could be construed as breaking bonds, as liberating from restraints or as removing obstacles were well received. Free trade, free banking, minimal government, and strict construction of the Constitution may all be viewed in this light. Above all, freedom to the Jacksonian meant freedom from modern institutions and their impersonal relationships, for these were the relations which Jacksonians found fraudulent, coercive, and degrading. The federal government's separation from the banking system, which the Independent Treasury Bill was to effect, was simply the aspiration of most individual Democrats writ large. According to the *Democratic Review,* the Administration was saying to the banks, "I seek not to injure you,—let me alone." Their stormy relationship had caused too much pain. The government was compelled to assert its independence and declare, "I will not again expose myself to the fluctuations, uncertainties, and hazards of this connection."[66]

Equality was almost as important as freedom to the Democrat. This principle formed the basis for many of the Jacksonians' attacks on modern institutions. They cited it when denouncing banks, corporations, tariffs, and internal improvements. In the hands of a rigorous Democratic philosopher such as William Leggett, equality seemed to preclude almost every modern institution and almost every attempt by government to encourage or regulate economic development. He pronounced equality of rights "the fundamental maxim of democracy and of political economy." Adherence to this maxim, Leggett maintained, repudiated the idea of energetic government. Following Jefferson, he believed equality implied only a "wise and frugal government, which shall restrain men from injuring one another, shall leave them otherwise free to regulate their own pursuits of industry and improvement, and shall not take from the mouth of labour the bread it has earned."[67] Equality had its modern aspects, of course, but one should not overlook the fact that it was often used by Jacksonians seeking to resist the dynamics of nineteenth-century life.

Localism was another important principle of Democratic policy. Jacksonians believed in the primacy of the more intimate environment. A belief in states' rights, despite Jackson's firm rejection of nullification, was more prevalent among Democrats. The state governments were safer repositories of the interests of the people, declared a speaker at a Virginia Democratic convention, because they were "more immediately under [the people's] scrutinizing eye, and directly responsible to them."[68] Moreover, against state governments, Jacksonians championed lesser jurisdictions and the private rights of individuals. The more distant the authority, the more suspect it became. This suspicion was in the first instance a rejection of the unseen, impersonal environment. This localism was a political attempt to wall off the local and the personal from the alienating influence of the distant and impersonal. Jacksonians yearned for the ways of the small community and sought to protect the remnants of such ways from the aggressions of a more cosmopolitan world.

Similarly, one can discover numerous attempts by Jacksonians to compartmentalize their lives in order to escape the inner conflict which resulted when their traditionalism was confronted by modernity. The appeal which "separation of church and state" or "separation of bank and state" had for the Democrat cannot be fully explained by rational arguments for their spiritual or economic desirability. Only when one realizes how more traditional religious forms were being challenged by the evangelical spirit and how more traditional economic practices were being undermined by the rise of capitalism in the nineteenth century can one understand why many Americans felt a strong need to isolate these spheres of their lives from the influence of others.

Democratic policies were designed to return to the laws of nature, not the artificial laws of man. Jacksonians believed in the spontaneous, the simple, and the natural—all characteristics of the age that was passing. John William Ward noted that nearly every characterization of Andrew Jackson eventually employed

such words as "natural" or "native," "instinctive" or "intuitive."
He also observed that the term "simple" was one of the key
political terms of the era. It was used by Jacksonians not only to
define their ideal society but also to describe the society that had
existed before "corruption" and "artificiality" entered the American Eden. Jacksonians longed for a world where individuals
instinctively knew their place, where human relations were not
hopelessly complex, and where the ties which bound people
together were based on something more than self-interest. To
avoid disaster, admonished a correspondent of the Boston
Weekly Reformer, Americans must "return to a simple and unso-
phisticated state of things."[69]

Democrats also sought to slow the rate at which the forces of
change were eroding the free, the equal, the local, and the
natural. The Jacksonian felt instinctively that the pace of
change—the pace of life itself— was dangerous. He spoke out
against the artificial stimulation of society by government and
against those who were too aggressive or too ambitious. "Where
is there now to be found the old fashioned importing merchant,
whose word was as good as his bond, and who was content to
grow rich, as our fathers did, by the successive and regular
profits of many years of patient industry," asked James
Buchanan. "Is not the race almost extinct? All now desire to
grow rich rapidly."[70] Life should retain a natural tempo. Individuals should not be so eager to get ahead that they would
destroy the old ties of community. This desire was at once a
description of the Jacksonian's ideal world—one that was slow to
change—and a symptom of the anxieties which he experienced
in adjusting to the new world which was emerging. Change was
coming too rapidly for the Jacksonian to accommodate himself
to it. Those who sought to increase the pace of modernization
were feared because they thus increased personal anxiety, and
those whose policies promised to limit the influence of modernization were hailed as saviors.

It is ironic that these very Jacksonian policies, designed to slow
change, ultimately accelerated the change of both men and

institutions to modern forms.[71] Jacksonian demands for freedom and equality had the effect of withdrawing emotional
commitment from the bonds between the individual and society.
Democrats preached suspicion, distrust, even rebellion. They
were told to be on the alert for evidence of coercion or
oppression. Democracy could maintain its ascendancy only
through "sleepless vigilance and perpetual conflict," warned the
Vermont *Statesman.*[72] Jacksonians were also urged to resist with
an iron will both seducing temptations and the pressures of
obloquy. Such an outlook encouraged the individual to cut
himself off from the traditional sources of direction and to look
within himself for the proper guide to thought and behavior.

Some historians have noted that Democratic policies such as
free banking and general incorporation laws brought about the
proliferation of modern economic institutions.[73] But there was
more irony than intent in this development. The essential
Jacksonian was hostile to capitalist enterprise and the market
economy. It is true that within the Democractic fold there were
men such as David Henshaw, who, after Jackson vetoed the
charter of Nicholas Biddle's Bank of the United States, sought to
replace the "monster" with an even bigger bank controlled by
Democrats. There were also, as Bray Hammond has demonstrated, state bankers who supported the destruction of a
national bank because they wanted to expand the operations of
their own banks.[74] The Jacksonian attack on monopoly did
indeed attract some individuals whose only objection to banks
and corporations was that there were not enough of them or
whose greatest desire was to get rich by creating a "monopoly" of
their own. But such men and such aspirations were not the
essence of Jacksonianism.

The heart of the Jacksonian movement lay with those who
would do away with all paper money banks and all acts of
incorporation. After the Panic of 1837 reinforced their fears of
these institutions, Democrats in western states effectively pursued such a policy. Free banking, general incorporation laws,
and other corporate reforms were primarily efforts by eastern

Democrats, faced with a more deeply entrenched corporate system, to eliminate some of the worst abuses of the system. The futility, as well as the political peril, of trying to destroy corporations entirely necessitated these compromises of Jacksonian principle. But even in the East there were Jacksonians who were not willing to compromise and who made life difficult for Jacksonians who were.[75]

Democratic acclaim for open economic competition was not an endorsement of the aggressive pursuit of self-interest but a condemnation of monopoly. In a proper world neither would exist. Jacksonians desired the peace and unity of an idealized past, not the ceaseless conflict of a capitalist future. But while Whiggish institutions and attitudes prevailed, Jacksonians were taught the virtues of competition rather than cooperation, resistance rather than reconciliation, and destruction rather than creation.

When Jacksonians accepted modernity, they felt themselves compelled by necessity rather than inspired by opportunity. Modern ways held a certain fascination for the Jacksonian, but it was a fascination he condemned others for exciting and himself for feeling. Modernity was a sinister temptation, a spider's web woven by the crafty to entangle him. The Jacksonian sought personal independence not to more freely engage modernity, but to extricate himself from it.

❧ 2 ❧

The Whig World

Solitude is impracticable, and society fatal. We must keep our head in the one and our hands in the other.

RALPH WALDO EMERSON[1]

The Whig social character was well adapted to the individualistic nature of the emergent American social order. More truly inner-directed than his Jacksonian opponent, the Whig was comfortable with rational, self-interested human relations. Feeling little frustration with his world, he expressed great confidence that both he and the country were destined to prosper. The Whig glorified American institutions and was impatient with those who questioned their beneficence. He extolled opportunity as if it were achievement itself, so sure was he of his own ability to succeed. Whig optimism, it is true, overlaid a substratum of dark fears about America's future, yet hopefulness was the prevailing sentiment among Whigs. Their fears, like their hopes, sprang from a sense that the possibilities of their world were unlimited; and their self-confidence ensured that these fears would engender enterprise and not despair.

Whigs had an intense desire for order, both in themselves and in society at large. Freed from the communal constraints of traditional society and solely responsible for their own well-being, these were men intent on bringing order to their lives. They saw both individual and collective progress as dependent on the willingness of Americans to exercise self-control. They

63

championed those institutions devoted to inculcating this virtue in the young and those remedial institutions responsible for disciplining adults who had not proven themselves capable of disciplining themselves.

Though committed to an individualistic ethic, Whigs were also dedicated to the task of uniting Americans for their common advancement. They were concerned lest the ability to act collectively be lost, now that it was no longer habitual or coerced. To facilitate this unity, Whigs preached that Americans shared a common destiny and that each man's efforts could not help but advance the well-being of the rest. Whigs also extolled the virtues of harmony, order, and stability for producing the kind of mutual confidence necessary among men if they were to unite their energies effectively. At the same time Whigs disparaged those who seemed to undermine their attempts to create this trust among Americans.

Whigs, like Jacksonians, also needed reassurance, but their need was of a different sort. They did not need to be convinced of their abilities, their equality, or their acceptance by others. Many of them, however, sought assurance that their individual striving ultimately benefited the community, that in some larger sense their individual actions served their fellow man. Moreover, they had to be convinced that the aggressive pursuit of materialistic ends would not endanger their eternal souls. Individualism, as Tocqueville realized, is not selfishness, but many Whig consciences found the distinction too subtle. Party rhetoric helped to persuade Whigs that their actions were neither selfish nor immoral.

Whigs could not admit that the persistent problems of American society revealed underlying flaws in the structure itself. The Whig message was that the vicissitudes of the age were the consequence of others' inability to make themselves over in the Whig image. They declared that the Whig political program, together with the institutions and values which promoted it, were necessary for the triumph of civilization over barbarism. Those who opposed their program must, therefore, be men unable or unwilling to exercise the enlightened self-control necessary to civilized life.

The legislation that Whigs advocated was designed to promote the development of the institutions and values of modernity. It sought to stimulate, facilitate, and bring order to individual striving. It had its roots in the character of Americans who did not fear the aggressive pursuit of self-interest or the impersonal institutions which inner-directed men created to advance these interests.

The Sense of Confidence

The Whig was characteristically confident of his capacity to succeed in life. Compared to the Jacksonian, he seldom felt manipulated, constrained, or scorned by others. He had great faith in the beneficent effects of modernization and boundless hopes that his own life would be swept forward on a rising tide of economic growth. The institutions of modern life which angered and frustrated Jacksonians were, to the Whig, engines for individual and collective advancement.

Daniel Webster struck the Whig keynote when he declared that all facets of American growth and development were richly beneficial, not just to the few but to everyone:

> There is no monopoly in science. There are no exclusive privileges in the workings of automatic machinery, or the powers of natural bodies. The poorest as well as the richest man in society, has a direct interest, and generally the poor a far greater interest than the rich, in the successful operation of these arts, which make the means of living, clothing especially, abundant and cheap. The advantages conferred by knowledge in increasing our physical resources, from their very nature, cannot be enjoyed by a few only. They are open to the many and to be profitable, the many must enjoy it.

Increased knowledge and scientific advance, booming factories and rapidly improving means of transportation were all part of

Webster's optimistic Whig vision of the American future. "The factories, the steamboats, the railroads, and other similar establishments," he held, were "general and popular in all the good they produce. The unquestionable operation of all these things has been not only to increase property, but to equalize it, to diffuse it, to scatter its advantages among the many, and to give content, cheerfulness, and animation to all classes of the social system."[2]

While Whigs extolled the widespread benefits of growth, they reminded Americans that their system opened to all the doors of opportunity. The Whig program, maintained the Troy (N.Y.) *Morning Mail,* furnished "a broad and unobstructed path to prosperity and honor." Whigs constantly reaffirmed their belief that no impediment blocked the way of any man whose character and hard work entitled him to succeed. "Every man starts fair in this country," said the New York *Enquirer.* "Every pursuit in life should be and is, open to all," asserted the Springfield *Republican.* "No man in America is doomed by the necessity of his circumstances to die in the same condition, in which he was born," Calvin Colton declared. On the contrary, "he may . . . become rich, and important, and great, if he has wit and virtue, in spite of any body, and of every body."[3]

The institutions which the Jacksonians found oppressive, monopolistic, and aristocratic, the Whigs perceived in an entirely different light. Corporations were not soulless monsters to the Whig. They were beneficial devices, said the Boston *Courier,* which enable men "of the smallest means, . . . to originate and carry on undertakings which, without the power, credit and facilities derived from such acts [of incorporation], would either not be undertaken at all, or only by individuals of great wealth and for their sole benefit." The effect of acts of incorporation was "not to favor the rich at the expense of the poor, but . . . to place those who are in pursuit of wealth on a level, as men of business, with those who are already in possession of it."[4]

Nor were the banks inherently irresponsible or monopolistic. To Henry Clay, they were merely "organized agencies for the loan of money and the transaction of monetary business; regulated agencies acting under the prescriptions of law, and subject to a responsibility, moral and legal, far transcending that under which any private capitalist operates." Daniel Webster denied that banks benefited only their stockholders while cheating the rest of society. "Banks, everywhere, and especially with us, are made for the borrowers," he maintained. "They are made for the good of the many, and not for the good of the few." Even the Bank of the United States, which Jacksonians called the "Monster," was, said Calvin Colton, "an institution that proved most important to the Government, and most useful to the country. No party ever lost any thing by it, and all parties were benefited."[5]

The credit system, in the Whig mind, was not a form of fraud built on deception, but "a good thing—that is often necessary to the welfare of the industrious and enterprising poor man . . . one of the most powerful levers by which such a one is enabled to raise himself to independence." Whigs admitted that banks sometimes favored the interests of particular individuals and that some paper money was of dubious worth, but these were correctable flaws in a generally beneficial system. "It is to this system of sound credit currency," argued Calvin Colton, "that, as a nation, we owe our unrivalled march to prosperity and wealth." Banks and paper money were essential to the success of the credit system and thereby to the hopes of the poor. Horace Greeley invited his readers to "point to the country where poor men share any of the advantages of Credit—where Credit is generally diffused, and we will show you a country which cherishes Banks and Paper Currency."[6]

The tariff, too, was represented by Whigs as a device to enhance the opportunities of the common man. They denied that it was useful only to capitalists and corporations, or that its inevitable consequence was to depress the interests of labor. "For *one* benefit to those capitalists," asserted the Washington *National Intelligencer,* the tariff laws "confer hundreds of benefits on the working classes." The tariff, by protecting the American worker from the competition of poorly paid Europeans, enhanced the position of labor. Daniel Webster maintained that "whatever enhances wages, whatever increases the price of labor, is expressly for the benefit of labor." Even in the South, where one might expect regional interests to dampen enthusiasm for the tariff, Whig papers such as the Fayetteville (N.C.) *Observer* and the Augusta (Ga.) *Chronicle and Sentinel* praised the tariff for conferring untold benefits upon the American working class by protecting them from "European pauper labor."[7]

If the Jacksonian was an individual who, however successful, viewed himself as an outsider, the Whig was an individual who, however unsuccessful, considered himself an insider. Only those who had faith in themselves and who trusted the workings of impersonal institutions could be drawn to the Whig cause. There was considerable evidence to support Democratic contentions that the Whig program was sometimes expensive, partial, monopolistic, and fraudulent. Credit bubbles burst, banks and businesses went bankrupt, individuals were ruined, but Whig faith in the system continued—even among many of those who were ruined. The Whig was the man who believed that he, and the country, would bounce back.

Yet such buoyancy was not unmixed with doubt and anxiety. As William R. Taylor has observed of the Whigs, "Beneath a surface of seemingly imperturbable optimism and dogmatic certainty ran a strong undercurrent of fear and uneasiness."[8] Whigs were agonizingly aware that the liberated individual was free to do evil as well as good, to fail miserably as well as to succeed famously. If Whig hopes were utopian, their fears were apocalyptic. Beneath the harmony and union of the Constitution, lurked revolution and anarchy. While the credit system maintained prosperity and progress, powerful attempts to dismantle it threatened poverty and barbarism.

The antipodal possibilities within the individual were equally stark. Edward Everett believed that men were endowed "with a capacity . . . of perhaps infinite improvement." Their intellect, if "trained and instructed, strengthened by wise discipline, and guided by principle . . . ripens into an intelligence but a little lower than the angels." Without such instruction, however, "this divine principle all but expires, and the man whom it was sent to enlighten sinks down, before his natural death, to his kindred dust." If education is neglected, man "is launched upon the world a benighted being, scarcely elevated above the beasts that perish; and all that he could have been and done, for society and for himself, is wholly lost."[9] Even so, the Whig was less distressed by the depths to which he and his society could sink than he was inspired by the heights to which they could rise. His confidence surmounted, though it never obliterated, his fears.

Democrats were aware that the Whig was a different kind of person and that his self-assurance was one of the principal characteristics which distinguished him. "The truth is," said the New York *Evening Post for the Country*, "that the Whigs are sanguine, confident, and boastful by temperament." The *Democratic Review* acknowledged that "they are naturally fond of splendor and strength—large and sweeping action—bold and brilliant energy of enterprise." The Whig businessman, complained the Washington *Globe*, never worried about the uncertainties which troubled the Democrat: "The idea of owing more than he can ever reasonably expect to pay, does not rob him of a wink of sleep, or disturb his repose for a moment. . . . [H]e lives as if the world were at his command." In the same vein, a Democrat writing in the Boston *Morning Post* described the Jacksonian view of the typical Whig constituent: "If you feel that you are sharper than most others—if you think that without capital you can compete with capital—if you have sufficient confidence in yourself, to suppose that you are an overmatch for knowledge, experience, and wealth— why, then join your labors to the opponents of the democracy—it is not to such *strong* men that I write."[10]

The Problem of Self-Control

Although the Whig looked confidently out on individualistic America, he was troubled when he looked within himself. The greatest threat to his well-being was not the tyranny of others, but the tyranny of his own inner drives. Cut off from his fellow man, the inner-directed individual found in the flaws of his own character the chief obstacles to his ambition. Thrown back on his own resources, he had to discipline his passions if they were not to pose a threat to the achievement of his long-range goals. Excitement and extravagance had to give way to equanimity and moderation. Caprice and rashness had to submit to regularity and system. Individual progress and, ultimately, social progress, now depended on the willingness of individuals to exercise a virtuous self-control.

The Whig, beset by his own problems of self-control, saw the character defects of individuals as being at the root of social problems. It was a commonplace of Whig thought that "the greatest obstacle to the perpetuity of good institutions, is doubtless in human nature itself." Neither the cause of nor the solution to these problems lay primarily in the structure of society, as Democrats seemed to believe. Greeley's *Tribune* asserted that "no improvement in the constitution of Society, or in any institution whatever, can make the idler, the prodigal, the drunkard, the libertine, either respectable or prosperous, without a transformation of his character." American conditions made such character transformation imperative. Each American would have to develop a new set of inner controls to replace those which society at large no longer exercised. The American government itself mirrored the private situation of individuals. It too was "a system by which *man should govern himself,* unshackled on the one hand by a despotic power which he could not control, and wisely guarded on the other against the sudden tumults of his frail and erring passions."[11]

The Whig ideal was the man who had brought his passions under control and whose will, while it mastered his inner drives, was not yet a law unto itself. Seward eulogized Webster for his ambition, but reminded his listeners that Webster's was an ambition "generally subordinate to conventional forms, and always to the constitution." Similarly Lincoln, in a eulogy of his idol, Henry Clay, noted that "his will was indomitable"; but he also warned his audience that in lesser men "this quality often secures to its owner nothing better than a character for useless obstinacy." Americans had to rule themselves by the force of their wills, but will itself had to be controlled by the forms of a free society. No Whig doubted that Andrew Jackson had a strong will, but they feared that it was ungovernable. "That strong and unbending will, which is the best qualification to lead an army," declared Calvin Colton, "is the worst possible to preside over a true democracy, where the will of all is to be consulted; that despotic authority which is necessary in the field, is most unsuitable in the Chief Magistrate of a free people; and that impetuosity which bears down a foe, in the onset of battle, will carry away the pillars of a republic."[12]

Self-restraint was the mark of a moral man, a man truly fitted for self-government. Whig policy on Indian affars, on relations with the French, and on the Mexican War demonstrated that self-restraint had public as well as private dimensions. It was in the best Whig tradition that the party showed as much concern for the Indian nations when they became "helpless and dependent" as they had when they were "mighty." The same theme was evident when, in a dispute with France, Henry Clay reminded Americans that their demands that France fulfill her treaty obligations would have more force if the United States "could say to France that, in all instances, we had . . . adhered faithfully to every obligation which we had contracted, no matter whether it was entered into with a powerful or a weak people." During the Mexican War, the Fayetteville *Observer* charged that the war showed that Democratic doctrine maintained "The Right of the Strong to Plunder the Weak," and it insisted that honor should be given to him "who has mercy on the weak, who forbears to exact more than his just due." There was no virtue in dealing justly with those powerful enough to compel fair treatment. Civilization was preserved by those dedicated to abstract justice and who paid no heed to the relative strength of the parties to a dispute.[13]

Since Whigs knew that self-restraint and self-discipline did not come easily, they championed those institutions committed to helping individuals to achieve self-mastery. Whigs expressed warm support for the institutions which shaped the character of young Americans: the home, the church, and the school. They also banded together in voluntary associations to advocate self-control among their peers. Finally, they promoted remedial institutions responsible for reforming individuals who were unable to exercise the self-discipline necessary to make their own way in society.

Because the family was responsible for maintaining moral order in a fragmented world, Whig feelings about that institution bordered on worship. Arguing that it was an organization of "divine ordination," Daniel D. Barnard declared that "the Family must be held sacred." Since Whigs believed that strong character was essential in an individualistic society and that character was formed early in life, the home became the first line of defense against the chaos and disorder always threatening to overwhelm both the individual and society. The task of the family was to instill values conducive to self-reliance and economic success: honesty, industry, frugality, and temperance. But most of all, the family was a school for self-control. "It is only by this institution," Barnard argued, "that the turbulence of outrageous passion is calmed down." The essence of character for the inner-directed Whig was the taming of his inner drives, and that battle began in the home.[14]

The formation of character was most particularly the work of the women of the home, whose special moral and spiritual qualities were thought to fit them for the task. Catherine Beecher, whose *Treatise on Domestic Economy* was a popular handbook on how to run the home, believed that woman's role was of paramount importance to democracy because the values internalized in early childhood would determine whether America's open society would prove a blessing or a curse. Of the three most important habits that Beecher thought necessary to the formation of character, two— the "submission of the will" and "self-denial"—were habits of self-control. Sarah Josepha Hale, for forty years the editor of *Godey's Lady's Book,* a monthly devoted to American home life, was equally intent on shaping the character of the young. For Hale, as for Beecher and all Whigs, character meant "restraint, self-control, self-discipline." Her long and influential career spent advocating these values led William R. Taylor to acclaim her the "mistress" of "the house of Whiggery."[15]

Beyond the home, the church, by which most Whigs meant the institutions of evangelical Protestantism, was the primary agency responsible for assisting Americans to gain control over their passions. Whigs championed religion for its inculcation of morality, which in practice was little different from building character. Virtue was to be attained by strengthening the forces of reason or conscience so that they could wage effective war on the "bad passions" of human nature. Particularly important was the moral training of the young which the churches carried on. Whig newspapers such as the Albany *Jeffersonian,* the Marshall (Mich.) *Western Statesman,* and the New Orleans *Picayune* all praised the sabbath schools for encouraging correct moral notions in the rising generation. To the Whig, "the *morals* of the people, purified by the spirit of the Christian religion," was one of "the pillars on which rests the temple of freedom." Social order and political stability alike depended on the moral restraint of the people, and organized religion was committed to instilling such moral restraint in Americans.[16]

Where Whigs had their way, both character and virtue were also fostered by the public schools. Whigs championed public education for many reasons, but one of the most salient was the school's potential for disciplining the young in the habits of self-control. To the Whig, far more than intellectual development was involved in a proper education. The teachers in the common school system of New Hampshire were reminded by the school's commissioner, Charles Haddock, that they were to "make MORAL instruction a prominent object." They were enjoined to impress upon their students the virtues of "sobriety,

industry and frugality; chastity, moderation and temperance."
This emphasis on obedience, discipline, and order in the schools
of the era was dictated not merely by the requirements of the
educational process, but by the future well-being of the students
and of the social order as well. Discipline and self-restraint were
necessary for the success of the self-reliant individual and for
the peace of an individualistic society.[17]

Whigs also threw their energies into many voluntary associations designed to promote self-discipline. The temperance movement was the largest and most representative antebellum reform,
and historians agree that the Whigs were the party of temperance. Temperance enlisted the interest of Whigs for the same
reason that they showed a special concern for the home, religion,
and education. They opposed drink because it reduced a man's
ability to exercise self-control. Under the influence of alcohol a
man became a slave to his own passions. As one recent historian
has put it, "Giving in to it meant destruction of one's autonomy."
The young Abraham Lincoln hailed the "temperance revolution"
as a greater event than the political revolution by which national
independence had been obtained. "In *it*," Lincoln declared, "we
shall find a stronger bondage broken; a viler slavery, manumit-
ted; a greater tyrant deposed." He looked forward hopefully, he
said, to that happy day when, "all appetites controled [sic], all
passions subdued, all matters subjected, *mind*, all conquering
mind, shall live and move the monarch of the world." Even such
legendary tipplers as Henry Clay and Daniel Webster assured
their fellow Whigs that they solidly supported the temperance
cause, though, like a great many members of their party, they
opposed legislation on the subject.[18]

The Whigs' insistence that individuals govern themselves can
also be observed in the asylum movement which gained most of
its political support from the Whig party. The asylum movement
gave birth to some of the most significant institutional reforms
of the age: the penitentiary, the insane asylum, the almshouse,
and the juvenile reformatory (house of refuge). Each of these
institutions was designed to help the individual discipline him-

self and bring his passions under control. The "bywords of asylum management" were certainty, regularity, order, and precision. All such institutions were supposed to remove the individual from the uncertainties and the temptations of nineteenth-century society until he had developed a character strong enough to cope with them. "The object is not alone to make the boys behave well while in our charge," explained a reformatory worker, "that is not difficult. . . . [But] any discipline . . . which does not enable the boy to *resist temptation* wherever and whenever he finds it, is ineffectual, and the whole object of houses of refuge is a failure." At the core of the reformer's boundless optimism, said David J. Rothman, historian of the asylum movement, was the belief "that a daily routine of strict and steady discipline would transform inmates' character."[19]

Reformers believed that the source of deviancy and dependency, the two social problems that these institutions sought to alleviate, was the extreme fluidity and openness of American society.[20] Without proper childhood training, the individual would be too weak to resist the temptations America presented to wrongdoers. Without properly disciplined work habits, families would be forced to rely on public charity. Indeed, without a firm inner sense of order, the chaos and flux of the world could actually drive one to insanity. The task of the penitentiary, the asylum, the almshouse, and the house of refuge was to gather up all whose circumstances demonstrated their inability to cope with the demands of an open society and to inculcate the order, the discipline, and the industry lacking in their lives.

Neither the accuracy of the reformers' diagnosis of social problems nor the effectiveness of their cure is relevant here. What is significant is their notion that many individuals were suffering from a society which was too open and too mutable. In sharp contrast to the Jacksonians, whose constant complaint was that the individual was hedged about on all sides by restrictions and controls, Whigs were convinced that Americans were plagued by an absence of order and limits in their lives.

Whigs assumed that others suffered from a lack of discipline because they realized how difficult it was for them to attain mastery over themselves. Many believed it was only a "wholesome" discipline instilled early that distinguished the supervisors from the inmates of an asylum. Theorists of insanity reminded Americans that "the barrier between normality and deviancy was very low. . . . [N]o one who stood on one side of it today could be sure he would not cross it tomorrow." One minister, contemplating the temptations experienced by the typical wayward youth, asked his audience: "Who of us dare to say that if he had been exposed to the same influences, he would have preserved his integrity and come out of the fiery ordeal unscathed?" Those concerned about America's youth were sure of one thing: they would need "a healthy moral constitution, capable of resisting *the assaults of temptations,* and strong enough to keep the line of rectitude through *the stormy and disturbing influences by which we are continually assailed.*"[21]

Whigs sometimes criticized and sometimes attempted to aid those who seemed incapable of keeping sufficient rein on their natural impulses. Such interest in the behavior of others served several purposes, but two are particularly relevant here. First, their condemnation of uncontrolled impulse, from the contempt for the passionate nature of Andrew Jackson himself to their attacks on the unruliness of Jackson's followers—especially the Irish—served to reinforce their own efforts at self-control. By their professions of the importance of this characteristic and their efforts to help others realize its benefits, Whigs found the strength to fight their own internal battles against the natural human propensities to self-indulgence, intemperance, and sloth. Second, they believed that the success of the American experiment in self-government was dependent upon the willingness of individuals to exercise self-control in their private lives. If too many Americans fell prey to their passions, if too many succumbed to ignorance, prejudice, and licentiousness, they would destroy the moral foundations of a free society.

Some historians have advanced the now familiar argument that the essence of Whig reform was not "self-control" but "social control."[22] David J. Rothman, for example, represented the reformers of the asylum movement as men and women fearful of modernity, trying to restore an eighteenth-century world where "men were to take their rank in the hierarchy, know their place in society, and not compete to change positions." Much of the evidence for this interpretation derives from the rigidly structured, authoritarian nature of life within the asylums and penitentiaries which reformers created. According to this view, these institutions were designed to function in two ways: first, to teach each inmate to know his place; second, to reawaken public respect for order and authority in America at large.[23] This perspective, however, mistakes the real nature of Whig reform.

The notion of order and authority to which the Whigs were committed was a thoroughly modern one. While traditional society had been ordered primarily by external social pressure brought to bear on the individual, nineteenth-century Whigs looked to a social order that was a consequence of the voluntary determination of free men to regulate themselves. While authority in traditional society had been largely personal, being fixed in certain individuals at birth, Whigs supported an authority that was impersonal and based on consent. Far from wishing to alter the dynamic and voluntaristic character of modern society, Whig reformers were attempting to help Americans to cope with it. The desideratum was not acquiesence to the demands of the community but inner strength to resist social pressures. As to those unfortunates who were already too dependent on external circumstances or who succumbed too blatantly to their passions, they must be made to become masters of themselves.

Both the means and the ends of Whig reform demonstrated a commitment to the individualistic world in which they found themselves. They rejected the coercion and brutality that had been the customary means of dealing with the deviant and the dependent. Moreover, since dependence of the many upon the few was a commonplace of traditional social thought, the Whig concern to eliminate dependence was itself a modern notion. The reason why Whig poor relief programs often seemed hesitant and niggardly is because the reformers feared lest they turn able-bodied citizens into permanent dependents. None of their most typical institutions was designed to house inmates permanently. The pentitentiary and the asylum were not intended to be permanent refuges for society's outcasts, but rather temporary way stations on the road to a life that was both self-fulfilled and self-controlled. Whig reformers made no attempt to impede the ambitious or to set limits on the capable; their purpose was instead to enable the deviant and the dependent to compete with the rest without resorting to crime or losing their sanity.[24]

The Whig party sought to build a social framework within which free men could achieve their own ends, and Whig reformers sought to enable men to cope successfully with such a world. The reformer's stress on self-control and self-reliance is entirely consistent with their allegiance to the party which created the idea of the self-made man. Neither Whig politicians nor Whig reformers were attempting to restore a fixed social order in which each individual "knew his place." Whigs, whether as a result of philosophical conviction or acceptance of the thrust of historical change, rejected the notion of social control. They believed that the social order in the making had to be based on the willingness of Americans to gain mastery over themselves. They did not believe, as did their Jacksonian counterparts, in slowing progress to reduce the discomfort of individuals. Too convinced of the beneficial effects of modernization, they sought through the family, the church, and the school—and in the event that these institutions failed, through the asylum and the penitentiary—to enable Americans to adapt themselves to the world of individualism.

Individualism and Interdependence

Self-assurance came easier to Whigs because they were men whose feelings were already turned inward. Having left behind

the traditional social context of life, they were more confident
that they could do battle with an impersonal and uncaring
world. Although the Whig was no longer bound emotionally to
his fellow man, he did not seek to isolate himself. On the
contrary, having been thrown back upon his own strength, the
Whig was acutely aware of his need for others. He was deeply
concerned with creating new relationships which would unite
independent individuals for collective benefit.

These new bonds, however, would not be like the old. They
were to be ties of self-interest uniting the energies and resources
of freely contracting individuals. They were no less important
for their limited nature. Whigs believed that individuals could,
by the proper combination and organization of their efforts,
give to their individual powers an expansive force that far
surpassed the productivity of those working in isolation. Each
individual could, without sacrificing his independence, work in
harmony with others to realize more fully his personal ambitions.

Such cooperation was not easily achieved in the age of
Jackson. Those intent on escaping dependent relationships
listened skeptically to Whig celebrations of the interdependence
of individuals. Those who felt the need to be defiantly detached
did not thrill to Whig praise of harmony and union. Those
uncomfortable with Whig notions of order became restive when
Whigs extolled the benefits of stability, regularity, and system.
Desiring to draw people together, confident of the benefits
which they would reap as a consequence, and yet frustrated by
Jacksonian resistance to their programs, Whig rhetoric was
often one long paean to the virtues of collective effort.

Whigs readily accepted the interdependence of individuals
and interests. They applauded Daniel Webster's constant re-
minders that "we are all embarked together, with a common
interest and a common fate." They nodded agreement when
Henry Clay told them that "every portion of the republic is
indirectly, at least, interested in the welfare of the whole, and
that they ever sympathize in the distresses and rejoice in the

happiness of the most distant quarter of the Union." William Seward expressed a deeply held Whig sentiment when he said that

> so unwavering are the laws of Providence which punish human vices, and reward human virtues, that every vice indulged, and every crime committed, not only brings danger and suffering on the delinquent, but works injury to his country and his race; while very virtue practised, and every generous effort made for even self-improvement and elevation, is followed by personal advantages not only, but by benefits, to society, and to mankind.[25]

This kind of interdependence did not imply homogeneity. The Constitution, said Webster, was "for certain purposes, to make us *one people,* though not," he hastened to add, "for all purposes." Diversity was essential to the well-being of individual and nation, but it was not to be forgotten that differences should blend together harmoniously, complementing and not conflicting with one another. Webster argued that "the interests of the different parts of the country, though various, are not the opposite; flowing, indeed, in diverse channels, but all contributing to swell the great tide of national prosperity." On another occasion he quoted Alexander Pope to illustrate the way in which the states related to each other under the Constitution:

> Not, chaos-like, together crushed and bruised,
>   But, like the world harmoniously confused;
> Where order in variety we see,
>   And where, though all things differ, all agree.[26]

Whigs believed that diverse interests would attain such harmony only if Americans recognized and accepted their common destiny. Calvin Colton warned that "if the great law of mutual dependence in society be overlooked or violated, in the policy and measures of Government, . . . the most fatal consequences must unavoidably follow." Much Whig rhetoric was dedicated to demonstrating that Whig policies, which often appeared to benefit only a certain class, a certain interest, or a certain geographical region, actually, because of "the great law of mutual dependence," benefited everyone. Hence, John Quincy Adams argued that "the great interests of an agricultural, commercial, and manufacturing nation are so linked in union together that no permanent cause of prosperity to one of them can operate without extending its influence to the others." Henry Clay asserted that "the Cumberland road is a great national object in which all the people of the United States are interested and concerned." And Webster said of the tariff that "this is not, in a society like this, a matter which affects the interest of a particular class, but one which affects the interest of all classes. It runs through the whole chain of human occupation and employment, and touches the means of living and the comfort of all."[27]

The Whig was told to take a broad, elevated view of public affairs so that he might perceive the comprehensive effect of Whig policy. He would not understand the beneficial workings of the whole if he restricted his gaze to his immediate surroundings, nor would he be likely to support effective public policy if he defined too narrowly his own self-interest. Addressing himself to the problems of his native New York, William Seward declared that "it is to be desired that every citizen of the state engaged in public affairs should be intimately acquainted with all the different portions of its territory." Such a comprehensive vision alone would give "a just conception of the greatness and power of the whole state, and the unity and harmony of its varied interests. . . . He would no longer fear that the improvement of one section would impair the prosperity of another; nor longer doubt the ability of the state, with judicious and well-directed efforts, to accomplish the desired improvements of the whole."[28]

In the interest of the common good, the Whig had to overlook the way government sometimes distributed its benefits unevenly in society. "In a country so widely extended as ours, so diversified in its interests and in the character of its people," Daniel Webster admitted, "it is impossible that the operation of any measure should affect all alike." But if legislation attempted to affect all Americans in precisely the same way and to the same degree, nothing could be done by government to promote the country's progress. For Webster, a statesman anxious to advance the development of all of America's diverse interests, a broader perspective had to be taken. "In such cases," he reasoned, "it has always appeared to me that the point to be examined was, whether the principle was general. If the principle were general, although the application be partial, I cheerfully and zealously gave it my support."[29]

The great danger, Whigs believed, was that men could not see this general principle or that they would not accept it. Unable or unwilling to view comprehensively America's diversity, they would fail to observe that their own interests were ultimately dependent on the interests of others. If distance or differences were allowed to divide Americans into insignificant little bands, each dedicated only to the preservation of its own local interest, all progress would be halted. The gulf between individuals, classes, interests, and sections would widen, and hostility and suspicion would pervade their relations.

Whigs always took pride in their own efforts to create harmony among Americans and they castigated their opponents as sowers of hostility and suspicion. William Seward spoke for all Whigs when he maintained that "the public welfare is best promoted by mutual harmony and confidence," not by hostility and suspicion. The virtue of the Whig party, boasted the *American Whig Review*, was that "it has never done anything to kindle passion, to favor discord, to stir up faction, to excite class against class, interest against interest, or section against section. . . . Its whole influence has been harmonizing, elevating, and redeeming." The New York *Tribune*, meanwhile, counseled resistance to Jacksonian attempts to "array the Poor against the Rich, the Laborer against the Capitalist, and thus embroil Society in one universal network of jealousies and hatreds." In

Montgomery, Alabama, a Whig meeting resolved "that any attempt to divide the people into classes, distinguished by birth, by wealth or poverty, or by profession, or occupation, is . . . subversive of the true principles of our political institutions; and ought to be discountenanced."[30]

Like harmony, order was a prime Whig value because it reduced discord and distrust, thus enabling individuals to transcend their differences and work together for their mutual benefit. Greeley's *Tribune* declared that its reverence for order was "based on the conviction that through Order alone is any real and enduring Progress attainable." Feeling the tenuous nature of the ties which bound Americans together, Whigs supported efforts to increase their confidence in each other and resisted Democratic efforts to unsettle society. Whigs condemned Jacksonians for introducing disorder into the economic transactions of the country by their interference with the credit system. In the wake of the Panic of 1837, the Petersburg (Va.) *Intelligencer* asked, "Where is now that confidence among men which formerly prevailed? . . . Gone. Instead of confidence we have doubt and distrust." The *Intelligencer* did not doubt that the "disordered exchanges" and "tottering banks" were produced by "the unskilful interference of the Federal Government with the financial affairs of the country." The Albany *Daily Advertiser* also lamented the fact that "the essential ingredient in all fiscal and commercial transactions, *mutual confidence,* had been annihilated by the vindictive policy of the General Government."[31]

The order which created mutual confidence among men, Seward declared, was guaranteed by "a conservative support of tried institutions and laws." Whigs deplored the way in which Jackson's vetoes and his theories of the Constitution had unsettled America's fundamental law. They attacked Democratic willingness to make "experiments" with government. By arguing that laws were "contracts" between the generations, they resisted the spread of the Jacksonian notion that law was merely the desire of a current majority, which could be changed readily without disastrous effects on society. If the great compromises of the past could be overturned by temporary majorities, particularly sectional ones, such majorities would create, argued the Boston *Atlas*, "a spirit of incurable distrust; they will be looked upon as men and communities whom no promises can bind." This sort of attitude would destroy America, since "fidelity to agreements is the very corner stone of society."[32]

The conservatism of the Whigs lay not in any special reverence for the past. "Our Conservatism is not of that Chinese tenacity, which insists that the bad must be cherished simply because it is old," explained the New York *Tribune*. "We insist only that the old must be proved bad and never condemned merely because it *is* old; and that, even if defective, it should not be overthrown till something better has been provided to replace it." Still less was their conservatism based on any resistance to dramatic economic and social change. At the heart of Whiggery lay a dynamic conception of national growth and individual mobility. Whigs were conservative only in the sense that they accepted the current constitutional and legal system as a sufficient framework for American development. "I know of no happiness for my country so much to be desired," said Daniel D. Barnard, "as that she should be left, under the guidance of wise and unambitious counsels, to the natural and easy development of the proper advantages of her position, just as it is, and of her institutions very much as they are, for at least one whole generation." Even here Whigs did not oppose necessary change; they merely wanted legislative progress to be cautious and sure-footed. If it became necessary to make a fundamental social change, Henry Clay counseled, "it should not be sudden, but contracted by slow and cautious degrees."[33]

Moderation and compromise would ensure that society retained the peace and stability it required. Whigs believed that "there ought to be some bounds to human controversy. Stability is a necessary want of society." Henry Clay always put himself and his party in the forefront of any effort to settle political differences peacefully. In Clay's mind, it was "the great principle of compromise and concession which lies at the bottom of our

institutions; which gave birth to the Constitution itself, and which
has continued to regulate us in our onward march, and conducted the nation to glory and renown." He reminded Americans that there had been many great epochs of compromise in
their history: "The adoption of the Constitution was a compromise; the settlement of the Missouri question was the second
epoch; the adjustment of the tariff was the third." At the time of
this statement Clay's contribution to the Compromise of 1850
still lay in the future.[34]

To the Whig, nothing justified compromise so much as the
preservation of the Union. To maintain it "in all its integrity and
vigor" was, said Clay, "the paramount desire which has influenced me throughout my whole public career." The Union
"comprehended peace, safety, free institutions, and all that
constitutes the pride and hope of our country." Daniel Webster's
rhetoric on the importance of the Union reveals the Whig need
both to draw individuals together and to establish a stable
framework for their unity:

> The Union is not a temporary partnership of States. It is the
> association of the people, under a constitution of Government,
> uniting their power, joining together their highest interests, ce-
> menting their present enjoyments, and blending, in one indivisible
> mass, all their hopes for the future. Whatsoever is steadfast in just
> political principles, whatsoever is permanent in the structure of
> human society, whatsoever there is which can derive an enduring
> character from being founded on deep laid principles of constitu-
> tional liberty, and on the broad foundations of the public will—all
> unite to entitle this instrument to be regarded as a permanent
> constitution of Government.[35]

Those seeking to re-establish ties between individuals found
satisfaction in Webster's use of words such as "association,"
"uniting," "joining," "cementing," "blending," and "indivisible."
Those who sought to stabilize the framework for those relationships were delighted with his use of the words "steadfast,"
"permanent," "enduring," and "deep laid principles."

All this was public rhetoric designed to address the great public issues of the day. No doubt some well-informed Americans of the era accepted it on that level alone. But most Americans, whether consciously or not, must have translated it into the idiom of their private worlds. The language of interdependence, unity, harmony, and order would have had greatest appeal to those for whom such words had personal meaning. Individuals cut off from their fellows, troubled by notions of independence which allowed only suspicion and competition between individuals, found fulfillment in the Whig message. It was a theory dedicated to uniting equals peaceably through the self-interest of each. It promised order and harmony without sacrificing personal freedom and ambition or limiting America's rapid growth. Whether it could really have produced this utopia or not is another question. Nevertheless, this was the nature of the Whig vision, and those who found it particularly satisfying formed the constituency of the Whig party.

The Need for Reassurance

It is hard to imagine that a Whig might stand in need of reassurance. Some years ago, Marvin Meyers expressed the general view when he said of the Whig that "the fulfillment of liberal premises in capitalist progress was for them entirely natural and unproblematic."[36] Yet this statement is misleading. It is true that Whigs readily accepted the development of a modern capitalist economy and eagerly sought to accelerate its growth. It is also true that individually they suffered less than their opponents from frustration and inadequacy in the competitive individualistic society that developed along with it. One cannot say, however, that their adjustment to a changing society was untroubled. The Whig message, like that of the Jacksonians, was in part a message of reassurance for men beset by anxiety.

In 1839, the Boston *Courier* observed that "if the poor need encouragement, the rich sometimes need justification." While

Jacksonians were not necessarily poor and Whigs were not necessarily rich, the statement nonetheless makes an important point. Indeed, one of the most pervasive themes in Whig rhetoric has to do with the reassurance of men who needed to believe that self-interested striving need not be selfish and that good business need not involve bad ethics. To do this, Whig spokesmen were sometimes remarkably willing to give a great deal to the Jacksonian position. Thus, the New York *Tribune* declared that "no clear-headed man can doubt that the 'influences' surrounding a life in Trade are less wholesome, that the temptations to departure from the narrow path of rectitude are more frequent and specious, than in a life of Productive Labor." The conclusion drawn from this admission, however, was distinctly unJacksonian. For the *Tribune* went on to declare that "a man may live as righteously and usefully by Trade as by any other vocation." What was necessary was that trade "be revised and conformed to the spirit of Truth, Justice, Christianity and Philanthropy."[37]

Whiggish concern about the morality of modern commerce can be seen in numerous articles on the subject that appeared in *Hunt's Merchants' Magazine* in the late 1830s and early '40s. With titles such as "Mercantile Character," "The Moral Law of Contracts," and "The Morals of Trade," these articles sought to delineate the moral responsibilities of those tempted by the seductive opportunities to gain wealth presented by a modern economy. They argued that modern commerce provided too many opportunities to do wrong, and that the law allowed too much latitude to go wrong. A higher ethical standard than law was required. While acknowledging the ethical problems which beset the modern merchant, however, these pieces stressed the fact that the merchant also possessed a great power for good. A life in trade, when conducted with a proper attention to conscience, was a high calling. One writer could not see "why a man may not engage in trade from as pure and high motives as we suppose him to have who preaches the gospel." There was "a nobleness of character in the right course," maintained another.

"The aspirings of youth, the ambition of manhood, could receive no loftier moral direction than may be found in the sphere of business."[38]

Time and again Whig leaders reminded the rank and file that it was not only lawful but praiseworthy to strive and compete, although this must be within the context of a morally sensitive life. "It is . . . neither a sin nor a shame to feel within us, the workings of an active and enterprising disposition," declared one Whig moralist. What was "both sinful and shameful" was "to feel nothing else." Horace Greeley's *Tribune* announced, "We regard the ambition to heap up riches as groveling and despicable." But it quickly added that "few men can be truely independent or greatly useful without *some* property, and no man can innocently take upon himself the responsibilities of a husband and father without striving to provide for those who have a right to expect of him a subsistence." Another Whig agreed that "true passion for money, the mere desire to accumulate . . . is . . . demoralizing and debasing in itself." On the other hand, however, "the search after competence is unquestionably one of the best springs of action in a community, at least it is one whose good effects is [sic] apparent in the industry, the *employment,* and consequently the morals and happiness, of the great proportion of society."[39]

Messages like these were received gratefully by Whigs because the apparent conflict between the new individualism and the old communal virtues troubled many of them. In contrast with their Jacksonian contemporaries, Whigs felt themselves largely independent of coercive social pressures, although this did not exempt them from the need to believe that their lives had social meaning and value. It is necessary to bear in mind that, while the inner-directed man will be highly flexible as to means, his fundamental convictions have been determined by the internal moral gyroscope that keeps his life on course. In the case of the Whigs, their gyroscopes had been implanted by parents and role models whose own social norms were formed in a pre-industrial age, less attuned to the philosophy of individualism. Their children could be comfortable with the aggressive pursuit of self-interest only so long as they could persuade themselves that their activities were beneficial to others as well.

The Whig was quick to deny Jacksonian accusations that his party was dedicated to selfishness. Such accusations typically resembled that of the *Bay State Democrat* which charged that Whiggery was composed of men "who have little patriotism, little or no philanthrophy, and a large share of self-sufficiency, who worship at the shrine of mammon." But the Whig was stung by such criticism, nonetheless. His party did defend the pursuit of self-interest and glorified its contributions to the onward march of civilization. Yet within the Whig a firm commitment to individualism warred with the moral precepts of an earlier age. One Whig deplored in the pages of the Boston *Courier* that "our homes are too much locked up. We are too much intent on our own happiness, and sympathize too little with those around us." The *American Whig Review* also lamented the American propensity to give "too exclusive devotion . . . to the narrow circle of our own operations."[40]

Whigs needed to believe that their efforts ultimately benefited others. The most obvious manifestation of this need was the prominent participation of Whigs in the many movements for benevolent and humanitarian reform. The Whig belief in social interdependence described earlier was a more subtle manifestation of the same need. If all were tied together, then every constructive individual act could not help but redound to the benefit of others. Edward Everett's contention that "the interest of the capitalist is identical with that of the community" enabled him to argue that "whatever selfish objects" great investors may have, they cannot obtain them without "supplying the demand of the people for some great article of necessity, convenience, or indulgence." Such a belief allowed the Whig to go about his business of self-advancement happy in the thought that his efforts had social benefits.[41]

So, too, Daniel Webster's celebrations of union and Henry Clay's appeals to compromise carried conviction to Whigs precisely because they needed so much to believe that a society grounded upon individualism need not be characterized by strife and contention. Jacksonians, of course, were similarly troubled by the evidence of social discord around them. But while Jacksonians often seemed willing to forgo the advantages of modernity in order to recapture social harmony, Whigs— more convinced of the benefits of the new order—struggled to reconcile the new ways with the old morality.

Whig rhetoric, then, was not aimed at men whose accommodation to their age was entirely untroubled. Whigs harbored within themselves moral notions which they found difficult to reconcile with the individualistic values that dominated their lives. For the chief inhibition upon Whig aims was neither society nor institutions but the chastening effects of their own consciences. As David Riesman has observed, "We may sum up much that is significant about inner-direction by saying that, in society where it is dominant, its tendency is to protect the individual against the others at the price of leaving him vulnerable to himself."[42]

The Search for Understanding

Whigs, no less than Democrats, needed to comprehend their world. They needed an interpretation of the events of their time which would be consistent with their distinctive notions of how and why things happen. The rhetoric of the Whig party provided them with that interpretation.

Whigs were convinced that they had developed a blueprint for social progress. Since God had blessed Americans with a broad land, rich in natural resources, the question was how best to exploit the opportunities presented. Clearly, the situation called for citizens who were both free and enterprising, men who aggressively pursued their own interests but who willingly united their energies to promote collective interests. Equally important, these citizens must be enlightened and moral, aware that knowledge and self-discipline were essential ingredients in individual and social advancement. Furthermore, an energetic government, run by wise men of broad vision, should act as an auxiliary to individual effort. Such a government would recognize its responsibility not only to preserve order but to stimulate the productive activities of its citizenry as well. Since Whigs believed that America already possessed all these qualities to a large degree, its position was "unspeakably grand." It represented "the very greatest hope that the world has for the future of true progress." Indeed, Whigs perceived signs in their own time of the fruition of this hope. "History could not point to an instance of more rapid growth than had been realized by these United States," the Albany *Evening Journal* declared. All the elements of nineteenth-century progress had "united to convert a vast wilderness into a land of peace and plenty."[43]

But there were also grounds for grave apprehension. The election of Andrew Jackson to the presidency threatened to undo all that had been accomplished. Almost immediately he began to dismantle the framework for economic and social development that the national government had erected in the previous generation. The national bank, the protective tariff, and federally sponsored internal improvements all came under attack. It seemed to the Milledgeville *Southern Recorder* that Jackson was waging "war" on "the growing prosperity of the nation." The revolution in commercial policy introduced by Jackson and his followers, Calvin Colton maintained, broke up all the "established relations of the different parts of the community toward each other, and left all in a mass of confusion and ruin." Though Democrats claimed they were acting in the name of reform, Whigs saw nothing constructive in their policies. They were rather, as Thurlow Weed labeled them, "the Architects of Ruin at Washington." "Our adversaries," complained Horace Greeley, "inveterately do nothing, dare nothing, urge nothing for the good of mankind." It was bad enough that Democrats withheld from business the fostering hand that it was "their sacred duty to extend," but they seemed determined to undermine all efforts at civilized advance. "The opposition," asserted the *American Whig Review*, "is simply a destructive party."[44]

Whigs entirely rejected the Jacksonian contention that men required only the relaxation of artificial social constraints in order to realize their full potential. Not that Whigs believed, as had the Federalists of an earlier era, that human potential was severely limited. On the contrary, Whigs characteristically enlarged upon the untapped possibilities within each person. The realization of these possibilities, however, was another matter. Nature was less important than effort and education. William Seward expressed the Whig position succinctly. "Nature," said Seward, "has left all the human faculties in one sense incomplete, to be perfected by training for special and distinct pursuits." Success in any vocation was "proportioned to the measure of culture, training, industry, and perseverence brought into exercise."[45]

Whig views of man were, not coincidentally, akin to those of the evangelists of the day who promised that all could attain salvation if they were but willing to seek it. God no longer arbitrarily sanctified some and damned others, but offered salvation to any individual whose faith and actions demonstrated his worthiness. Similary, Whigs promised that all could be independent, even rich, with the proper character and industry. Of course they knew that all would not attain wealth; experience had shown that everyone would not exercise the self-mastery that ensured success. Spiritual and worldly possibilities were unlimited, but both required much of the individual to attain them. No mere lifting of restraints and ending of monopolies would beget paradise, either here or in the hereafter.

A more "natural" social order—the professed goal of Jacksonian policy—held no charm for Whigs. Indeed, the yearning of their opponents for a simpler, arcadian past appeared to them as the chief obstacle to a happy and prosperous republic. The alleged social advantages of mere liberation from social constraints Whigs viewed as both illusory and pernicious. The state of nature, Calvin Colton reminded his fellow Whigs, was "a state of *despotism and wretchedness*."[46] Without those artificial contrivances of human ingenuity that carried society forward to a higher state, Whigs believed that there could be no real progress. The Democrats' attempt to return to nature seemed to Whigs to threaten the very institutions and values upon which civilization depended. Whig rhetoric grew frantic in contemplation of the possibilities. The Albany *Evening Journal* claimed to believe that, in a Jacksonian world, "all the civil and religious institutions shall be swept away." In a similar vein, the Philadelphia *World* charged that the Jacksonian object "seems to be anarchy, the prostration of all government, the disturbance of the whole order of society." The fate of religion hung in the balance. "They would make a nation of Deists, Atheists and Barbarians," declared the Mobile *Advertiser and Chronicle*. "They are at open war with the morals and religion of the country." Education itself would not be long safe, for, once the churches were demolished, "our schools, our academies, our colleges, and seminaries of learning, will be assailed." Wicked as all this was, what alarmed Whigs most was the Jacksonian onslaught against the credit system.[47]

In the Whig mind, the credit system was as much symbol as fact, and on it rested their hopes for both the material and the moral advancement of America. Had the Jacksonian view prevailed earlier, maintained the *American Whig Review*, it "would have checked all national progress, and left us at the moment at the rear instead of the front of civilization. We should have had no canals, no railroads, no progress, and hardly a national existence." Were it to prevail now, "the grand enterprises of the country must be abandoned—and with them the spirit of improvement must cease." The destruction of the credit system, Calvin Colton insisted, will "destroy a people."[48]

The matter of credit also had serious implications for the moral fiber of society. When Calvin Colton declared that "credit is morality," he was expressing a typical Whig sentiment. Since credit was based on mutual confidence, the cornerstone of civilized life, those who sought to undermine it were in effect undermining the only basis for social order. Thus, the Milledgeville *Southern Recorder* argued that Jacksonians were attempting "to destroy the public morals by persuading people that no man is to be trusted." Similarly, the Detroit *Daily Advertiser* declared that Jacksonianism assails credit because "it is built up upon the hypothesis that there is no such thing as personal integrity."[49]

The Jacksonian attack on all that Whigs deemed essential to progress in all its forms angered and perplexed them. That a few perverse men might oppose the march of civilization they could understand, but that widespread support for such destructive programs should develop among the citizenry genuinely puzzled them. Most exasperating was the deep attachment so many Americans felt for Andrew Jackson, "a poor old superannuated President—in his best estate, but an ignorant and uneducated man of moderate capacity." The New York *Enquirer* declared that "the infatuation of the people of this country in their purblind devotion to General Jackson is utterly astonishing, and will be looked upon in a generation or two, as one of the most prominent delusions of the nineteenth century." Whereas the Jacksonian message had to explain why Whigs seemed set upon subverting the natural order which Democrats found so attractive, the Whig message had to explain why Jacksonians seemed determined to dismantle the institutions of progress so painstakingly built up.[50]

Whigs decided that they had found their answer in the nature of the Democratic constituency and the unscrupulousness of the Democractic leadership. Since, in their own estimation, the Whig position stood for enlightenment and progress, it followed that the opposition must be rooted in ignorance and debasement. For this reason, Whigs pointed in consternation to the illiteracy and provincialism of the Democratic rank and file. "IGNORANCE AND LOCOFOCOISM GO HAND IN HAND," shouted the headline on a Boston *Atlas* article reporting high rates of illiteracy where Democratic votes prevailed. They found no cause for surprise in the fact that immigrants, particularly those from the most backward nations of Europe, succumbed to Democratic blandishments. The Irish, in particular, fell into the ranks of the Democracy, Whigs believed, because "their minds have been so thoroughly subdued by their former depressed condition, that they seem utterly incapable of recovering elasticity, and of managing well for themselves." That so many of these, too, were Catholics, the Whigs found comprehensible, since the Church had always demanded intellectual dependency and subservience. Catholics were easily formed into masses and wielded by demagogues, asserted the Richmond *Whig*, a trait "resulting from the absolute control of the Priesthood over the ignorant classes."[51]

Taking advantage of this situation was the Democratic party, an organization, said Horace Greeley, run by a "race of hollow demagogues whose heaven is a majority." Seeking nothing but power, they used the public purse to enlist salaried officers in a political army whose "trained bands" of "misguided followers" were "ever ready to obey their smallest commands." Appealing to the passions and prejudices of the ignorant, manipulating those unaccustomed to think for themselves, and bribing the greedy with the spoils of office, Democratic leaders taught the people "to play the part of automatons at their own elections." A Democrat "is not allowed to think for himself," charged the Springfield *Republican*, "but his thinking must be done out by the wire pullers. If he presumes to do it, he is immediately lashed into the traces, or excommunicated from the church of 'the democracy.'" According to the Whigs, their opponents constituted a dangerous amalgam of political knaves and servile masses.[52]

Such a view of the opposition satisfied the mentality of the Whigs even as it worried them. It was the sort of interpretation calculated to appeal to men confident of themselves, in control of their own lives, and willing to face the uncertainties and temptations of modernity. Even the concerted opposition of half the country did not suggest to the Whig that there might be some defect in his vision of America. Opposition to a Whiggish future could come, he thought, only from those unable or unwilling to understand the benefits of improvement, those whose personal characters were debased by poverty and ignorance or corrupted by power and greed. Such men, it appeared, wanted to halt America's progress and return the country to the wilderness which it had once been. The Whig party and its program for political action were designed to see that this calamity did not occur.

The Roots of Policy

Whig policies were shaped by Americans who willingly embraced the modern world. They were confident of their ability to cope with it and optimistic about the benefits that they expected it to bestow on themselves and their children. Its complexity, artificiality, and impersonality held no terrors for them. They disciplined themselves enthusiastically to the requirements of an individualistic social order. By means of government and voluntary associations they sought to unite their countrymen by ties of self-interest in pursuit of ends beyond their individual capacities. Self-advancement and social progress were their goals and they saw no contradiction between the two.

Believing that government was a powerful and indispensable auxiliary to private effort in the advancement of civilization, Whigs had no hesitation about expanding the scope of its operations on all levels. As inner-directed men they had little fear of the distant and impersonal. As insiders they were not worried about energetic government becoming oppressive. Bolstered by the constitutional philosophy of broad construction, they encouraged energy and resourcefulness on the part of the federal authority. In Henry Clay's "American System," the Whigs proposed a sweeping plan for economic development. A national bank provided capital for entrepreneurial activity, and a circulating medium to facilitate trade among Americans spread over a vast land. A protective tariff encourged the development of a manufacturing interest which would complement the existing interests of agriculture and commerce. Federal aid to internal improvements promoted a comprehensive network of transportation and communication. Thus, the Whig agenda was broadly nationalistic, geared to drawing together the disparate localities, states, and regions of the young Republic.[53]

While the Whig program was national in orientation, much of it was intended to be carried out in the states. Whig state legislators were far more likely than their opponents to grant corporate privileges to banks, businesses, and non-profit associations, and they were far less likely to favor restrictions on paper money. Whigs expected state governments to do their part in furthering the transportation and communication network of the country by authorizing and subsidizing internal improvements. Moreover, Whigs looked to the state governments for a wide range of social and humanitarian endeavors, including the construction of schools, asylums, and poorhouses.[54]

Unlike their opponents, Whigs felt no special need to insulate from government either their religion or their economic relations. The slogans of "separation of church and state" and "separation of bank and state" had no appeal to them. While they recognized the right to freedom of worship and had no inclination to revive the idea of an established church, they did consider the moral notions of Christianity one of "the pillars on which rests the temple of freedom." Believing that the country would be well served if the people entertained "a profound respect for religion," they expected government to do its part to foster such respect. And the idea that government should separate itself from banks, key agents in producing economic prosperity, was sheer folly. Aside from individual enterprise, said the *American Monthly Magazine*, the chief element in national greatness was "a disposition on the part of government to foster, to encourage, and assist that enterprise."[55]

Whigs did not share their opponent's fear of accelerating the pace of change. They wished to put no limits on the growth of transporation, communication, manufacturing, commerce, and agriculture. Modernity and the countless benefits which they thought would accrue from it could not come too rapidly for them. As the Fayetteville *Observer* rhetorically asked its readers, "Do we grow too fast? Is our enterprise too great? . . . Are our comforts and enjoyments so multiplied that a sound policy requires that they be curtailed?"[56] Whigs were, however, wary of making frequent alterations in the constitutions and laws. But this conservatism was often actually a consequence of their desire to promote rapid economic advancement. Legal instability created uncertainty and distrust among individuals seeking to plan for the future. It made men unwilling to take the risks which a dynamic economy required.

Whigs were anxious to further economic growth because their notions of freedom and equality, the fundamental principles on which democracy rested, required a prosperous America. Freedom required prosperity because, Whigs maintained, a people degraded by poverty must ever be slaves.[57] No man could think or act for himself if he were dependent upon the favors of another for his survival. Hence, the American people could preserve their freedom only so long as economic abundance could be spread widely among the populace. Freedom for the Whig, then, did not require liberation from the institutions of modern economic development, as it did for his Jacksonian opponent. Its preservation was crucially dependent upon the benefits they bestowed.

Equality, too, was for the Whig a consequence of prosperity. In the Whig mind, equality did not imply any parity of wealth. It meant the equal opportunity to acquire wealth. This type of equality was not compromised by a disparity of fortunes in society. So long as a diversified, dynamic economy kept wealth circulating and continued to open new avenues of prosperity to the ambitious, Whigs were satisfied that equal opportunity existed. The real threat to equality was posed, they believed, by

Jacksonian economic notions which imperiled the possibilities for individual advancement which Whig development presented.

Whigs admitted that the fast-paced world to which they were committed made severe demands upon the individual. Progress multiplied temptations as fast as opportunities. Individualism increased one's vulnerability even as it eroded the community to which one would naturally look for support. Because they were more detached from their fellow men and because they knew at first hand the temptations and isolation of nineteenth-century America, they were particularly sensitive to the personal stresses of their times. It was for this reason that three institutions bulked so large in Whig thought—the family, the church, and the school. These were the institutions devoted to helping Americans build the kind of character which their age demanded. Only the school could receive financial support from Whig governments, but all of these institutions received moral support from Whigs. For the Whig was convinced that they were essential to the prosperity, even to the continued existence, of the American government.

In sum, there is much truth in Edwin C. Rozwenc's observation that Whigs were more successful than their opponents "in creating a party ideology that was applicable to the changing social conditions of the Jacksonian era."[58] The strength of the Jacksonian movement, however, is evidence that many Americans were reluctant to surrender the comfortable security of an older way of life. Perhaps it was best that so many were reluctant, since Whig policies were ultimately influenced by the Jacksonian's justifiable concern with the consequences of modernity. Indeed, the thinking of the entire Jacksonian generation was shaped by a distinctive Democratic-Whig dialogue regarding the nature of an individualistic society.

PART TWO:

The Dialogue of Parties

A culture achieves identity not so much through the ascendancy of one particular set of convictions as through the emergence of its peculiar and distinctive dialogue.   R. W. B. LEWIS

The differing world views of Jacksonians and Whigs informed their dialogue over the major issues of the age. Though some of the issues may have seemed remote to many Americans of the Jacksonian generation, they became immediate and compelling when they were discussed within the context of individualism. Each public issue necessarily became part of a national dialogue on the proper nature of the individual's relations with his fellow men. Some of the most important issues that the parties addressed concerned the individual's relationships to the public sphere, the rule of law, and the social hierarchy.

Jacksonians and Whigs differed sharply over the propriety of enlarging the public sphere. They debated whether energetic government enhanced or diminished the well-being of Americans. They disagreed on whether men could exercise power over others without becoming corrupt or tyrannical. Finally, they argued about the degree of unity that was necessary for the nation and about what effect geographic expansion would have on the ties which united Americans.

While both parties desired a peaceful and orderly society, they saw different roles for the rule of law to play in achieving such a society. They could not agree on how best to ensure widespread adherence to the law or on what degree of adherence was desirable. Underlying their disagreement lay a more fundamental conflict over whether legislation enlarged or constricted the realm of personal freedom. All of their differences were best revealed in their reaction to challenges to the abstract rule of law and in their attitudes toward America's highest law, the Constitution.

Jacksonians and Whigs also took different views of the economic inequality which marked their age. Though both sides acknowledged the theoretical legitimacy of a disparity of fortunes, they clashed over whether the actual disparities they observed were justifiable. More important, they engaged in a profound debate over the effect this inequality would have on the rest of American life.

❧ 3 ❧

Private and Public:
The Individual and Society

The best government is that which governs least.
                                        Democratic Review[1]

*The legitimate object of government is to do for a community of
people, whatever they need to have done, but can not do, at all,
or can not, so well do, for themselves—in their separate, and
individual capacities.*   ABRAHAM LINCOLN[2]

Alexis de Tocqueville feared that as individualism spread, men
would forget those common concerns, interests, and purposes
which constitute the sphere of public activity. Ultimately individualism could lead to a society in which all virtue had been
destroyed and people were "absorbed in downright selfishness,"
but Tocqueville believed that, at first, it "only saps the virtues of
public life."[3] When each individual is free to follow the dictates
of his own will, when he readily leaves others free to pursue their
own ends in their own ways, it becomes difficult to discover what
if any ties still bind him to that collective identity we call society.
The very existence of society is called into question. Even more
problematical is the individual's relationship to the state, for, as
the coercive agent of society, government has a unique power to
define and enforce the individual's responsibilities to his fellow
man.

The disposition to consider oneself alone, to deny one's relationship to the whole, has been a recognizable strand in the American character.[4] Although Americans have seldom isolated themselves completely or denied the legitimacy of public obligations, they have been prone to place severe limits on the public sphere. In their ideals and actions they have questioned the contention of the ancient Greeks that man's ultimate satisfaction comes from association with his fellows in the public arena. Americans have expanded the private, more intimate sphere of life in a manner that has threatened at times to deny the public sphere entirely.

The political problems posed by such an attitude were first manifested during the Jacksonian era. How was a public sphere to be created, perfected, and perpetuated among a people disposed to consider themselves as standing alone, unconnected in their interests or destiny? Was such a public sphere even necessary? What were one's duties within it and where were its limits? What was the proper relationship between this public and the apparently more important private sphere? These were some of the questions which an individualistic society raised for public life. The two great political parties of the day were at the center of the controversies which such questions engendered and, whatever the variations among individuals, characteristic party positions in these controversies can be observed.

The Democratic tendency was to limit the extent and the power of the public sphere. The Jacksonians' great party newspaper, the *Globe,* announced at the head of each issue: "The World is Governed too much." According to the *Globe,* the proper language for a "proud freeman" to speak to the general government was "PROTECT ME and LET ME ALONE." It disparaged the fact that "some of our people are not content with *liberty.* Instead of looking to government for *protection* only, they ask for *aid.*" The Columbus *Democrat* was proud that "we don't look to Government for relief—we don't call on Hercules to help us— we rely upon our honest industry and frugality alone to release us from all our embarrassments."[5]

Democrats were not to be taken in by appeals to the time-honored concept of the "public good." The *Democratic Review* characterized that phrase as one "to which the lives and fortunes of millions have been wantonly sacrificed." "The great object of government," the *Review* went on, "is to secure every man in the enjoyment of his rights. Beyond this, it should not meddle with the affairs of men." That "the affairs of men" should have so little connection with government was a novel conception. Democrats denied that government was a vehicle for human advancement, that it had any responsibility to do good. Each individual was to seek his own good in his own way, neither hindered nor helped by public power. Democrats chastised those who believed that "human nature must be fostered, fondled, or stimulated to exertion by legislative interposition." The public management of men's affairs was not only unnecessary, it was wrong. "Understood as a central, consolidated power, managing and directing the various interests of the society, all government is evil, and the parent of evil." The democratic basis of this public power made little difference to members of Jackson's party: "A strong and active democratic *government,* in the common sense of the term, is an evil, differing only in degree and mode of operation, and not in nature, from a strong despotism."[6]

Whigs, on the other hand, believed that there was such a thing as the public good and that it was the responsibility of the government to promote it. They were not averse to asking the government for aid; indeed, they believed that it was for such aid that government had been created. Governor Seward of New York declared that "it is the object of republican institutions to encourage and stimulate improvement of the physical condition of the country, and to promote the moral and intellectual advancement of its citizens." The *American Whig Review* asserted its belief that "the people are entitled to demand from the general government its aid in advancing the great popular interests, commerce, manufactures, agriculture." "There is no shallower cant," John Pendleton Kennedy maintained, "than this cry of 'let us alone.'"[7]

Horace Greeley, the Whig (and later Republican) publicist, wrote tellingly of the differences between the Whigs and their opponents on the proper role of public action. Whigs, he said, believed that government had "great *affirmative* functions and uses" and was not simply "a social engine for the repression of outrages and crimes." Greeley traced the Democrats' theories of government back to Thomas Paine's axiom that "society is the manifestation of the Virtues of Man; Government of his Vices," and he was certain that such ideas of government were destructive of all civilized advance. He charged that "on every great question of the day," the *Democratic Review* "takes ground in direct opposition to the cause of National and Social Progress. . . . On no single point is the spirit of the *Review*, constructive, creative, hopeful of the future." His vision of progress depended on associated activity encouraged, regulated, and enforced by the state. Greeley rejected the Jacksonians' rush toward "a savage and jealous individual independence, regardless of social and general well-being"; he championed the Whig cause, whose purpose was, he said, "to harmonize and cherish all interests, and bind them in the silken bonds of mutual advantage and general welfare." He argued for "*positive legislation* which will advance the highest interests, and promote the permanent well-being of our great nation." The people, he said, "look for action; they require that something shall be *done* for their good, and that all patriotism and all republican spirit shall not evaporate in empty words."[8]

The Whig willingness to use public power for collective purposes must, of course, not be exaggerated. Sidney G. Fisher spoke for many good Whigs when he argued that "it is a mistake to suppose that the supreme authority of the State should be an all-pervading power, regulating the pursuits and watching over the interests of individuals. These may be safely left to the impulse of personal interest, and to the guidance of personal knowledge." Government interference was to be limited, but Whigs believed that there were some "objects essential to the existence and happiness of society, to the attainment of which individual exertion is incompetent." Such a conception was a far cry from a planned society where government not only regulates but directs the activities of individuals. Whigs could accept a larger sphere for public action because they believed that the limited public programs which they advocated—including, for example, currency regulation, a protective tariff, aid to internal improvements, and public education—would facilitate rather than impede the individual's pursuit of private ends. The action might be public, but the ultimate test of its legitimacy was its ability to advance private interests.[9]

It may seem paradoxical that Whigs, the most individualistic of Americans, should see a great role for collective action, while Jacksonians should be concerned to remain independent of public purposes. In fact, there is no inconsistency in these party orientations.

There were three reasons why Whigs were more willing than Jacksonians to give comparatively large scope to public action. First, being more confident of their abilities and more secure in their independence, they were more sanguine that an expanded public sphere would enhance their own lives. Second, experiencing the relative weakness of the isolated individual in the face of the new economic and social forces, they were more conscious of the need for aggregating the powers of men behind projects beyond their individual capacities. Third, many Whigs had been brought up on an older communal ethic which required each person to concern himself with the welfare of the whole. Now, though the typical Whig's feelings had, in Tocqueville's words, "turned towards himself alone," his values still demanded that he involve himself in a larger common purpose. Whig public policy enabled many men to seek their own ends while enjoying the idea that they were simultaneously assisting others to pursue theirs.

Jacksonians, on the other hand, were not as secure in their independence and were thus more jealous of it. Jacksonians were disturbed by Whig efforts to draw them into an ever-widening world. They resented those who continually sought to expand the sphere of their social obligations through broad definitions of "common interests" and "common destinies." To Jacksonians, collective action was justified only to protect them from still further collective involvement. The Democratic party drew individuals together to resist the efforts of Whigs to compel their greater participation in the institutions of modernity.

The Jacksonian's attempt at self-direction, to act in his own ways for his own purposes, was threatened by the Whig notion that his destiny was connected with that of society as a whole. But the threat was not only psychological. Whigs were in some cases prepared to use government to force the individual's cooperation. It is little wonder, then, to find in Jacksonian rhetoric a bristly independence, a sometimes extravagant denial that the individual has obligations toward others, and an unwillingness to surrender any portion of independence to achieve larger public ends. One who feels only half free does not readily compromise that freedom which he enjoys. He who feels cheated conducts transactions reluctantly and suspiciously. An outsider is rarely confident that the "welfare of the whole" has anything to do with him.

Private and Public

One of the most fundamental problems of public life in the age of Jackson was to determine the proper relationship between the public and private spheres of human activity. Whigs saw no distinct line separating the public from the private. They not only accepted the possibility that the two spheres might overlap, they argued that government had a responsibility to advance private interests. In the Jacksonian mind, however, public and private were two distinctly separate spheres. As Orestes Brownson put it, "Where the rights and duties of the individual begin, there end those of the state; where those of the state begin, there end those of the individual." Moreover, Jacksonians wanted to restrict the public sphere in order to allow private affairs the greatest possible latitude. The Democrat was "jealous of power, and always interprets all doubtful questions so as to increase the power of the people, rather than of the government." Democrats, especially ones with economic interests in government projects, did not always act in accordance with this maxim, but it was central to the meaning of the Jacksonian movement.[10]

Freedom to the Jacksonian meant freedom from government authority. American liberty, Orestes Brownson asserted, "is not the power to choose our own form of government, to elect our own rulers, and through them to make and administer our own laws." Rather, it was each man's ability to exercise all his God-given rights without government interference. Brownson wished to "throw around each individual a bulwark of sanctity, and not permit society to break through it." This sacred private sphere was to be an immense realm. The rights Brownson wanted to protect were not merely those enumerated in the Bill of Rights. They were not just "the rights of citizenship or certain private rights," he argued. "They stretch over nearly the whole domain of human activity." The private sphere was not to be broached on any pretext. "We may not control a man's natural liberty even for the man's good," Brownson declared. "So long as the individual trespasses upon none of the rights of others, or throws no obstacle in the way of their free and full exercise, government, law, public opinion even, must leave him free to take his own course."[11]

But in the mid-nineteenth century this ideal was still unrealized and Jacksonians saw great and growing obstacles in the way of its attainment. There were "two antagonistic tendencies at work; one to individual freedom, . . . the other, a tendency to centralization, to the merging of the individual in the state, in the mass." Brownson called the latter "the only dangerous tendency in this country." Democrats were urged "to contend manfully for individual rights, and resist at the threshold every encroachment of power." True democracy, said Brownson, "takes care not to lose the man in the citizen."[12]

Such care was especially necessary when government threatened to become more centralized. In the age of Jackson, the

Democratic party feared efforts to shift the balance of public authority from the states to Washington. The Democrat's "first duty" was "to watch that the Federal Government does not swallow up the State governments." The "central character" of the capital caused it "to engross as much of the public business of the country as possible." The states' rights concept was an important bulwark against the widening distance between individuals and the ever-dangerous public sphere. When authority becomes centralized, "the individual finds the government so far from him, and his own share in it comparatively so insignificant, that he soon comes to feel himself individually of little or no importance, and when he so feels he ceases from all manly defence of his rights, and loses himself in the mass."[13]

Democrats were intent on maintaining a strict separation between the public and private spheres. In the Jacksonian mind there could be no policy—apart from the need to protect each individual from the aggressions of others—that could serve both public and private ends. The merest hint that legislation resulted in private gain was enough to convince Democrats that such laws could not be in the public interest. This idea is evident in Jackson's Bank veto message. Because the capital of the new Bank was to be greatly increased, it was obvious to Jackson that the Bank was designed "not for public but for private purposes." Because the Bank paid a bonus to the government for its charter, it was clear that "exclusive privileges were given for private, not public benefit." That legislation could serve both private interests and the general public simultaneously was inconceivable. When the *Hampshire Republican* boasted of the Democratic party—"So general and disinterested are its principles, that they are incapable of subserving mere private ends"— it was giving the highest praise.[14]

The separation of church and state served as a model and a rallying cry for Jacksonian efforts to disengage public power from what they considered purely private areas of life. The party was able to use the issue effectively against Sabbatarian laws, proclamations of Thanksgiving and fast days, and occa-

sionally penetrations by religion into public education. Early in
his second term as President, for example, Jackson refused to
name a fast day because he feared to "disturb the security which
religion now enjoys in this country, in its complete separation
from the political concerns of the General Government."[15] But
the real battles for separation of church and state had already
been fought. The applications of this principle in the Jacksonian
period were usually matters on which reasonable men might
differ and few Whigs ever considered restoring public support
to particular denominations.

The war against Whig financial institutions, however, was not
over, and the separation of church and state became a model for
the separation of bank and state. When the Panic of 1837 struck,
there were already many Democrats who, like William Leggett,
viewed the bank policies of the Jackson Administration as "but a
period of transition." Jackson had destroyed the national bank,
but he left the federal government more closely tied to the state
banks than before. "We desire the [complete] divorcement of
politicks from banking," wrote Leggett. "We believe that nothing
but evil has hitherto flowed from the connexion of bank and
state; and we believe that nothing but good will result from their
complete separation." To the *Democratic Review,* a state bank
system was nothing but "the lesser of two kindred evils." It, too,
was an "unnatural" alliance which the writer looked to Van
Buren's Independent Treasury scheme to bring to an end.[16]

In the wake of the panic, radical Jacksonians called upon
government at all levels to divorce itself more completely than
ever from private interests. The *Democratic Review* argued that
the separation of the federal government from the banking
system was "an immense achievement for a single step—yet that
step has been but across the threshold of Reform." The underlying principle had next to be applied to the state governments.
As a general rule, "government should have as little as possible
to do with the general business and interests of the people."[17]

By the early 1840s radical Jacksonian papers such as the *Bay
State Democrat* were ready to put this principle into effect. They

fought for the separation of government from all banks, all corporations, all business interests, no matter what public services they were alleged to perform. In a convention address of 1841, Democrats in Massachusetts were told to "separate business and state as jealously as you would church and state. . . . Law-made wealth and law-made religion are equally obnoxious." Radical Jacksonians found justifiable no instance of government involvement in the economy. To them, "the idea that the General Government should undertake to regulate the exchanges, is as absurd as it would be to declare that the General Government should transport the produce of the farmer to market." They opposed state support for railroad building because "if a State may build a rail-road, there is no conceivable enterprise having the least claim to be called *public*, to which it may not extend its patronage."[18]

To the Whigs, a government which did not involve itself in economic life would be shirking its duty. It had an obligation to foster private enterprise, said Greeley's New York *Tribune*, "to encourage every development of it, and to lend it all the assistance properly in its power." In the Whig view, since government had an obligation under the Constitution to regulate the currency, it had an implied obligation to regulate the banks which issued it. Whigs thus objected strenuously to Van Buren's Independent Treasury, which was designed to separate the federal government entirely from the currency transactions of the private citizen. To Daniel Webster the policy was "a rash dereliction of duty, a sort of headstrong refusal to execute plain constitutional obligations." Both Webster and Horace Greeley observed that Andrew Jackson, even in his most irresponsible moments, had never gone so far as to deny the obligation of the government to provide a sound currency for private transactions.[19]

Whigs rejected absolutely the view that there was an inevitable antagonism between the public and the private spheres. In former times, when the great mass of the people had no voice in their government, they admitted that this might have been the case. Under the republican form of government that existed in nineteenth-century America, however, the Whigs believed that the power of government could safely serve the interests of all. The New York *Enquirer* expressed its impatience with Democratic insistence upon a "broad line . . . of distinction between the Government and the People." So, too, did Ralph Waldo Emerson. As he so often did, Emerson caught the spirit abroad among many of his countrymen: "I confess I lose all respect for this tedious denouncing of the state. The state is our neighbors; our neighbors are the state. It is folly to treat the state as if it were some individual arbitrarily willing thus and so." This was the Whig view—that the state could have no interests distinct from the welfare of its members.[20]

This being so, the Whigs sought to create closer bonds between the people and the government. Here they confronted the reality behind Tocqueville's observation that, in an individualistic society, "it is difficult to draw a man out of his own circle to interest him in the destiny of the state, because he does not clearly understand what influence the destiny of the state can have upon his own lot." The average American, immersed in his private affairs, had little notion of how legislation, conceived in support of broad public purposes, might help him. Thus, the task of Whig orators and publicists was to attempt to convince the individual that ultimately his welfare and prosperity were dependent upon the welfare and prosperity of the whole. "Whatsoever promotes communication, whatsoever extends general business, whatsoever encourages enterprise, or whatsoever advances the general wealth and prosperity of other states," Daniel Webster told an audience in Bangor, Maine, in 1835, "must have a plain direct and powerful bearing on your own prosperity." The crux of the matter was that legislation be framed with a view to serving the public good. That some private interests might benefit more than others in the process was in itself no objection, so long as these contributed to the general advance of all.[21]

The most controversial public issue of the era, the relation of government to the banking system, demonstrates the Whig approach to the relationship between the public and the private spheres. In a rejoinder to Jackson's Bank veto message in 1832, Daniel Webster dismissed the President's objection that the national bank benefited private investors with the observation that the very "object aimed at by such institutions is to connect the public safety and convenience with private interests." Moreover, "if a [national] bank charter is not to be granted, because to some extent, it may be profitable to the stockholders, no charter can be granted. The objection lies against all banks." In an 1837 attack on Van Buren's Sub-Treasury plan, Henry Clay went further. "In making war upon the banks," said Clay, "you wage war upon the people of the United States." He urged his listeners to remember that "we are all—People—States—Union—Banks, bound up and interwoven together, united in fortune and destiny." Three years later, he returned to the same theme: "The divorce of the state from banks . . . is not the only separation it [the Sub-Treasury plan] makes; it is a separation of the government from the constituency; a disunion of the interests of the servants of the people, from the interests of the people."[22]

In their efforts to convince Americans that private self-interests depended upon an enlargement of the public sphere, Whigs were again testifying to something that Tocqueville had noted about democracy in America. "When men are no longer united among themselves by firm and lasting ties," he wrote, "it is impossible to obtain the co-operation of any great number of them unless you can persuade every man whose help you require that his private interest obliges him voluntarily to unite his exertions to the exertions of all others."[23]

By the mid-1830s many Americans were relatively untroubled by human relations based upon mutual self-interest and were confident that public authority could be exercised in such a way as to serve generally beneficial purposes. Such people tended to support Whig efforts to pursue rapid national development with the aid of the state. But there were also many others who resented the creation of an impersonal world and who resisted the aggressive use of public authority which threatened to transform even their private sphere of activities. They tried to separate themselves from this new world, to compartmentalize their lives in order to preserve what they could of a simpler past. Because of the way they perceived the changes they were experiencing, they doubted both the efficacy and the purity of collective efforts to guide and shape the new social order.

The Efficacy of Public Action

Although the nineteenth-century is generally considered "the high noon of laissez-faire," in Jacksonian America there were strong pressures on government to promote national development.[24] There was a pressing need for a national economic infrastructure—a skeletal framework of transport, currency, and credit that would facilitate commercial exchanges and provide a general basis for economic growth. But despite agreement on the need for such an infrastructure, there was strong disagreement about the role government should play in creating it. In the age of Jackson, the chief contests over the proper scope of public authority were fought on an economic battleground.

Whigs advocated the energetic use of government authority to promote rapid economic development, while Democrats generally opposed the use of public powers for such ends. Democratic objections to government involvement in economic life were several, but perhaps the most significant was that Jacksonians simply did not believe that such involvement could have the desired effect: the greatest possible economic well-being for all Americans.

Government action, Democrats believed, could in no way improve upon the undirected action of individuals in the economy. The New York *Evening Post* was convinced that men were "the best judges in their own affairs" and believed that they "should be permitted to seek their own happiness in their own way, untrammeled by the capricious interference of legislative bungling." The Columbus *Democrat* declared simply that Democrats "believe they can work out their own prosperity better than any one can do it for them." The *Globe* agreed. "Nothing is better attested by experience," it insisted, "than the doctrine that individuals will manage their private affairs with most success when *let alone.*"[25]

Government attempts to facilitate the combination of individuals for productive purposes were ill-advised. The *Boston Quarterly Review* reported that "the spirit of association is fast giving way to the more powerful engine of progress, individuality." Previously, the power of the lone man had been "divided, subdivided, and weakened through multiplied associations." Now, however, the *Review* observed, "The great idea, that the whole is best served by the perfection of the parts, is becoming more and more the ruling sentiment." Moreover, Jacksonians maintained that associations, particularly those with corporate privileges granted by the state, tended to restrict opportunity and limit freedom. Such associations could only impede, they could not further economic development. In light of this fact, the Boston *Morning Post* argued that "competition, instead of combination, is what the public good requires."[26]

Stimulation of economic enterprise, Jacksonians believed, was unnecessary and counterproductive. Since Americans were "notoriously, a moving, stirring people," the *Globe* maintained, there was "more danger that we should do too much, than we should do too little." There was no need to increase incentives to get ahead, said the *Democratic Review*. The desire to get ahead was built into human nature. "The injunction to labor there written," said the *Review,* is already "far more imperative than Human law could make it." It was the conviction of the *Globe* that America's progress had been "trammelled and obstructed, rather than impelled and facilitated, by the excess to which our system is so liable." William Leggett eloquently summarized the Jacksonian view of Whig economic stimulus in 1836: "They dug canals, where no commerce asked for the means of transportation; they opened roads where no travellers desired to penetrate; and they built cities where there were none to inhabit."[27]

Jacksonians wanted capital left in private hands where it would do the most good. Public control of it was necessarily inefficient. How could Americans benefit when their tax dollar was given back to them "after a year's detention" and "with a deduction of twenty cents to pay collectors and clerks who have been employed to take it away and bring it back?" Even the best-intentioned efforts to expend public funds were bound to be unfruitful. Public charities, said the New York *Evening Post,* "are founded on erroneous principles, and do infinitely more harm than good." The *Evening Post* professed to be aware of many New York charities "founded in the most amiable and benevolent motives, that annually add very largely to the sum of human misery, by ill-judged exertions to relieve it." Americans were best served when the government left "every man to take care of himself, and of those who have a natural claim to his protection."[28]

Rather than such misguided legislating for the general good, which was, according to the New York *Evening Post for the Country,* "altogether too general to be perceived or felt by individuals," Jacksonians wanted most human relations left to the regulation of nature. The *Democratic Review* believed that if government limited itself to "a system of administration of justice between man and man . . . the floating atoms will distribute and combine themselves . . . into a far more perfect and harmonious result than if government, with its 'fostering hand,' undertake to disturb, under plea of directing, the process." This freedom to associate according to the "laws of nature" the *Review* called "the fundamental principle of the philosophy of democracy." If the world were not yet perfected, it was because this principle had been imperfectly applied, "all human society having been hitherto perpetually chained down to the ground by myriads of lilliputian fetters of artificial government and prescription."[29]

The party of Jackson was convinced that "legislation has been the fruitful parent of nine-tenths of all the evil, moral and physical, by which mankind has been afflicted since the creation of the world." Certainly no regulation of the economy was required, since "the laws of trade, having been enacted by God himself, . . . cannot be resisted with impunity." "Commerce unshackled with tariffs, and Banks unconnected with the Government, will gradually regulate each other—or rather individual interests in the community will regulate both." In fact, little else was required "to carry a state to the highest degree of opulence, but peace, easy taxes, and a tolerable administration of justice; all the rest being brought about by the natural course of things."[30]

Whigs explicitly rejected the Jacksonian principle that mankind's affairs would attain their highest development if they were left free to order themselves. They denied the existence of any "natural" social order which would result in anything other than fierce competition, disorder, and violence. Even if these evils could be averted, the principle of "let alone" would lead only to backwardness and stagnation. In the Whig mind, the vital functions performed by the public sphere made the difference between barbarism and civilization. If Jacksonian principles were consistently applied, Whigs maintained, national wealth and progress would be destroyed and the country returned to the wilderness it had once been.[31]

While the Jeffersonian vision of a nation of farmers still appealed to many Jacksonians, Americans who rallied to the Whig standard believed that "a merely agricultural community always must remain in a rude and stationary condition." They acknowledged the value of a rural population, but they feared that such a population would remain at "a dead level of mere material comfort, unless it be surrounded and interpenetrated, by centres of more varied industry and enterprise: places where the genius for other pursuits, which will inevitably appear in almost every family among this population, may find its legitimate sphere of action, instead of chafing in uncongenial pursuits, or rusting in inactivity." "Sure I am, as sure as I am of any principle, moral or political," said Daniel Webster, "that, if there is such a thing as benefiting the agriculture of the country, it is to be accomplished by urging forward manufactures and the mechanical arts."[32]

At the center of Whig thought was a profound appreciation of diversified economic growth and the wondrous ways it had transformed the lives of Americans. Progress, they believed, was dependent upon retaining and accelerating the changes which had already taken place in the production of material prosperity. But such progress could be achieved only if government stepped in to stimulate, regulate, and harmonize the forces which capitalism had set loose in the world.

Whigs spurned the Jacksonian notion that isolated individuals were more productive than those who combined their efforts. They sought to use the state to consolidate the powers of individual citizens by its public policies and to facilitate the aggregation of capital and men through its creation of private corporations. To a much greater extent than Jacksonians, they believed in the necessity and the beneficial consequences of bringing together individuals who could accomplish little as long as they remained separate. As Webster noted, "There are many objects, of great value to man, which cannot be attained by unconnected individuals, but must be attained, if at all, by association." And though Whigs were disposed to use voluntary associations for many of their efforts, they also agreed with Webster that for many objects "government seems the most natural and efficient association. Voluntary association has done much, but it cannot do all." Whigs believed that unaided private efforts were not up to such massive projects as the building of major roads, canals, and railways. "To wait for individual enterprise to accomplish such improvements," William Seward told New Yorkers, "is to delay them for a subsequent, perhaps a remote, generation." The New York *Enquirer* agreed, proclaiming its belief that these "are projects of too vast moment and too universal an interest, to be left to the unaided efforts of individuals. It considered them as "falling within the legitimate province of State legislation."[33]

Whigs did not share the Jacksonians' unqualified faith in the virtues of economic competition. They acknowledged the merits of competition as a spur to effort, but then extolled the superior virtues of harmony, cooperation, and mutual benefit. After the nation experienced its first real depression in 1819, Henry Clay expressed pain that "our people present the spectacle of a vast assemblage of jealous rivals, all . . . jostling each other in their way," to compete for a place in foreign markets which were already glutted with goods. He believed that government, through appropriate legislation, could transform competitors into men bound together in a harmonious system of mutually beneficial endeavors.[34]

Clay's American System, which was designed to further the growth of diverse but complementary economic interests, was supposed to create such harmony. The tariff would integrate city and country, industry and farming in a mutually beneficial cycle of growth. The farms would feed the cities and the cities supply the farms with industrial goods. Internal improvements would open markets to remote farming areas, taking the strain off those lands with easy access to current markets. At the same time, good transportation would stimulate urban growth by facilitating the movement of necessary agricultural products into the cities. A properly regulated currency system—which provided a uniform, readily acceptable, and easily transferable unit of exchange—would facilitate trade between widely distant individuals and markets. And trade, after all, as Calvin Colton said, was "mutual help for mutual benefit."[35]

Productivity was as important as diversification in the attempt to mitigate the evils of economic competition. If the economy was not sufficiently productive, if it was unable to provide ample opportunity to the enterprising, then competition would become destructive rather than beneficial. When Whigs looked to England and saw the "gigantic and horrible evils resulting from the competition among laborers for the same employment," they felt they had "discovered the pitfall of modern civilization, the inevitable doom of unrestricted, of *unadjusted* competition." Unless this pitfall was avoided, there could "be no continuous progress for the race," and "modern civilization, like the ancient,

must fall into ruin." In his own country Henry Clay had seen the
same problem after the Panic of 1819. It was a time, he then
said, when "the existing occupations of our society, those of
agriculture, commerce, navigation, and the learned professions,
are overflowing with competitors, and . . . the want of employment is severely felt."[36]

The Whig remedy to this problem was government-stimulated
economic growth. If Americans were not to compete destruc-
tively, there had to be ample demand for their labor and sufficient opportunity for their ambition. Deeply impressed with the
expansive forces of the age and the fierce ambitions of a free
people, Whigs sought to use government to assure lucrative employment for all Americans. As William Seward observed,
"Action is the condition of our existence." As governor of New
York, he knew that if his state did not sufficiently accommodate
the aspirations of its citizens, they would "seek other regions
where society is less tranquil, and where ambition enjoys greater
freedom, enterprise higher motives, and labor richer rewards."[37]

Whiggery, through devices like Clay's American System, attempted to combine harmony with opportunity. Clay himself
declared that "wise legislators" would have as "a prominent
object . . . to multiply vocations and extend the business of
society." "By creating a new extensive business, then," he continued, "we should not only give employment to those who want
it, and augment the sum of national wealth by all that this new
business would create, but we should ameliorate the condition of
those who are now engaged in existing employments." It was
this powerful ability to stimulate growth and create opportunity
which in the Whig mind justified the use of public power. Such
public power did not limit the private sphere, but rather gave it
an expansive force which it could not have attained on its own.
As Clay said, "The truth is, that the System *excites* and *creates*
labor, and this labor creates wealth, and this new wealth com-
municates additional ability to consume, which acts on all the
objects contributing to human comfort and enjoyment." While
the Jacksonian *Globe* disparaged those who ask for "a course of

legislation which shall create pursuits, or make those existing more lucrative," the Whigs called "the encouragement of industry, by affording at all times a ready demand and a fair reward for labor, . . . the first great object in political science."[38]

The size of the public sphere did not concern Whigs as long as its actions were beneficial to the people it was meant to serve. When Whigs complained about public spending, it was not about the magnitude, but the manner in which monies were spent. "The question," one Whig explained, "is not—How many dollars and cents has the Government collected from the People and expended?—but, has the money been wisely expended, and have the People received its full value in benefit to them—to the country?" Public money, if properly spent, could create wealth. In 1838, Horace Greeley declared that five million dollars expended on public improvements "would, in the long run, increase rather than diminish the National resources, and even as a mere matter of revenue policy, be found to bring more into the Treasury than is subtracted therefrom."[39]

To the Whig, then, the state was an indispensable ally in the attempt to promote national development. It could draw people together for constructive endeavors and give their efforts an expansive force they could never have on their own. It was capable of ordering and harmonizing the economy as well as stimulating it. Jacksonians, for their part, feared to see numerous self-interests brought together into powerful combinations. They denied that government efforts to order and harmonize economic striving would have the desired effect; rather they would upset the order and harmony of nature. Most of all, they believed that attempts by the state to stimulate economic enterprise would only interfere with the natural growth of the economy. Always mixed with doubts about the efficacy of government action, moreover, were their fears of corruption and oppression. Hence the second great debate on the public sphere: even if government could sometimes produce beneficial material conditions, could a government of men possess such power without perverting it to selfish ends?

The Purity of Public Action

Party differences over the scope of government were matters of both principle and practicality. Jacksonians wanted to restrict government because it was right to do so and because the common good could best be achieved by leaving individuals alone. Whigs disagreed on both accounts. Another dispute emerged over views of the purity of government. The Jacksonian was unable to imagine a powerful state which was not corrupt. Whigs acknowledged the dangers of corruption, but they were more optimistic about the possibilities of restraining it.

The essence of the Jacksonian view of government was distrust. By its very nature the state was suspect. The *Democratic Review* argued that "there exists in every government, no matter how constituted, whether representative or not, a difference of interests between the *governing* and the *governed*." And government was, the *Boston Quarterly Review* added, "invariably administered for the good of the governors." No man who wielded power could be trusted. Human nature was simply not capable of coping with the temptation of either power or money. The Winchester *Virginian* declared that the chief objection to a national bank did not lie in the Constitution of the United States, it "lies in the constitution of human nature!" The bank simply represented "*too much power* to be concentrated in a few individuals; *Man* is not competent to its faithful discharge." It was always dangerous to confer power on men because "it is in the nature of man to abuse power."[40]

As we have seen, the first Jacksonian impulse was to deny government power over private interests so that there would be no temptation to abuse it. This struggle to limit power was unending, since there was always a tendency in government to expand its authority. A strange spell seemed to overcome a man when he became a legislator: "He is all at once wiser in the affairs of his neighbors than they are themselves; he sees that they do not always manage their own business properly; his fingers itch to arrange it for them, and his head teams with admirable and useful schemes of legislation for obliging them to attend to their own interests." For this reason, the New York *Evening Post* reminded its readers, "Men cannot watch with too narrow scrutiny the movements of their legislative agents."[41]

In order to limit the power of their representatives, Jacksonians supported a policy of rotation in office. In his first annual message to Congress, Jackson called this policy "a leading principle in the republican creed."[42] Democrats believed that no man should remain long in office or he would certainly be corrupted. Time alone would wear away any resistance to temptation. A hard crust developed over those in power which made them forget principle and their dependence on the people. The more secure an officeholder, the more his interests would diverge from those of his constituents. He would begin to see his position as a species of property which belonged to him and not to the people.

Jacksonian suspicion of those who exercised power was not confined to Whig legislators; they were nearly as suspicious of their own leaders. The *Democratic Review* declared, "We have no great faith in professional politicians, whether self-styled 'Democrats' or 'Whigs,' when too long entrusted with too securely established a power." It hastened to add that "as a general rule, a Whig politician is much less safely to be entrusted with power than a Democrat, from the different directions of the natural tendencies of their respective systems of opinion." But Democrats were suspect too, for it was obvious that some Jacksonians were using the party in an opportunistic way. The *Bay State Democrat* announced "unhesitatingly that there are men with us who are not of us, and who act with the democratic party only because they can make more money by so doing." Likewise, the *Ohio Monitor* complained, "Very many ambitious men have placed themselves in the democratic party solely because it was the only party which could promote them."[43]

To maintain popular control of government, Jacksonians adhered to the principle of instruction. Instruction was the right of the people to dictate their views to their elected representatives, and the duty of their representatives to abide by that dictation. The right of instruction inhering in the people was "the only control they retain over their agents; if this is lost, their *government* is lost." The Jacksonian representative was to give "an unvarying obedience . . . to the will of his constituents," to reflect accurately and immediately their current desires. He was not to be a leader seeking to anticipate their needs, or a man of superior judgment allowing his conscience to propose actions inconsistent with the will of those whom he represented.[44]

Democrats had no faith in great men. For public office, they wanted, according to the *Hampshire Republican*, "servants not masters; agents who will execute their will and not dictators to control it." The representative himself was not important: "The individual is nothing; his individual merits or demerits nothing. It is only as a faithful representative of the prevailing feelings and principles of his fellow men, their interests and their wants, that he is invested with distinction and entrusted with the exercise of power." George Sidney Camp, a Democratic theorist, considered it a "subject for congratulation rather than chagrin" that in the United States men "of the most shining abilities" were not chosen for office. Talented men were too apt to be independent thinkers, too sure of their ability, too proud of their position, too ready to feel superior to those whom they represented. Moreover, with the people constantly instructing the representative of their will, there was no need for knowledge, wisdom, or discerning judgment. There was the need merely for sympathy with his constituents, a receptivity to their views, and a willingness to be bound by their decisions.[45]

Jacksonians chided Whigs for their subservience to superior men. According to the *Hampshire Republican,*

> [Whigs] feel great reverence for high birth, wealth, and station; and delight to do homage to some political idol. Their leaders are, often, men of powerful intellect, ardent feelings and lofty ambition. They are never hampered by the instructions of their constituents, who are content to submit themselves to the direction of those whom they appoint to office.

To the Democrat, the superior abilities of the Whig leaders could only mean that they distrusted the capacity of the people for self-government. Whigs' attraction to great men was an indication that they regarded "government as a matter too important and too intricate to be trusted to the integrity and capacity of common people."[46]

To insure that the legislator remain within his proper bounds, Jacksonians urged that the honors and emoluments of public office be on a modest scale. Legislators should not, the *Globe* argued,

> be raised by distinctive marks or unusual incomes, above their fellow-citizens. No extraordinary dignity should be attached to their stations. . . . They should not be thought the superiors of other citizens. Nothing of show or parade should be expected of them beyond what is customary among private citizens with moderate incomes. Their *business* should not be considered as conferring greater consequence than any other honest calling.[47]

Nor was government policy to become so complex that only the gifted might comprehend its intricacies. Even the common man must be able to keep watch over his representatives and be competent to judge the wisdom of their actions.

Another source of concern to the Jacksonians was the added distance between the people and their representatives where the central government was involved. Sheer geographical distance and the difficulty of communication separated the central government from the citizen. It also multiplied the number of individuals and interests to whom the representative was responsible and whom he had to please. The individual voice in decision-making grew fainter with each step up the governmental ladder. As the individual constituent felt diminished, so the representative's sense of his own importance would increase—a prospect much to be feared. As the voice of the people became confused, the legislator would be prone to elevate his own judgment as the final arbiter of their true desires. Jacksonians also feared that even if the people's agent were not actually corrupt, he would, at such far remove from their everyday lives, misconstrue the interests and intentions of those whom he represented through ignorance. The *Globe* explained that

> the same government, from the nature of the human mind which controls it, cannot know and appreciate the local wants and interests of distant territories which its members never saw. If its territories be small, it may be well managed. In proportion as it enlarges, will its local interests be neglected; and when its territories become very extensive, the distant provinces, instead of renewing its fostering care, will almost certainly be taxed and plundered to enrich and adorn the residence and the vicinity of the court.[48]

Believing that distance and complexity led to corruption, Jacksonians desired government that was local and simple. Believing that human nature could not handle temptation, they sought to remove temptation from government. According to the *Democratic Review:*

> It is always to be presumed in government that every man will consult his own interests without reference to any rights which the law has not provided protection for. The State always contains men enough willing to misuse discretionary powers and ready to use any means to possess them, to make this principle a canon of political science. The only protection which the people have is to limit those powers by law, and then the exercise of them cannot be abused.[49]

Wherever government was able to control men's private affairs, partiality and corruption ensued. The principle of distinct separation between the public and private spheres was based on a solid foundation of experience. Internal improvements were "pushed on the log-rolling system," and money was "lavished upon favorite districts, and in favorite neighborhoods, to enrich partisans and retain power." The principal feature of the tariff system was "to build up a certain class, by laws made in their favor." It said to the rest of men, "You must bear additional burdens, that certain of your neighbors may thrive." The distribution by the federal government to the states of surplus land revenues was nothing less than "a grand bribery fund, to be expended in moulding the popular will to an unnatural acquiescence in the schemes, plots and plans of aspiring demagogues, and to make the people look with less abhorrence upon acts of legislative enormities." When government legislated on private interests, temptations of the strongest kind came into play. It seemed merely a fact of life that "men of every party find the temptations to profligacy too importunate to be resisted." The only way to avoid such corruption was to deny government the ability to act on private interests. Even if government power was capable of doing some good, the *Democratic Review* insisted, "it ought to be abolished for fear of the evil it is sure to do."[50]

Those most likely to profit from private legislation—the rich and those who enjoyed corporate privileges—had special opportunities to influence government. The rich were "constantly on the alert to obtain advantages for themselves," and because they were a small group able to act in concert, they could "direct their united energies to a particular object." Located primarily in the cities, controlling the professions—especially the law—and having greater access to newspaper publicity, they constituted a cohesive force threatening to overawe government and to direct legislation toward their own selfish ends. Those in possession of corporate charters also found it easy to bend public authority to their desires. Although the attainment of corporate privileges was often the end toward which corruption was aimed, these privileges, once achieved, became powerful means to effect further inroads on public power. If corporate charters were to be modified or the interests of a corporation regulated, these matters would be pressed "upon the legislature until some action is obtained." When the interests of unincorporated individuals were to be acted on, however, they had to "petition from without" and their petitions would be "read and laid aside."[51]

The worst fears of Jacksonians were realized in the chartering of the Bank of the United States. It was too large, too powerful, too distant, and too complex in its workings. It allowed the public sphere to penetrate far too deeply into the private business affairs of the country. Worse still, the public powers which it exercised had been delegated to a corporate body only marginally and indirectly responsible to the people. It violated nearly every principle of the Jacksonian code for the proper use of public power and was therefore inordinately prone to corruption. Jacksonians had many objections to the Bank of the United States, but fear of power alone would have justified seeking its destruction.

Whigs were far more optimistic that government could promote private interests without corruption. It can be argued that, since their legislative program required broad government action, it was necessary for them to take this view. Had they admitted that the state could not possibly legislate without sinking into a mire of bribery, deception, and self-interest, their cause would have been lost. But whatever pressure circumstances exerted on their view that government was capable of exercising broad powers responsibly, they were in fact far more ready to trust others with their interests and far more optimistic about man's capacity to resist temptation.

Whigs, as we have seen, had great faith that individuals could be trained to control themselves. The home, the church, and the school were designed to inculcate virtue—which to Whigs was largely the capacity to resist temptation. Self-control, self-denial, and service to others distinguished the ideal Whig legislator. Men of character, if the people had the wisdom to elect them to office, could be trusted to serve the interests of the whole. As Webster remarked, "It is in the character of the officers, and not in the strength of bars and vaults that we must look for the security of the public treasure."[52]

Whigs, however, worked at cross-purposes with Jacksonians in their attempt to elect superior men to office. To the alarm of Democrats, they wanted government service to remain an honored calling that would attract men of character and discernment, who could be trusted to devise statesmanlike legislation without fear of corruption or narrowness. Since Whigs saw greater scope for government action, they saw greater need for wise men to administer it. Since they encouraged government to promote diverse and complicated private interests, they wanted leaders with the knowledge and the education to oversee complex affairs. To combat the tendency of legislators to concern themselves only with selfish local interests, Whigs advocated the election of individuals with elevated views, cosmopolitan leaders aware of the world beyond their constituencies and able to take a broad, detached view of public affairs. As the Boston *Atlas* observed, society was a "complicated system" which "to produce its just, equal and beneficent effects must be directed by great practical wisdom, discerning foresight, patriotic integrity."[53]

It was inconceivable that men of such quality could be persuaded to run for public office under the doctrine of instruction. The Detroit *Daily Advertiser* dismissed the concept as "one full of mischief." Whigs, of course, believed it was "the duty of every Representative to shape his official action in general conformity with the wishes of his constituents." But the Whig officeholder reserved the right to act on his own convictions. He "must answer to his own conscience, his country, and his God, for his official conduct," said the Albany *Evening Journal.* Whigs rejected the absolutist Jacksonian doctrine of instruction because it tended "to make their officers the mere *automata* to register the edicts of popular fanaticism." This doctrine would "preclude every bold and upright man from office, and make its robes merely the livery to be worn by menials and parasites." High-minded statesmen were rare in their age, Whigs maintained, because it seemed that in order to obtain office "a man has to give up his own self-respect" and once there, "no upright, independent man can feel at ease, or hold his own assurance that he makes his own opinions the basis of his public acts."[54]

Whigs also condemned the elevation of party allegiance over individual character and over the interests of society as a whole.

Dedication to party, like the doctrine of instruction, dangerously narrowed the views and the independence of the legislator. To the Whig, "when a REPRESENTATIVE, instead of regarding the welfare of his constituents and the honor of his country, becomes the slave of party or the minion of power, he degrades himself and abuses the Republic." Whigs distinguished between "those who take office, or enter into political life or political contests, with an honest and hearty desire to sustain what they regard as valuable principles, and promote what they regard as the highest good of the community . . . and those who trade and traffic in politics, who fetch and carry, and plot and pander for party or for men."[55]

One of the chief symptoms of the desire "to trade and traffic in politics" was the spoils system. While to the Jacksonian the spoils system was merely the healthy principle of rotation, to the Whig it was the corrupting "principle of claiming a monopoly of office by the right of conquest." This practice, by proclaiming "that political contests are rightfully struggles for office and emolument," had the effect, the Whigs asserted, of stimulating "the basest passions to the pursuit of high public trusts." Whigs argued that "to the victors do not belong the spoils, for there are no spoils, unless parties confess themselves thieves and plunderers of the public purse." Even worse, the practice led to the distribution of offices on the basis of party allegiance rather than individual capacity and personal integrity. Webster feared that "the same party selfishness which drives good men out of office will push bad men in. Political proscription leads necessarily to the filling of offices with incompetent persons, and to a consequent malexecution of official duties." Henry Clay was sure that America's free institutions could "be preserved in their purity and excellence only upon the stern condition that we shall for ever hold the obligations of patriotism paramount to all the ties of party."[56]

The Whig predilection for broad, elevated policies often led them to prefer legislation by the federal rather than by state governments. Whigs did not share the Jacksonian fear of the central government. They believed that on some issues the general government was likely to adopt more enlightened and liberal policies than were many of the states, which sometimes took narrow and selfish views detrimental to the whole. Furthermore, Whigs trusted the national government more than their opponents did because they had more faith in the mechanisms which the framers of the Constitution had devised to "oblige it to control itself." They believed that separation of powers, checks and balances (though Jackson had made them skeptical of the veto power), and especially the bulwark of the Supreme Court and the Constitution were capable of limiting the power of government to do evil. And beyond the government itself lay the ever-effective remedy of the ballot box. If they were not satisfied with their representatives, the people were periodically given the opportunity to remove them and replace them with men capable of achieving those ends for which government was instituted.[57]

The parties, then, differed sharply on the ability of government to avoid corruption and on the practices which would enable it to remain pure. The suspicious Jacksonian believed only a small, simple government, one incapable of acting on private interests, could be trusted. And he had faith only in the representative who was tightly shackled to the will of those he represented. The more trusting Whig put his faith in a large government capable of promoting broad, comprehensive programs serving diverse private interests and in the men of great capacities and elevated views who were required to administer such a government. Apart from the powers of the executive, which had been inflated under Jackson, and the sordid influence which partisan political corruption had on public life, Whigs were relatively complacent about the evils which might flow from government influence on the activities of the people. They were determined that Jacksonian fears of power not end all attempts to use government as an agent of progress. The New York *Enquirer* reminded its readers that "there is nothing human which may not be abused . . . yet [this is] no ground to

refuse all action where good policy and propriety demand it."[58]
If evil flowed from government, it was not a necessary consequence of government's existence, but the result of mistaken
attempts to hinder its uniquely comprehensive powers to
achieve great public purposes.

Unity and Union

Nineteenth-century America lacked the natural forms of cohesion which had bound together nearly every earlier society.
Americans did not share a common ethnic background, language, or religion. Their common history, even for those who
were not recent immigrants, could be encompassed within the
lifespan of a single individual. America could function as a social
unit only if it could artificially create among its people some
sense of collective purpose, some unifying vision capable of
drawing together diverse men immersed in individualistic striving. The federal Union became the symbol of this attempt. Both
Democrats and Whigs claimed to be staunch defenders of the
Union, but the Union they defended did not hold the same
meaning for both parties.

The Democratic view of the Union had little to do with the
concept of unity. In the Jacksonians' ideal state, "institutions and
the organized machinery of government" did not exist to draw
men together. Their function was primarily to keep individuals
from getting in each other's way. The Union was to be preserved
in order to ensure that every individual might be left "free to
pursue his own happiness in his own way." Insofar as it was able
to serve this purpose, the Union would receive the voluntary
support of every American. "This," said the *Democratic Review*,
"is the true principle of cohesion." In the Democratic mind the
nation had "the love of liberty for its means, liberty itself for its
own reward, and the spread of free principles and republican
institutions for its end."[59]

There was little positive substance to the Democratic conception of the Union. In Jacksonian eyes the state was to be respected and supported less for what it did than for what it did not do and for what it did not allow others to do. The sole purpose of the state was to secure freedom by maintaining order. Because such a government was incapable of acting on private interests, it also lacked the ability to unite individuals behind any collective interest. Democrats opposed strenuously Whig attempts to invest the Union with a sense of corporate purpose. The most advanced stage of civilization was not collective but individual. As the *Democratic Review* explained, "The course of civilization is the progress of man from a state of savage individualism to that of an individualism more elevated, moral, and refined. Personal separation and independence were the beginning, as they will be the end, of the great progressive movement."[60]

Jacksonians feared that collective purposes would not be their purposes. As outsiders, they could not allow the dominant values to become the only values. They could not allow themselves to become submerged in the whole by denying the significance of those things which set them apart from others. Understandably, then, Democrats felt the necessity to undermine collective action by emphasizing the ways in which government activity and Whiggish institutions distributed their benefits unevenly in society. They distinguished the situation of the worker from that of his employer. They emphasized the differences of rich and poor, banker and farmer, city and country, Whig and Democrat. Jacksonians warned their followers not to allow themselves to be convinced that these distinctions were unimportant, lest they be hoodwinked into approving grand schemes in which they had no real interest. Always there existed the underlying assumption that unity could only be achieved at the expense of their own way of life.

Concern to defend the independence of the parts from the aggressions of the whole, the individual from the encroachments of society, led Jacksonians to reject Whig notions of harmony. If the weak became passive, they would be overrun by the strong. Jacksonians had to fight to retain their freedom and dignity. If the Democratic party were to cease to exist, even with the simultaneous dissolution of the Whigs and the creation of a new "Era of Good Feelings," the inevitable consequence would be the domination of America by Whiggish types, who required no political party to attain their ends. Only the Jacksonian needed to remain conscious of his special place in society and only the Jacksonian needed to resist attempts to unify and thereby pacify public life.[61]

To the Whig, however, union had strong connotations of unity. The Whig Union was not merely a collection of individuals united only by the principle that each should refrain from interference in the lives of the rest. It was a Union rich with possibilities for collective purposes. Whigs envisioned an energetic state drawing together the efforts of countless individuals in order to achieve comprehensive public ends beneficial to all. In this sense, the coordinated positive activities which were the consequence of union were practically the definition of civilization itself.

To the Whigs who advocated unity and corporate purpose, there was no contradiction between union and individual independence. "The highest civilization," observed Henry C. Carey, "is marked by the most perfect individuality and the greatest tendency to union."[62] The distinction between this conception and that of the Democrats may be subtle, but it is real. It is the difference between Americans who felt that they could unite their efforts without sacrificing their individual ends and those whose experience told them that the ideology of collective action merely obscured the fact that some were using the concerted power of the many for their own purposes. Necessarily, then, Jacksonians could not share the Whig faith that a positive notion of union held little threat for individual independence.

The idea that unity could be achieved within the whole without sacrificing the autonomy of the component parts was an important strand running through all Whig thinking. As we have seen, Whig partisans viewed membership in voluntary organizations as enhancing the possibilities of the individual, not as limitations on his freedom. At the public level the same idea can be seen in arguments that a compact, cohesive Union, integrated by a dynamic federal government, was compatible with the independent integrity of the states. Hence Webster could say of the states that they were "sovereign, but connected communities." Clay argued that "all was homogeneous" in that there was a "happy distribution of power which exists between the Federal government and the State governments. . . . The States had their institutions for local purposes, and the general government its institutions for the more general purposes of the whole Union." That separation could lead to homogeneity posed no problem for the Whig mind. Seward proclaimed happily that "the Union exists in absolute integrity" and that the states flourished "without having relinquished any part of their individuality."[63]

Whigs emphasized the similarities among Americans, not their differences. Rather than dwell on the personal, the local, or the sectional, they drew attention to those causes in which all were bound together. The Union was not the only example of this strand of Whig thought, but it was the most pervasive, the least divisive, and it held the most symbolic value for individuals troubled by the distance they had put between themselves and their fellows. The language often referred to the nation, to the states, to political communities, but the underlying meaning for most Americans was personal and individual. It is easy to perceive individual concerns in statements like the following one from the *American Whig Review:*

> The Whigs have ever asserted that union is the grand source of popular elevation. Without it, we should have been a collection of powerless communities, ever conflicting and mutually retarding each other's growth. Under its influence our interests become one, and commerce, agriculture, and manufactures are its natural fruits.

Such a statement had a powerful emotional impact on the Whig mind, as did the proclamation of Webster that the theme of his entire career had been to make Americans "*one people,* one in interest, one in character, and one in political feeling."[64]

Whigs were angered by Jacksonian attempts to put greater distance between individuals in American society. This effort to divide people frustrated the Whig desire to unite Americans behind projects of mutual interest. After Jackson's death, Clay lamented the baneful effects of the Old Hero's leadership on the country: "War and strife, endless war and strife, personal or national, foreign or domestic, were the aliment of the late President's existence. War against the Bank, war against France, and strife and contention with a countless number of individuals." If progress were to be made in America, such strife had to cease and individuals had to be brought into more harmonious relations with one another. Webster's speech on Jackson's removal of the public deposits from the Bank of the United States is a classic Whig statement on the effects of Democratic policies:

> Everything is now in a false position. The government, the Bank of the United States, the State banks, are all out of place. They are deranged, and separated, and jostling against each other. Instead of amity, reliance, and mutual succor, relations of jealousy, of distrust, of hostility even, are springing up between these parties. All act on the defensive; each looks out for itself; and the public interest is crushed between the upper and the nether millstone.

The wonderful harmony of mutual self-interest inherent in their American System was being reduced to "jealousy," "distrust," and "hostility." Cooperation and unity were giving way to an America in which "the public interest is crushed" because men act on the defensive and "each looks out for [himself]."[65]

Although they realized full well the independent-mindedness of individuals in nineteenth-century America, Whigs could not accept the Jacksonian notion that Americans must therefore remain isolated from each other. As Calvin Colton declared, "It gives us pain and anxiety, whenever we hear people of one part of the Union boasting, that they can do without the other." Whigs were prone to view the Union as "a family of States," where the harmony of familial relations must reign.[66] Individuals were reminded of the interests, the history, and the collective destiny which they shared, while the differences which divided them were minimized. Whig efforts to draw Americans together often relied on appeals to naked self-interest, but especially when they discussed the union, Whigs also appealed to loyalty, to faith, and even to the sacredness of the ties which bound the states to one another.

But it is possible to lay too much stress on the extent to which Whigs believed in corporate purposes. Perhaps even more than Jacksonians, they recognized the value of diversity in modern life. As Major Wilson has perceptively observed, the Whig view of progress was qualitative, designed to produce rich and varied opportunities for the individual, while Democrats tended to envision primarily the quantitative expansion of a Jeffersonian nation of farmers.[67] The conformity which Whigs desired did not extend to the details of life, but was primarily concerned with the underlying commitment to the institutions and values of nineteenth-century America. If they seemed concerned with the values and behavior of other Americans, it was largely to help them voluntarily to adapt themselves to the requirements of a peaceful and productive individualistic order.

The chief corporate ends advocated by Whigs were concerned with facilitating the efforts of Americans to discover common interests and purposes. Internal improvements were pressed as a means of allowing distant Americans to communicate, to meet, and to trade with one another. In an address of 1836 to the Plymouth County Agricultural Society, a Whig minister extolled the unifying and progressive virtues of modern systems of transportation and communication:

> The different sections and remote regions, by modern improvements in the arts of locomotion are brought into the neighborhood of each other, the products of one division are exchanged for those of another; the imports and manufactures of the east for the growth of the west, the riches and skill of the north, for the precious products of the south. Thus the parts are bound together by a

golden chain of mutual benefits into a beautiful whole, and the links that connect us are becoming more strongly cemented every day.[68]

Threats of disunion could be dissipated merely by allowing Americans to discover their mutual needs and desires. As Abbot Lawrence wrote to Henry Clay, "A railroad from New England to Georgia, would do more to harmonize the feelings of the whole country, than any amendments that can be offered or adopted to the Constitution." It was certainly proper in the Whig mind that the state should see to it that the means for broad social intercourse existed in society. "All things which aid in ensuring mutuality and contented union, should be encouraged, and brought into use and effect," the Richmond *Compiler* insisted. "Rail roads are a most practical and efficacious agent, in producing effects so desirable, and so essential to the harmony of the confederacy. . . . Truly are rail roads bonds of union, of social, of national union."[69]

In a similar fashion a sound national currency facilitated commercial ties among Americans. Whigs decried the loss of a nationally supervised medium of exchange because it weakened the network of commercial exchanges which was doing so much to tie together distant and disparate individuals and sections. To Webster, "The constitutional power vested in Congress over the legal currency of the country was one of its very highest powers, and . . . the exercise of this high power was one of the strongest bonds of the union of States." The disruption of the Bank of the United States and the consequent disorganization of the currency of the country tended to disorganize society itself. It bred uncertainty and distrust in the commercial relations of all Americans. If "the chain of common currency, a common standard of value, a common medium of exchange" were broken, it would "make a shipwreck of our highest interests." Money was the common fluid, the lifeblood whose circulation united and energized all the diverse interests of American society. If its circulation was "disordered or corrupted, paralysis must fall on the system."[70]

Even Whig support for the corporate form of business enterprise should be understood as an attempt to facilitate the
aggregation of men and money for productive and humanitarian purposes. Whigs readily accepted the shift to general incorporation laws because their intent in chartering corporations
was not, despite Democratic charges, to create monopolies or to
limit opportunity, but to encourage men to unite their efforts
behind good causes.

Given the parties' differing positions on the need for unifying
isolated individuals and the differing conceptions of the Union
which resulted, it is not surprising that Whigs and Jacksonians
had different ideas about how rapidly the Union should expand
its boundaries. Democrats were always strong expansionists—it
was John L. O'Sullivan, an editor of the *Democratic Review*, who
coined the term "manifest destiny"—while most Whigs agreed
with Daniel Webster that there is "danger of too great an extent
of territory" and "that there must be some boundary, or some
limits to a republic which is to have a common centre."[71]

Since the Jacksonian notion of progress was quantitative
increase within a primarily agrarian way of life, the Democrat's
chief concern was to extend American territory and to make
free land accessible to ever greater numbers. Freedom to the
Jacksonian was primarily a function of space. Wherever individuals were gathered too closely together, independence and dignity suffered. This view was expressed by Z. P. Flowers, an Ohio
Democrat, in a Fourth of July oration in 1839:

> Man while pent up in narrow limits, breathing the pestifforous [sic]
> air of cities, and daily accustomed to the pomp and show of the
> vanities of his fellows, loses the fresh exuberance of nature, and his
> mind as well as body, becomes enervated and predisposed to be
> enslaved by vicious habits or dependent from circumstances; while
> he who inhales the invigorating forests [sic] air, feels elasticity of
> limb and freedom of mind, that cannot be controled [sic] but by
> reason and laws to which he has given his consent.[72]

In the city, density of population and impure air alone seemed to erode freedom.

But what Jacksonians primarily objected to in the densely settled areas was modern life itself, with all of its consequent institutions and relationships. The Milledgeville *Federal Union* encouraged America's expansion because "the larger our dominion the . . . more restricted will be the interference of the General Government." Moreover, such expansion would allow Americans to hinder the Whigs' attempt to "cover the country with monied corporations." Whiggery, asserted the *Federal Union,* wanted "to keep the people crowded on a small space, that wealth might overshadow and subdue their energies." The *Hampshire Republican* preferred life in the country because the farmer "is not obliged to get his living under the eye, direction, or control of another; to eat, get up, and to lie down at the ring of a factory bell—nor is he called upon this or that hard, disgusting, or immoral action, at the beck of clients, patients, and parishoners, as lawyers, physicians, and clergymen sometimes are."[73]

Democrats were particularly outspoken against incipient industrialization. According to the *Democratic Review,* it was "almost a crime against society to divert human industry from the fields and forests to iron forges and cotton factories." The *Globe* encouraged the poor of the eastern cities to move to "the wide West, where nature invites them to enjoy the profusion of her richest bounties." The Boston *Weekly Reformer* thought urban mechanics should "exchange their confined apartments in the narrow alleys of cities in which they are cooped up; for the broad horizon and healthy air of the country." Freedom and independence were not possible in densely populated cities, nor could one be truly free under the commercial and industrial institutions of modern America. Nature, confided the *Democratic Review,* "has told us to remain planters, farmers, and woodcutters—to extend society and cultivation to new regions." "If an increasing population be cramped and confined," the *Review* later added, "in too small space either by artificial or natural restrictions, it will necessarily bring on those evils so prevalent in other countries." Jacksonians preferred pastoralism to the dangers of a civilization like that of Europe.[74]

To the Whig argument that dispersion would weaken the Union, the Jacksonians replied that the opposite was the case. The *Democratic Review* argued that "the multiplication of the States and the extension of the territory of the Union, far from having any tendency to break the federal bond, have always appeared . . . to be among the causes which have operated, and were likely to operate, most favorably upon its continuance." James K. Polk, the greatest Democratic expansionist of all, declared in his Inaugural Address that "as our boundaries have been enlarged and our agricultural population has been spread over a large surface, our federative system has acquired additional strength and security." Polk believed "that our system may be safely extended to the utmost bounds of our territorial limits, and that as it shall be extended the bonds of our Union, so far from being weakened, will become stronger." The "true principle of cohesion" was the guarantee of freedom provided by the state. "Distance and climate can have no influence on this bond," argued the *Democratic Review*. "It is wholly independent of them. There need be no fear of the effect of any possible extension of territory."[75]

Whigs, however, did fear the effects of expansion on national unity and the future of America. Webster believed that, in America, "political society exists and coheres, and must exist and cohere, not by superincumbent pressure on its several parts; but by the internal and mutual attraction of those parts; by the assimilation of interests and feelings; by a sense of common country, common political family, common character, fortune and destiny." It seemed obvious that such coherence could not exist if geographic expansion outstripped Whig efforts to provide the means for Americans to interact with one another. Webster feared "that extension often produces weakness, rather than strength; and that political attraction, like other attractions, is less and less powerful, as the parts become more and more distant."[76]

The Whig vision of America required greater collective efforts, more cooperative development than the Jacksonian vision. Whigs called for the qualitative development of all of America's resources—human and material—not just for the quantitative expansion of a simple, agrarian way of life. Government was to play a positive role in creating a fuller life holding new possibilities for the individual. A compact and dynamic Union was to be the vehicle for Whig progress. "Instead of aiming to enlarge its boundaries," said Webster, "let us seek, rather, to strengthen its union, to draw out its resources, to maintain and improve its institutions of religion and liberty, and thus to push it forward in its career of prosperity and glory."[77]

Whigs required a nation held together by something more than "subjective feeling," something more than "popular affection sustained by a scrupulous observance of the covenant of freedom." As Clay believed, "Union is our highest and greatest interest. No one can look beyond its dissolution without horror and dismay." Whigs used every means at their disposal to preserve the Union, including making the Union almost a religious cult with the Constitution as the sacred ark of the covenant. Yet their primary attempt, and the one to which Jacksonians were most opposed, was, to use Major Wilson's phrase, to "thicken and objectify the bonds of Union" with the aid of Clay's American System.[78]

Thus the apparent agreement between the parties on the importance of the Union disguised profound differences on the meaning of that union. While to the Whig the idea of union implied important elements of unity and coherence, to the Jacksonian it merely meant a guarantee of the right to be left alone. While the Whig concept implied a strong central government capable of strengthening the bonds between individuals, the Jacksonian believed positive governmental activity could only destroy the fragile bonds of affection which united the nation. He agreed with Andrew Jackson that "in thus attempting to make our General Government strong we make it weak." "Its true strength consists in leaving individuals and States as much as possible to themselves."[79]

The origin of these antithetical views of union lay in the character of the individuals who held them. The large question of the unity and coherence of the nation was important to most Americans, but not nearly so important as their relations with others in their own communities. The Whig, concerned about the tenuous nature of his ties to others, responded positively to programs which promised to "thicken and objectify" the bonds of Union. He worried more about the vulnerability of the Union because he worried more about the vulnerability of his ties to other individuals. The Whig also believed in the power of men united by common interest. Convinced of the beneficial effects of economic development and realizing the need for aggregating men and money behind great projects, he praised governmental efforts to draw Americans together for productive purposes.

The Jacksonian, feeling already bound too tightly by the self-interested connections by which the Whigs sought to unite Americans, resisted their efforts to inject unity into the concept of union. His primary concern was to break free from such ties. He opposed Whig attempts to integrate the nation's individuals and institutions because, as an outsider, he assumed this integration would be achieved at the expense of his way of life. He was more suspicious of government and less convinced that economic development of the type envisioned by Whigs would enhance his position in society. He preferred the opportunities of the open West and the stability of the simpler way of life which his fathers had known. To the Jacksonian, a man deeply troubled by his relations with the modern world, union meant little more than the opportunity to seek escape from such relations altogether in an ever-expanding American landscape.

4

Public Order: The Individual and the Rule of Law

The opponents of Democracy, now, as heretofore, have seldom condescended to argue with the humbler portions of society. They have been uniform in appealing to strong measures.

Washington *Globe*[1]

Arbitrary power procures the performance of duty only by the terror of penalties. Laws relying on that motive alone will be ineffectual, whether written in the statute-book in blood, or engraven in the rock by even an Almighty hand.

WILLIAM H. SEWARD[2]

All societies, in order to ensure their continued existence, must produce some degree of conformity among the people who live in them. Traditionally, this conformity was produced by consensus, deference, or coercion. Most commonly, some consensus on the range of acceptable behavior was built up gradually over time and subsequently exercised a powerful influence on those who were reared within it. Its full impact was rarely felt, since long before conflict came into the open, it had been quietly averted by the gentle shaping of each individual to "fit in." Where authority vested in a superior class was accepted, elites set down the proper patterns of behavior for those who customarily deferred to them.

145

Where consensus or deference failed to achieve the necessary degree of conformity, rulers used coercion to force their ideas about behavior on a reluctant populace. In each of these cases—consensus, deference, or coercion—the source of social conformity was more or less conscious and explicit, just as it was more or less effective. Nevertheless, throughout history, these have been the usual ways in which societies have produced the conformity that makes social life possible.

Modernity, however, posed difficult new problems of social order. When men became part of larger human systems populated by individuals with different interests, behavior, and values, they needed to find some new mechanism to govern their interactions. To fulfill this need modern societies have turned to the rule of law. It is this which provides the only structure within which the individual can interact with others confidently, knowing, as he does, that they subscribe to the same rules and will be held accountable for any breach of them. He cannot assume every individual with whom he deals will share the same religious values or moral code. But as long as the law functions, he has reason to think that others will at least function within the broad limits of human activity which is legally permissible.

After the Revolution, adherence to the rule of law became a matter of grave importance to Americans, since they sought to establish society upon a new foundation, largely abjuring each of the traditional means of maintaining order. Through legal and constitutional change they consciously destroyed the consensual basis of the community, while the expanding nation and its dynamic economy undermined even more surely the communal basis of social order. At the same time, Americans repudiated the hierarchical notion of society which allowed those with social authority to dictate the terms of human interaction. Finally, the long colonial experience of "salutary neglect" by British authority and a revolution bent on preserving such a "hands-off" approach by government, produced a national ideology of minimal government and the emasculation of government's coercive powers.[3]

It was in the Jacksonian era that Americans first came to grips with the problem of maintaining order in a society based on individualism: that is, the problem of preserving an essential foundation of conformity without consensus, without deference, and without the undue use of coercive force. By the 1830s the impact of throwing off these ancient forms of restraint was being felt. Certainly there were healthy effects: the much-praised energy of Americans and the surprising degree of individual initiative which the new freedom allowed to flourish. But there was a darker side as well: confusion, conflict, and mob violence. In such a context it was perhaps inevitable that political controversy should erupt over the rule of law.

Whigs and Jacksonians entertained different ideas about law and order in American society.[4] Their differences were most clearly revealed whenever the rule of law was threatened. Whigs demonstrated intense concern about breaches of the law. Jacksonians were more complacent, appearing to agree with Jefferson that an occasional rebellion was good for the country. Of course, these differences were not absolute, nor were they always in evidence. Nevertheless they were real, and one can observe their effects in many political conflicts of the Jacksonian era. The origins of the parties' divergent views on this issue can, once again, be found in the social character of the parties' memberships.

The Whig's intense concern for social order was an outgrowth of his search for order within himself. The inner-directed Whig had been rendered freer from community pressures, freer from deference to authority, and less fearful of coercion by others. But such freedom created its own problems. Whigs felt that their lives suffered from a lack of direction and restraint and they read this feeling into the problems of their age. When Whig leaders spoke of the need for some restraint upon the excited agitation of American society, it struck a responsive chord in listeners attempting to bring their own restless energy under control. Certainly they did not want to repress entirely their own passions, but they did want to direct them into constructive and socially acceptable channels. Whigs felt that the tumult of the age was destructive to society and to them individually. The freedom, indeed the incentive, to act in antisocial ways caused severe psychological strain in those with a strict moral upbringing. By regulating such temptations, the proper ordering of individual activities could reduce anxiety within the individual and thereby liberate his full energies for constructive action. The Whig conception of order, then, involved a system of restraints which aimed not at limitation but at liberation.

To the Jacksonian, restraint could have no positive connotations. Because his more traditional character already caused him to feel constricted and thwarted by modern relationships, any new restrictions on his actions could only be viewed as harmful. Seeing deception and oppression in existing laws, he necessarily saw any attempt to add to these artificial rules as a step taking him farther from the natural world to which he longed to return. Breaches of decorum or even occasional violations of law were as often hailed as condemned by Jacksonians. In the Jacksonian mind, only liberation from the constraints of law would produce a truly health-giving, natural order. The burden of this chapter—the first conscious attempts to come to terms with the problem of order in an age of individualism—must, therefore, be primarily the story of Whig thinking on the subject.

Coercion vs. Voluntarism

The Whig conception of order has often been misunderstood because the Whigs have seldom been considered to be within the mainstream of the American tradition of individualism. That is, until quite recently, historians have been reluctant to admit that Whigs had given up the traditional modes of social control: consensus, deference, and coercion. Whig attempts to harmonize American life have been viewed as attempts to homogenize it—to re-establish the restrictive consensus of the colonial community. Their desire to place men of energy and talent in positions of power seemed evidence of a lingering commitment to hierarchical notions of society, and their pleas for an orderly populace seemed appeals for derence to such men. Their advocacy of energy in government appeared to be but a prelude to reasserting the coercive force of governmental powers long since rejected by the American people. But all these impressions are false.

In fact, whatever individual exceptions may have existed, Whigs accepted diversity, equality, and limited government as fundamental conditions of American life. They did not demand excessive homogeneity; they did not seek to create a new aristocracy; and they did not believe in a system of law which required coercion as its primary mode of enforcement. On the contrary, Whigs were acutely aware of the voluntary basis of the American legal system. They knew that with the minimal coercive powers which government retained in America, no law could be enforced effectively unless the overwhelming majority abided by it of their own accord.

There are many ways of securing obedience to law. The threat of punishment against those who are tempted to disregard the obligations imposed by law is only the most obvious method. To be sure, so central has this approach been to traditional legal theory that for over a century Anglo-American legal philosophers found the key to the understanding of law in the notion of "orders backed by threats." Legal philosophy today, however, recognizes that, in many societies, most people adhere to law not from fear but out of a dedication to the rule of law itself. They may obey because of moral or religious scruples, economic interest, or countless other motives, but in each case the fear of coercion is likely to be secondary or even non-existent. Of course in every society, some men behave lawfully solely from fear of retribution, but if this number becomes too large, society will be disordered because there will not be enough people who obey voluntarily and support the system itself to coerce those who obey only out of fear.[5]

Rejecting coercion, and yet seeing an important role for law in ordering and enhancing individual energies, Whigs were intent on discovering how the greatest degree of voluntary obedience to law could be secured. They had little faith in the natural harmonies among men alleged by Jacksonians. They felt that unless strong rational control was exerted over the passions, men could not live together in peace. Of course, Whigs knew that Americans would adhere voluntarily to law if they believed it was in their own self-interest to do so. Hence Whigs constantly sought to convince the public that the law benefited and liberated them, giving them security and opportunity. They sought to combat Jacksonian notions that the law was primarily coercive and inhibiting, a restrictive device which shut off opportunity and smashed hopes.

Jacksonians, too, of course recognized that obedience to law might arise from self-interest, but they also felt that very few specific laws could win acceptance on that basis. These were such as benefited all equally by restraining one man from injuring another. Aside from this fundamental category, legislation otherwise tended to treat men differentially, profiting some at the expense of others. Appeal to self-interest here might win the adherence of those who hoped to gain some particular advantage for themselves, but not of others who might stand to lose. In the Jacksonian mind, the only common denominator that would insure the widespread allegiance of Americans to the rule of law was the universal self-interest in personal freedom.

Whigs argued for a conception of self-interest in relationship to law which was broader than that of the Jacksonians. Similar to Tocqueville's concept of "self-interest rightly understood," it suggested that one's interest should not be construed too narrowly. "Self-interest rightly understood," Tocqueville observed, "produces no great acts of self-sacrifice, but it suggests daily small acts of self-denial. By itself it cannot suffice to make a man virtuous; but it disciplines a number of persons in habits of regularity, temperance, moderation, foresight, self-command." Whigs emphasized that it was important to realize that the individual's well-being was ultimately dependent on the well-being of the entire social order. They presupposed a society in which men, acting independently, would realize that their actions could not fail to affect others. It was not that Whig principles expected the individual to sacrifice his own interests to those of his betters, but rather that all must discipline themselves to the exigencies of an impersonal social order which would ultimately lead to the greatest good of the greatest number. Although one was required to control his immediate longings, he was also assured that in some larger sense he was yet serving his own interests. Adherence to law, then, though it required "small acts of self-denial," "ultimately reaped personal benefits in peace, order, freedom, and material abundance."[6]

The Whig ideal, however, was neither the man who obeyed the law out of a fear of punishment nor the man who restrained himself out of an enlightened self-interest. It was the man who, though he might be unaware of the law, always acted within the law because his own inner controls did not allow him to act in ways detrimental to his fellow man. Such control did not come easily. Special training was necessary to enable the individual to check his natural impulses and to cultivate behavior appropriate to civilized life. Those whose lives were properly disciplined in the home, the church, and the school, need never fear, or even feel, the constraints of the law.

The greater the number of those who controlled their own passions by internal controls, the less outward control had to be exerted by society. It was this idea which lay behind much of the Whiggish stress on education and moral training. If wisdom and morality could be instilled when individuals were young, little coercion would be necessary when they were adults. The Whig tendency to see a connection between education and morality on the one hand, and the political world on the other, was largely the result of their intense desire to see free government work and to create and maintain an orderly society with the least possible coercion of individuals. Again the words of Tocqueville express the Whig position precisely: "Educate, then," said

Tocqueville, "for the age of implicit self-sacrifice and instinctive virtues is already flitting far away from us, and the time is fast approaching when freedom, public peace, and social order itself will not be able to exist without education."[7]

The Whigs' zeal for order was a powerful motive for their commitment to public education. William B. Shephard, in an address before the literary societies of the University of North Carolina, maintained that if the state were to educate every citizen, lawlessness and disorder would disappear. "Let the understandings of the people . . . be correctly cultivated," Shephard argued, "and our fair land will no longer be convulsed by those schemes of turbulence and violence, which threaten disgrace, if not destruction, to our institutions." Without proper education, however, the wild passions and vicious propensities which are "engendered by pride and fostered by ignorance" would take root. If that was allowed to happen, it was "absurd to expect order, sobriety of deportment, and all the virtues of a good citizen."[8]

More prominent Whig leaders such as William Seward and Daniel Webster were equally adamant in their advocacy of education to avoid disorder. Seward, who spoke often about the necessity for educating young Americans, reminded his listeners that democracy was no cure-all for lawlessness. "There can . . . be no security against error in communities," he declared, "other than what protects individuals against it, habits of virtue and cultivated intellects." If Americans were properly educated, he believed, "vice and crime would no longer obtrude themselves everywhere among us; mutual truth, justice, and forbearance in society would, more than human laws can do, protect us in all our personal rights." If all Americans joined Whigs in their commitment to education, Daniel Webster asserted, America would show its superiority over the Old World in protection against crime. "Other nations spend their money in providing means for its detection and punishment," said Webster, "but it is the principle of [the United States] to provide for its never occurring. The one acts by *coercion*, the other by *prevention*."[9]

Virtue was as important as knowledge in the Whig view of education. "That system of education which neglects the moral training of the mind," the Detroit *Daily Advertiser* declared, "is far worse than useless; it but enlarges the capacity of mankind for evil, and renders itself a curse instead of a blessing." A virtuous self-control was the end Whigs had in view. "The attainment of knowledge does not comprise all which is contained in the larger term of education," said Daniel Webster. "The feelings are to be disciplined; the passions are to be restrained; true and worthy motives are to be inspired; a profound religious feeling is to be instilled, and pure morality inculcated under all circumstances."[10]

The Whig suggestion that religious feeling could be a useful ally in the schools' attempts to inculcate virtue ran afoul of Jacksonians, who viewed it as a violation of the separation of church and state. But Whigs thought their opponents' fears of theological indoctrination groundless. Self-restraint and sound morals, not adherence to a particular faith, were the educational goals they wished to attain. Horace Greeley explained that "religion, in its theological aspect," was "precluded by the variance of views and creeds, from the proper range of school studies. It must be left to the Church, the Sunday School, the family fireside, and, where that is unlighted by the wisdom from above, to the kindly offices of the evangelical and pious."[11]

The Whig party's open support of religious values, whether in the public schools or in society at large, was based neither on narrow doctrinal points of theology nor on its inculcation of any detailed prescriptions for human behavior. Politically, religion was significant because the church was the primary institution in American society dedicated to the moral training of Americans. Whigs had no intention of creating a national church or of becoming involved in the doctrinal disputes of the various denominations. Americans, of course, had a special attachment to Christianity because it was the religious preference of the great majority. It was also peculiarly adapted to democratic times because it "speaks only of the general relations of men to

God and to each other, beyond which it inculcates and imposes no point of faith."[12]

Daniel Webster's comments on the value of Sunday schools can stand as a representative Whig statement on the general value of religion in maintaining the American social order. "The Sabbath School," he declared, "is one of the great institutions of the day." While Webster acknowledged its value as a school of religious instruction, he was primarily impressed with the sabbath school's contributions to civil society: "It leads our youth in the path of truth and morality, and makes them good and useful citizens." As a civil institution, he asserted that it "has done more to preserve our liberties than grave statesmen and armed soldiers." This was characteristic Whig thinking. Neither political institutions, however capable their leaders, nor coercive force, however powerful, could preserve American liberty if individuals did not show moral restraint in their behavior toward each other. Whigs knew religion was important to America because, as Tocqueville remarked, "religion sustains a successful struggle with that spirit of individual independence which is her most dangerous opponent."[13]

The kind of moral training which Whigs advocated would, of course, never wholly eliminate the need for coercion. Since in every society there are those who will violate the law, it is essential that the government discover and punish offenders. Whigs, however, were primarily concerned with the great majority of law-abiding citizens. They realized that free government worked only because most individuals voluntarily exercised the requisite self-discipline in the expectation that others would do likewise. But what if these expectations were to prove groundless? This misgiving, with its ominous implications for social order, was never far below the surface of Whig thought. In 1838, the young Whig Abraham Lincoln gave it expression in a now-famous speech to the young men of Springfield, Illinois.

With the revealing title "The Perpetuation of Our Political Institutions," Lincoln's speech called "the increased disreguard for law which pervades the country" the chief threat to political stability. He saw a "growing disposition to substitute the wild and furious passions, in lieu of the sober judgment of Courts." Lincoln worried about the consequences of this spirit in a "land so lately famed for law and order." His first fear was that "by instances of the perpetrators of such acts going unpunished, the lawless in spirit, are encouraged to become lawless in practice; and having been used to no restraint, but dread of punishment, they thus become, absolutely unrestrained." But the lawless were not his prime concern.[14]

What Lincoln feared most was that "good men, men who love tranquility, who desire to abide by the laws, and enjoy their benefits" would "become tired of, and disgusted with, a Government that offers them no protection." Such men, he said, "are not much averse to a change in which they imagine they have nothing to lose." By this means "the strongest bulwark of any Government, and particularly of those constituted like ours, may effectually be broken down and destroyed—I mean the *attachment* of the People." If those who cannot rule themselves are not restrained by the coercive powers of the government, "the feelings of the best citizens will become more or less alienated from it; and thus it will be left without friends, or with too few, and those few too weak, to make their friendship effectual." Lincoln's thinking on law and order questions, like that of most Whigs, is characterized not by a desire for massive coercion, but by a recognition that if the most unrestrained are not brought under control, the naturally law-abiding will not be encouraged to exercise that self-restraint essential to social stability and, ultimately, to them as individuals.[15]

Similar ideas about the maintenance of order can be seen in Whig economic thought. The Whigs' belief that there must be some regulating authority with the power to coerce those who fail to discipline themselves lay behind their desire for a national bank. Horace Greeley insisted that "*a Currency of Bank Paper without any National regulation or central energy is not a WHIG Currency.*" Some control was imperative if local banks were to be able to act responsibly and to coordinate their efforts with an understanding that other banks would do likewise. After Jackson had smashed the Bank of the United States, Henry Clay observed that because the banks were without a head, "instead of union, concert, and co-operation between them, we behold jealousy, distrust, and enmity."[16]

Of course the Jacksonian tendency was to reject the idea that Whig restraints and controls were necessary, either for society or the individual. The coercive powers of government deemed needful by the Whigs were viewed by their opponents as evidence of the opinion that Americans were incapable of self-government, rather than, as Whigs saw the matter, expressions of their belief that where the unruly minority were forced to act responsibly, the great majority would act responsibly of their own accord.

Jacksonians, rejecting the Whig notion that freedom required special efforts to train individuals in self-discipline, found Whig attempts to instill morality in individuals as dangerous as outright coercion. To them, such efforts were sinister attempts to disguise evil purposes, to coerce the mind, to limit freedom of thought—which was the most fundamental kind of freedom. "In the eyes of many liberal Democrats," Rush Welter has observed, "moral reform was a partisan conservative device for curbing the people's will." While Whigs were prone to think that morality must precede the establishment of true freedom, Democrats were more likely to regard freedom as the groundwork of true morality.[17]

Jacksonians denied that education and religion should be considered auxiliaries of social order. Education was valued by Jacksonians for its role in freeing minds from constraints rather than for the purpose of inculcating sound moral precepts. As Rush Welter has shown, Democrats viewed education "negatively, as a means for defeating power." It was for them less "a vehicle of social betterment" than a means for "the protection of individual rights." As for religion, Jacksonians held that this primarily involved transactions between God and man and that it properly had nothing to do with the social order and nothing at all to do with politics.[18]

Each party, then, inflamed the other on its most sensitive point: the Whigs in their efforts to find new means to order Americans liberated from the traditional social fabric, the Jacksonians in their attempts to limit the imposition of any new fetters on Americans whose natural freedom was already endangered by modern institutions. While Whigs believed that Jacksonian resistance to their counsels of self-restraint was an effort to undermine social order and moral decency, Jacksonians believed the Whig desire for order was merely a desire to control others and subordinate them to Whig purposes. On the question of law and order, perhaps among all others, one can see most readily the inherent conflict between those Americans concerned about the degree to which modernity had liberated them and those concerned about the threat which modernity posed to their freedom.

Personal Will and the Rule of Law

More than thirty years ago in an important book on the age of Jackson, John William Ward called attention to the fact that the era was fascinated by the man with an "iron will." Even gentle souls such as Ralph Waldo Emerson expressed deep admiration for the personal qualities of a Napoleon. To many of Emerson's countrymen, Andrew Jackson exhibited the same energy and daring, the same indomitable will. His will was a symbol of their own resistance to the constraints by which society tried to limit their aspirations. Yet if Jackson was a "Symbol for an Age," he was an ambivalent symbol. Ward himself observed that in Jackson's image there was a "mixture of attraction and repulsion." At its best this iron will represented the triumph of the self-made man, but there was also "danger implicit in the man of iron will." It "might lead to one man's success but to society's failure." What has been commonly overlooked, however, is the different way in which Democrats and Whigs responded to the man with an inflexible will.[19]

Though the Democrat revered the isolated man determined to resist the influence of established society, the Whig was prone to fear the influence of those who resolved never to submit to the will of another. To a Democrat like George Lippard, the thought of Jackson's personal fight against the Bank was awe-inspiring:

> When I think . . . of that ONE MAN, standing there at Washington, battling with all the powers of Bank and panic combined, betrayed . . . assailed . . . when I think of that one man placing his back against the rock, and folding his arms for the blow, while he uttered his vow, "I will not swerve one inch from the course I have chosen!" I must confess that the records of Greece and Rome— nay, the proudest days of Napoleon, cannot furnish an instance of a WILL like that of ANDREW JACKSON.

Henry Clay too compared Jackson to Greek and Roman leaders and to Napoleon, but the inference he drew from the similarity was hardly positive. Rather he suggested that it was because of such men that the liberties of the ancient world had been lost and that, in the nineteenth century, a "vast fabric of despotism" had "overshadowed all Europe." He declared that, if Jackson's will were to carry the day, "it will be a triumph of the principles of insubordination."[20]

In the Whig mind the man of great ambition, the man of indomitable will, represented a powerful challenge to the rule of law. It was only the willingness of the great majority to be bound by the abstract laws and impersonal authority of a modern legal code which had allowed great numbers of diverse individuals to become politically united and to interact peacefully for their mutual benefit. Whigs feared that ambitious men, men of genius, would refuse to bow to any earthly power. Their talents would drive them to break free of the orderly habits and the constraints of law by which ordinary men were bound. In an earlier generation the energies of such men had been channeled into the creation of the American Republic. But in their own age, one charged with the responsibility of preserving the work of the Founders, Whigs such as Abraham Lincoln feared that even presidential power would not suffice to contain the ambitious:

> Towering genius disdains a beaten path. It seeks regions hitherto unexplored. It sees *no distinction* in adding story to story, upon the monuments of fame, erected to the memory of others. It *denies* that it is glory enough to serve under any chief. It *scorns* to tread in the footsteps of any predecessor, however illustrious. It thirsts and burns for distinction; and if impossible, it will have it, whether at the expense of emancipating slaves, or enslaving freemen.

While the Democrat might have thrilled to such a passage, Lincoln used it to awaken his listeners to the threat such a man might pose for the social order. He called on the people "to be united with each other, attached to the government and laws, and generally intelligent, to successfully frustrate his designs."[21]

It was this fear of the personal will of one man which lay behind the violent Whig reaction to Jackson's use of presidential power. In his vigorous use of the veto, his refusal to execute a decision of the Supreme Court, his declaration that every public officer has a right to interpret the Constitution in his own way, Jackson appeared to undermine the rule of law. "The co-ordinate branches of the Gen'l Government," the Montgomery *Alabama Journal* charged, "have been overshadowed and made subservient to the caprice, and the will of one man." The New York *Tribune* lamented the end of "the golden days of our Republic, when the strongest Will was not absolute Law." The party of Jackson, said the Alexandria *Gazette*, has "trampled upon the Constitution and laws of the country, and set up their own will, and their own selfish and predatory disposition in their stead."[22]

Whig concern about Jackson's freewheeling use of presidential power focused on his abuse of the veto power. Whig doctrine on the veto power was poor constitutional theory; the Whigs, it seemed, were virtually blind to the provisions in the Constitution which allowed the President to withold his assent from legislation.[23] Why did they have this blind spot? If one assumes Whigs were concerned only to perpetuate the Bank of the United States, then the simple explanation that they were frustrated by Jackson's effective challenge to their aim would be sufficient. Yet the issue of executive despotism and the self-willed resistance to law lasted far longer than the national bank issue consumed the electorate, and it held appeal for those who were unlikely to be emotionally committed to the Bank of the United States. The issue went deeper than this.

In the Whig mind it was not the Bank which was being assailed, it was the rule of law itself. The veto power symbolized for Whigs the challenge to abstract law which personal will always represented. It threatened the only basis for order in a society which denied the necessity of popular consensus, the legitimacy of any ruling class, and the wisdom of granting government any considerable power to coerce. Though Jackson's own actions might be constitutional, Whigs feared his example would be copied by ordinary Americans with no such authority. The voluntary acceptance of an impersonal legal system, the willingness to submit to law would be subverted if individuals were encouraged to set aside or interpret for themselves their legal obligations.

The assertion of Jackson's bank veto message which excited "deep alarm" among Whigs was his announcement that "each public officer who takes an oath to support the Constitution, swears that he will support it as he understands it, and not as it is understood by others." Of course Jackson's intention in this statement was to shore up his own right to dissent from the Whig notion that only the Supreme Court had the right to determine the meaning of the Constitution. But his expansive language lent substance to Whig claims that this vital authority was dangerously threatened by its wide distribution among petty government officers. "The general adoption of the sentiments expressed in this sentence," Webster feared, would dissolve our government. It would raise every man's private opinions into a standard for his own conduct; and there certainly is, there can be, no government, where every man is to judge for himself of his own rights, and his own obligations. Where every one is his own arbiter, force, and not law, is the governing power. . . . Standing as it does, it affirms a proposition which would effectually repeal all constitutional and all legal obligations.[24]

Webster linked Jackson's sentiments on the veto to the doctrine of nullification, another of the age's many "disorganizing" ideas which Whigs sought to discredit. Nullification, said Webster, held that a state could "declare the extent of obligations which its citizens are under to the United States; in other words, that a State, by State laws and State judicatures may conclusively construe the Constitution for its own citizens." This conception was bad enough. "But that every individual may construe it for himself is a refinement on the theory of resistance to constitutional power, a sublimation of the right of being disloyal to the Union, a free charter for the elevation of private opinion above the authority of the fundamental law of the state, such as was never presented to the public view, and the public astonishment, even by nullification itself."[25]

To apply this principle to statute law would result in even graver threats to social order. Neither public officers nor private individuals could be allowed to place their own meaning on public statutes: "Laws are to be executed, and to be obeyed, not as individuals may interpret them, but according to public, authoritative interpretation and adjudication." If society is to exist it must be ruled by law, and, if laws are to be effective, they must be fixed and known by all who are obliged to obey them. If the disorganizing principles of Jackson's message were accepted, Webster warned, "social disorder, entire uncertainty in regard to individual rights and individual duties, the cessation of legal authority, confusion, the dissolution of free government" would result. Henry Clay agreed: "We should have nothing settled, nothing stable, nothing fixed. There would be general disorder and confusion throughout every branch of the administration."

If the principles in Jackson's veto message prevailed, Webster summarized, it would mean that "the reign of law has ceased, and the reign of individual opinion has already begun."[26]

The Whig's special fear of the self-willed individual was a product of his efforts to discipline his own fierce ambitions. When Lincoln wrote the stirring passage on how ambition "*scorns* to tread in the footsteps of *any* predecessor," he was not just a country boy with a vivid imagination. In that speech one senses his struggle to attain mastery over the surging forces of his own inner drives. "Passion," he said, "has helped us; but can do so no more. . . . Reason, cold, calculating unimpassioned reason, must furnish all the materials for our future support and defence." In his attempt to substitute reason for passion he turned to the same aids, the same solutions, as all Whigs. "Cold, calculating, unimpassioned reason," said Lincoln, was to "be moulded into *general intelligence, [sound] morality* and, in particular, *a reverence for the constitution and laws.*"[27]

Lincoln's use of the word "reverence" in describing the proper attitude toward law was not accidental. Whigs were intent on lifting the rule of law above the realm of men. In every way possible they sought to impress upon their contemporaries the impersonal nature of justice. In an egalitarian age it was important to stress that submission to law was not submission to the rule of other individuals. Just as the economic market was an impersonal world, so was that of the system of justice. It was to be free of the arbitrary and particularistic notions of private opinion and personal will.

Because it is difficult to become strongly attached to abstractions, Whigs sought to tap the religious feelings of Americans and use their sense of the sacred to secure adherence to the impersonal rule of law. One can find few examples of this strand of Whig thinking better than the following passage, once again drawn from Lincoln's speech to the young men of Springfield:

Let reverence for the laws, be breathed by every American mother, to the lisping babe, that prattles on her lap—let it be taught in the schools, in seminaries, and in colleges;—let it be preached from the pulpit, proclaimed in legislative halls, and enforced in courts of justice. And, in short, let it become the political religion of the nation; and let the old and the young, the rich and the poor, the grave and the gay, of all sexes and tongues, and colors and conditions, sacrifice unceasingly on its altars.[28]

The law which Lincoln reverenced and held sacred was no particular law, created or enforced by no particular set of men and designed to benefit no known individuals in predictable ways. It was the abstract and impersonal rule of law itself to which Whigs were committed.

Alexis de Tocqueville was surprised to find how well Americans understood the impersonal nature of law. In the United States, he observed, "the people feel no animosity against police officers, tax collectors and customs officials." No shame attached to sheriffs for carrying out their distasteful duty of executing criminals who had been sentenced to death. A citizen explained to him that "the sheriff executing a criminal is only obeying the law in the same way as the magistrate who condemns him to death; neither hatred nor contempt clings to his profession." Agents of the law were themselves respected because of "the extreme respect in which the law itself is held."[29]

One cannot argue that only Whigs were committed to the rule of law. Democrats did not advocate anarchy. But their perception of the problem of law was quite different from that of Whigs. "There are two sorts of corruption," explained the *Democratic Review,* "the one when the people do not observe the laws; the other, when they are corrupted by the laws."[30] The Whigs feared primarily the former, the Democrats the latter. Existing laws, the Jacksonian thought, were artificial, too complicated, too numerous, and too partial in their operation.

The party of Jackson, ignoring Whig cries that they were seeking to subvert all law, attacked the American legal system throughout the 1830s and '40s. The *Democratic Review* asserted that in their age the law was "rotted to the heart by chicanery," that "its original beauty has perished, and by vicious usage its blessings have been turned into curses." Contemporary law was designed only to confuse and deceive the ordinary citizen. "It has no affinity with common sense—candor is its aversion, and simple truth its enemy."[31] Here was a very different message from the one which Lincoln hoped would "be breathed by every American mother, to the lisping babe that prattles in her lap!"

Jacksonians found the legal profession to be as corrupt as the law itself. Lawyers, said the *Review*, were men "permitted to exert their mightiest influence to warp the judges in their judgment." They "were actuated by the strongest motives of the human breast, to pervert the principles of justice, and defeat the intentions of honest complainants by some of the devices of their wonderful arts. . . . They held themselves in readiness, and sold their services to the highest bidder, to advocate even the most unworthy cause, and plighted their honor and reputation to prosecute it successfully." To the *Democratic Review* it seemed "but justice to remark, that the influence which long and confirmed habits of prevarication and artifice naturally exert upon the mind, renders the professional lawyer less worthy of public confidence than the plain and uncontaminated private citizen."[32]

The Jacksonian also showed no blind veneration for the judiciary, not even for the Supreme Court. The *Democratic Review* found disgusting the "prostrate submission" to the high court's "presumed infallibility." "This abject mental subjection to authority and assumption," it maintained, "is unworthy equally of our country and age." Of the judiciary in general, the *Review* observed that "from one extremity of the Union to the other, this branch of the government has forfeited the public respect, and instead of being looked up to with love and veneration, its movements are watched with jealousy and distrust." One Mississippi Democrat asserted that "the judiciary is more *grasping*, farther removed, and exercises more *dictatorial* and *despotic* powers, than any other branch of the government, and withal is the least responsible."[33]

Believing, then, that American corruption did not result from resistance to law, but from the corrupt influence of law itself, Jacksonians could not be the champions of law that their Whig opponents were. They could not be legal conservatives when so many aspects of law needed reform. Indeed, they asserted boldly that they did not "object to the appellation of 'Radical' when there is so much evil to be attacked at its *roots*—to that of 'Destructive' when there is so much that we are loudly called upon to destroy." Whigs were both incensed and frightened by such seemingly lawless declarations. They were the sentiments of the sort of man whom Lincoln warned against, a man so corrupted by ambition that, if there was "nothing left to be done in the way of building up, he would set boldly to the task of pulling down."[34]

Jacksonians looked forward to the day when they would "find out a way of simplifying our relations with our neighbors to that degree, that good sense and honesty combined, will be all that will be requisite in most of the differences between men, to decide righteously upon them." As far as the Whigs were concerned, however, this utopian desire to live under such a drastically simple system of law and government could be realized only under a despotism. "The simplest of all governments," the New Jersey *Freedonian* observed, "is that in which the will of one man is the supreme law." It was the Whig contention that under Democratic rule this was precisely the direction in which the country was moving. Against this they set themselves, taking their stand on the bedrock of law. If there was one thing about which Whigs were certain, declared the New York *Tribune*, it was that "the essence of freedom consists in the supremacy of *abstract law* over *personal will*."[35]

Higher Law and the Rule of Law

Whigs believed that the rule of law was being challenged from above as well as from below. Some men claimed a legitimacy for their breaches of law which emanated from a higher source of law—natural or divine—rather than from a narrower or lower source—private opinion or personal will. Nature or God was often believed to give men some inherent insight into perfect justice or into the shape of a perfect social order in which men should live. Such insights were a powerful stimulus to the resistance of laws, which, created by imperfect men, were themselves imperfect. Whig defenders of law had to fight these legal heresies on two fronts: the first against Jacksonian assertions of natural law, the second against assertions of divine law within their own ranks.

The distinction between Whig and Jacksonian views of higher law in American society can be greatly overstated. Though one can, with some justice, delineate partisan differences on this question, their conflicts stemmed more from divergent attitudes than from distinct legal philosophies. The age of Jackson, in any case, was not a time when theorizing flourished in any field. It was an essentially pragmatic age. The Jacksonian appeal to natural law, then, should be viewed in this light; it was more attitudinal than philosophical, more pragmatic than theoretical.

As previously noted, Jacksonians were more disposed to find in nature an ordering mechanism for human affairs which required little supplementation by human laws. As the *Bay State Democrat* observed, "The natural world seems to have been formed to administer to the comforts, and contribute to the progress and glory of man." The great tragedy of man, his "fallen condition," was due to the fact that his laws failed to copy the laws of nature. "Man has sought out many inventions," said the *Democrat,* and "the fundamental principles of mind and matter have been disregarded."[36] Jacksonian attacks on the "artificiality" of Whig legislation were attacks on the departure of man-made laws from the laws of nature.

The essence of natural law was absolute freedom and absolute equality:

Man is a *free*-man in the moral and natural world. Mind acknowledges no restrictions; Nature no monopolies. Exclusive privileges are alike repugnant to each. The laws of mind and matter operate equally upon every mind and all matter. The rich cannot escape from them with inpunity; the poor are not shut out from their benefits. Each have their rewards and their punishments, and each are administered on the principles of equity.

Because they saw in Whig measures fundamental departures from this rule of freedom and equality, Jacksonians looked upon much of contemporary law as corruption and usurpation. Their solution to disorder in society was not more law or better law, but the elimination of law. "We should look for perfection only in absolute unrestricted freedom," the *Democratic Review* asserted. "We belong to the school that looks upon LIBERTY as the main principle of reform to the action of which we should trust, in preference to the clumsy and too often corrupt operation of LAW."[37]

Democrats emphasized that man's natural rights were antecedent to the state and that these rights were dependent upon no "compacts, grants, or decrees of convention." Moreover, they were often inclined to deny that men gave up any of these natural rights upon entering society. The *Boston Quarterly Review* asserted that "the notion that individuals give up a portion of their natural rights to society, in order to secure protection for the remainder, is a false notion." The *Democratic Review* also maintained that "man surrenders none of his rights on entrance into society." But it later hedged a bit by arguing that men "do not so much relinquish their rights, as adopt new modes for their exercise, at once consistent with natural liberty and social order."[38]

Extreme readings of these natural rights could easily undermine allegiance to law. It would be difficult for any legal system to come up to the standards of absolute freedom and equality which Jacksonians found in nature, especially when judged by individuals naturally suspicious of law-makers. Those concerned about order in society might justifiably be uncomfortable with Orestes Brownson's view of natural rights:

Liberty, according to our definition of it, is freedom to do whatever one has a natural right to do; and one has a natural right to do whatever is not forbidden by natural or absolute justice. . . . The government that restrains in any sense, in any degree, the natural liberty, that is the natural rights, of any, the meanest or the guiltiest citizen, is tyrannical and unjust.

As a philosophical assertion of the American creed this statement is perhaps without fault, but as a practical program of action it leaves much to be desired. What is absolute justice? And what degree of "tyrannical" deviation from it merits resistance to law? Sometimes the "popular will" became the Jacksonian standard of judgment, and according to the *Democratic Review* this will could somehow be distinguished from laws enacted under the Constitution. "It is our faith to defy every consequence of popular sovereignty," the *Review* declared, "if the popular will is misrepresented in the laws. By virtue of that faith we also distrust every government just in proportion as that will is misrepresented."[39]

Vague notions of absolute justice, natural law, and popular will, used as yardsticks by individuals to measure the legitimacy of laws constitutionally enacted and administered, were profoundly unsettling to Whigs. Nature, to the Whig mind, was "a state of *despotism and wretchedness.*" Natural law was "indefinite and *unsettled.*" As for natural rights, one might appeal to them in emergencies, but, Daniel D. Barnard argued, "instead of being the best, or even good authority, in the social state, they are the worst and most dangerous possible. They are for extremities, as a necessity, not for common use." The only law with which men should be concerned, he said, was that "*fixed by society.*" Americans should "turn their regards to Society, and find the natural rights of men there, or they will find them no where."[40]

Whigs too acknowledged theoretical concepts of absolute justice—though their tendency was to find them in moral law or God's will rather than in natural law or the popular will—but in practice men were to adhere to the laws of the state, not to their conceptions of divine will. Daniel D. Barnard explained:

There is, as I hope we all very well know, a higher standard than this [the nation's laws]—a Supreme Rule of Right, which is the Will of God. So far as the laws of the State square with this Supreme Rule they are right absolutely; and so far as they fall short of its true spirit, all that can be said of the matter is, that they are positive rules in respect to human rights and human obligations which make the nearest approach to the Supreme Rule that the nation, as such has yet been able to attain. In this view they must command, and will command, the right respect of every right-judging person.

As Thomas S. Grimke put it, "*Theoretically*, the constitution is not faultless, in the opinion of any intelligent man of the millions whom it blesses; but *practically*, it is faultless; because you cannot prevail on the requisite majority to agree to any amendment."[41]

Both parties, then, acknowledged the existence of a rule of human existence more perfect than man-made law, and neither party denied the authority of positive law. But Jacksonians were more willing to use the more perfect standard to question existing law, while Whigs hesitated to undermine respect for the law by appealing to utopian standards of justice. Jacksonians were hardly anarchists, though Whigs often accused them of being so. It is also true that Whigs themselves sometimes questioned the operation of laws which violated their consciences. But the parties did differ on their willingness to appeal to higher law, and political controversies did arise in which the parties' divergent attitudes on this point played a significant role.

The minor local issue of Mississippi's handling of their bonded indebtedness took on national significance because it appeared to Whigs to symbolize their opponent's disregard for law. During the depression of 1837–43, Mississippi repudiated its debt on a series of state bonds which had been issued to finance a program of internal improvements. Since the Democratic party controlled the government of Mississippi, Whigs nationwide raised a howl of protest against this repudiation and advertised it as evidence of the "disorganizing" principles of the

Democratic party. It was a natural outgrowth of Democratic principles, said the Whigs, and it demonstrated their disrespect for law. It is interesting to note that in response to this attack the *Democratic Review* disowned the repudiation. In a statement that Daniel Webster could not have improved upon, it condemned the action for its tendency to "generate a disregard of the moral equity of contracts, the main principle of cohesion of all human society."[42] Far more revealing of their actual position, however, was the necessity the *Review* felt to soften this stand and defend itself against attacks from its own party for taking it.

In a long digression from its main point, the *Review* responded to the "remonstrances" of other Democrats who charged that it had deserted the party by speaking out against repudiation. First, the *Review* sought to justify repudiation by acknowledging the injustice of the laws which had created the bonded indebtedness. Those who reneged on such legal obligations were only expressing "a natural and righteous exasperation against the authors of these great public frauds, and against the system of which they are the natural fruits." Next, because they had advocated the fulfillment of legal obligations by public bodies, the *Review* had to defend itself against the imputations of its readers that by doing so it had fallen away from the former "elevated tone of its democratic principles." The *Review* was forced to deny that it had become imbued with "the contagion of the atmosphere of Wall Street," that it had come under the control of those "interested" in Mississippi bonds, that it had imbibed "'foreign sympathies' alien to the cause and the rights of our own country or countrymen," or that through some gross mistake a "stockjobber" or "financier" had been allowed to write on the question in the *Democratic Review*.[43]

Mississippi's debt repudiation gained national attention primarily as a symbol of the legal philosophies of the major parties. The Jacksonian sense that some laws were unjust, that they did not conform to a natural order which stood above the law, did not produce general lawlessness among Jacksonians. But when hard times hit, when it was difficult to pay a debt (much of it owned by foreigners), when that debt was contracted in a manner which did not conform to their ideas of natural justice, it became easier for Democrats than for Whigs to reject their legal obligations.

The Whig inclination to stick with positive law and established institutions and the Jacksonian inclination to prefer the claims of natural law was revealed again in the debate over the Dorr Rebellion in Rhode Island. There Thomas Dorr and his followers sought to found a revolutionary government to achieve an expanded suffrage. Throughout the country opinion split roughly along party lines, with Democratic sympathies enlisting in Dorr's cause, while Whigs generally supported the existing government which was operating under the restricted suffrage of the colonial charter of 1663. Both sides admitted that the issues involved went to the heart of party differences. The *Democratic Review* declared that the event afforded "one of the best tests that [has] been presented within the present generation of the true character and spirit of the Whig and Democratic parties respectively," and Henry Clay discussed its implications "to illustrate the principles, character and tendency of the two great parties into which this country is divided."[44]

Though the struggle in Rhode Island initially involved the question of suffrage extension, it attained national significance only after Dorr's party resorted to revolutionary tactics to obtain its object. Immediately, Whigs, even those sympathetic to Dorr's aims, rallied behind the charter government. To the Jacksonian, on the other hand, Dorr's cause was just and his tactics involved a principle which was "the very cornerstone of our whole political system." That principle was "the right of the people to organize and re-organize the constitution of the State, independently of the existing legal authorities." By this however, Jacksonians meant something other than the right of revolution. No American could deny the existence of the natural right on which the American nation is based. What Jacksonians wished to assert was a kind of "domesticated" right of revolution, a natural right to act outside the law which might be exercised in an orderly way within society. While they referred to this right as a right of revolution, they seemed to expect the constituted authorities to acknowledge the legitimacy of their actions, and they objected strenuously when the government of Rhode Island treated Thomas Dorr as a failed revolutionary.[45]

What Whigs rejected was this very domestication of what they considered exclusively revolutionary rights. They denied that there was any way to exercise one's natural rights within an existing society; natural rights were by definition the rights of man in a state of nature, and "all the arrangements and ordinances of existing and organized society" must be "prostrated and subverted" to get back to that state. Such an action was not to be taken lightly. "In such a lawless and irregular movement as that in Rhode Island," warned Henry Clay, "the established principles and distinctions between the sexes, between the colors, between the ages, between the natives and foreigners, between the sane and the insane, and between the innocent and the guilty convict, all the offspring of positive institutions, are cast down and abolished, and society is thrown into one heterogeneous and unregulated mass." He chastised those who could not see the unsettling implications of this process:

> And it is contended that the major part of this Babel congregation is invested with the right to build up, at its pleasure, a new government? That as often, and whenever society can be drummed up and thrown into such a shapeless mass, the major part of it may establish another, and another new Government in endless succession? Why this would overturn all social organization, make Revolutions—the extreme and last resort of an oppressed people— the commonest occurrence of human life, and the standing order of the day.[46]

Jacksonians were more complacent about the assertion of natural rights in society. The *Democratic Review* asked, "May you at any time take a census of all this body of persons [i.e., parties to the social compact], and if you can procure the consent of a majority of them to any scheme, does such a scheme, *ipso facto*, become the law of the land?" Their easy answer to this query expressed none of the horror with which Clay viewed the prospect. They replied merely that "if the people should choose to act in an irregular manner, it cannot be helped; that they have the ultimate power to act as they shall judge best." Of course the *Review* added its conviction that "the people of this country will never act in that manner."[47]

The Jacksonian generation was correct in thinking that reaction to the Dorr Rebellion exhibited the fundamental differences between Democrats and Whigs, but these differences were not founded on philosophical theories about the right of revolution; still less were they based on different views of an expanded suffrage. Whigs and Democrats viewed the assertion of higher law differently because they viewed their place in society differently. Individualistic Whigs felt the tenuous nature of the bonds which held nineteenth-century society together. A society in which men were united only by temporary bonds of interest and in which order was maintained largely by mutual forbearance seemed ever poised on the brink of dissolution. In such a situation the artificial ligaments which united and the artificial rules which ordered that society became immensely important. Being more liberated from the guiding influence of tradition, Whigs could not take social order for granted; they knew that society and the state were in some sense artificial constructions and that, if artificiality were rejected, both would be destroyed.

Jacksonians, on the other hand, who still felt the weight of tradition, found it hard to envision society as a chaotic mass of unregulated individuals. Because they retained stronger social feelings, Democrats assumed that such feelings must be instinctive. To liberate men from the artificial restraints of law was merely to allow these instinctive social ties their rightful precedence. Natural rights could be asserted in a piecemeal and orderly way in society because an invisible hand would automatically maintain all the necessary bonds during the process of reform. Feeling in their own lives the strength of "instinctive," "spontaneous," or "natural" ties among individuals, they did not share the Whig fear that the repudiation of artificial ties and obligations would produce a descent into the maelstrom of anarchy.

Although the general tendencies of the parties on this question seem clear, they were not absolute. There were Democrats who were staunch defenders of positive law, and there were Whigs who were willing to invoke notions of higher law—especially where slavery was concerned. This anti-slavery movement within the Whig party constituted a powerful internal challenge to Whigs' professed preference for constitutional procedures.[48]

No issue was more likely to evoke Whig statements about higher law than slavery. Although anti-slavery attitudes were not essential elements of Whiggery, northern Whigs were always more sensitive to the anti-slavery issue than were their Democratic opponents. The Whig penchant for individual and national improvement involved some northern Whigs in anti-slavery, just as it involved others in temperance or educational reform. Moreover, as we have seen, Whigs emphasized the importance of moral training which they believed would naturally lead men to act in accordance with the law. But some laws occasionally appeared to conflict so sharply with moral behavior that some Whigs were hard-pressed to show allegiance to them. As Emerson warned this generation: "Good men must not obey the laws too well."[49] Such men were haunted by consciences which caused them to suffer for the sins of the community as well as those of their own commission. Southern slavery, supported by the Constitution and the laws, became increasingly difficult for some "conscience Whigs" to bear.

But however strongly the consciences of some Whigs condemned slavery, Whig party policy was always to defend the Constitution's compromises on the institution against the assaults of those who would question them on moral grounds. Henry Clay was morally opposed to slavery and yet he rejected the inference that this justified taking political action against it:

If a state of nature existed, and we were about to lay the foundations of society, no man would be more strongly opposed than I should be to incorporate the institution of slavery among its elements. But there is an incalculable difference between the original formation of society and a long existing organized society, with its ancient laws, institutions, and establishments. Now, great as I acknowledge, in my opinion, the evils of slavery are, they are nothing, absolutely nothing in comparison with the far greater evils which would inevitably flow from a sudden, general, and indiscriminate emancipation.[50]

There was, to the Whig, far more at stake than the existence or destruction of slavery's evils—there was also the efficacy of the rule of law itself, on which depended the success of the American experiment.

Even the most celebrated Whig appeal to higher law, William Seward's speech rejecting the Compromise of 1850, used that concept to reinforce the Constitution, not to defy it. Although his words were misunderstood by many at the time and by many historians subsequently, there have always been those who have tried to set the record straight. The editor of the 1853 edition of Seward's *Works* declared that those who accused Seward of maintaining the existence of a higher law in opposition to the Constitution were guilty of "a flagrant misrepresentation of his language." Although Seward did acknowledge the existence of "a law higher than political constitutions and human legislation," he asserted that there was no contradiction between this law and the law of the Constitution in the case in question. Both God and the Constitution, Seward maintained, dedicated the western territories to freedom. His March 11 speech argued that "the Constitution regulates our stewardship; the Constitution devotes the domain to union, to justice, to defence, to welfare, and to liberty. But there is a higher law than the Constitution, which regulates our authority over the domain, and devotes it to *the same noble purposes*" (emphasis added). Hence, Seward was not seeking to undermine the Constitution's authority, which would

have run against the grain of Whiggery, but was rather attempting to reinforce a Constitutional obligation by the sanction of
divine law, which was a common Whig practice.[51]

Mainstream Whig opinion maintained that divine or moral
responsibilities would never justify overthrowing the established
framework for order in American society. The American's
prime moral obligation was to support the Constitution and the
laws. Calvin Colton denied that political abolition was within the
sphere of any American's duties, "however their *moral feelings*
may be so inclined." To violate the law, even to do a good act,
would be "to erect our individual *feelings* into a court to set aside
public law." No man, Colton insisted, could "plead conscience to
violate a *contracted* obligation, to go out on a mission of benevolence!" "A mission of benevolence, which might otherwise be
very commendable," he argued, "becomes a crime, when moral
obligations are trampled under foot in the enterprise."[52]

Most important of all, Whig leaders reminded would-be
abolitionists that to narrow one's field of vision to a single cause,
no matter how moral, would be to lose sight of those broader
ends on which the well-being of every American, both black and
white, was ultimately dependent. Clay, after once again acknowledging the evil done to the black race in America, reminded his
listeners in the Senate:

> Their slavery forms an exception—an exception resulting from a
> stern and inexorable necessity—to the general liberty in the United
> States—We did not originate, nor are we responsible for, this
> necessity. Their liberty, if it were possible, could only be established
> by violating the incontestable powers of the States, and subverting
> the Union. And beneath the ruins of the Union would be buried,
> sooner or later, the liberty of both races.

Abolition was wrong because "it is a power that mounts the
hobby of one principle to rule over all others—a sword that cuts
all ties, however sacred, for the sake of cutting one admitted to
be bad." Whigs rejected abolitionist arguments that they could

not be responsible for the effects which their cause might have on the laws, the Constitution, and the Union. Calvin Colton knew some abolitionists argued that "they are not responsible for consequences, after having done their [moral] duty." "But the very question of duty depends," he replied, "in part on a consideration of consequences." Horace Greeley emphasized the same point, declaiming that "it is the easiest thing in the world to shove off all responsibility by saying do your duty and let the results take care of themselves. Considering consequences and choosing the best way to do a good thing is the prerogative of human reason."[53]

To the Whig, the best way to do a good thing in nineteenth-century America was to support unfailingly the laws and the Constitution which gave, in their eyes, the greatest prospect for the advance of all Americans. Neither the revolutionary implications of natural rights nor a narrow construction of moral duty could justify imperiling this uniquely beneficial structure for social order. The important Whig principle which was challenged by these higher-law theories—from within as well as from outside their own party—was what William H. Seward called "the political gospel of Daniel Webster": "the duty of calling the American people back from revolutionary theories to the habits of peace, order, and submission to authority, and of absolute reliance on constitutional remedies for the correction of all errors, and the redress of all injustice."[54]

The Constitution

Among Whigs, the Constitution represented the highest expression of the rule of law. It marked a triumph of voluntarism over coercion, having been written, ratified, and preserved without military might and having achieved the peaceful ordering of more than a score of states and many millions of people. Its existence guaranteed the ascendancy of law over will—whether the will of the one or the many. The Constitution was a species of man-made, yet "higher" law, exercising a stabilizing influence on the ephemeral and sometimes tyrannical whims of statute law. It was also the fundamental basis of American unity. The twin conceptions of the Constitution and the Union were virtually inseparable in the Whig mind. By creating both social order and social bonding, the Constitution united the devotion to law and the concept of the public good into a powerful symbolic whole for Whigs. The supreme Whig fear was that the Constitution would be undermined or overthrown. They viewed its creation in the convention of 1787 as a miracle of compromise and restraint. They had no hope that their own age could improve upon or even equal its wisdom.

Although most Democrats had great respect for the Constitution, it was, in their eyes, less perfect, less complete. Moreover, the check that it imposed upon the popular will—which most recommended it to the Whigs—was viewed by Democrats as its chief failing. Jacksonians even denied at times its importance in maintaining the Union. That the nation was held together primarily by the artificial bonds of constitutional prescription was inadmissible to them.

Although Democrats acknowledged a strong sympathy with minorities, they were not disposed to find in constitutional complexities that security for private rights which lies at the heart of American jurisprudence. The "supreme tribunal" in the Democratic lexicon was not the Supreme Court, but "the public opinion and will." In a properly limited government, Jacksonians maintained, there was no danger of the majority absorbing the rights of the minority. The idea was "wholly destitute of foundation or strength. There is no danger to be apprehended from the people," the *Democratic Review* believed, "if left to themselves." Minorities, not majorities, were the chief danger to American liberty. According to the *Review*, "a minority is much more likely to abuse power for the promotion of its own selfish interests, at the expense of the majority of numbers . . . than the latter is to oppress unjustly the former." The *Review* argued that the majority of a free populace has no inducement to go wrong. They cannot long be deluded. They have no exclusive affinities to cloud their perceptions or warp their judgments. Their whole interest is on the side of order and right.[55]

Jacksonians had an almost childlike faith in the "true" popular will as opposed to the will of the people after it had been sifted through complex constitutional mechanisms to become law. Any policies which they opposed simply could not have been the true will of the people. Either the people had been temporarily deluded by conniving politicians, or the mechanisms of government itself had frustrated their wishes. As the *Democratic Review* said, "It is under the word *government* that the subtle danger lurks." Thus the provisions of the Constitution which refined or checked the people's will were, in Democratic eyes, more likely to destroy freedom than to preserve it. Government was to be manifestly a "simple machine." The chief value of the Constitution was not its ability to regulate and guide the popular will according to certain principles, but its ability to set absolute limits on government activity. Democratic adherence to "the school of the strictest construction of the constitution" was not indicative of any lack of faith in the wisdom or goodness of the people, but rather a skepticism about whether any government, no matter how carefully constructed, could give adequate expression to the people's will. Such views arose from that profound suspicion and distrust of impersonal institutions which lay at the heart of Jacksonianism.[56]

Jacksonians denied the necessity of conservative checks on the majority, which they equated with "anti-democratic" or "aristocratic" principles. They saw in the Constitution "aristocratic and monarchical features which were conceded to satisfy the views of the different parties represented in the Convention." The saving grace of the system was that "there was left a sufficient infusion of democracy to acquire, in the course of time, the ascendancy and control over the whole." They hoped that one day, the popular will would find little in the Constitution that could act as an impediment to its most direct and unrefined expression. In keeping with this desire, they suggested reforms which provided for the elimination of executive patronage, for annual presidential elections, and for an elective judiciary— each of which was designed to enhance popular control over branches of government now distant from the people. Democratic policies of rotation in office, the doctrine of instruction, and strict constitutional interpretation were also efforts to mitigate constitutional limitations on the direct assertion of the popular will. Even a provision in the Constitution such as the executive veto, which hardly appeared to be "democratic," came to be seen as a popular device to circumscribe government rather than as a check on the will of the people. Democrats "knew that [democracy] would and must become the animating spirit of all [the Constitution's] forms and checks, which it would conquer, in succession, to itself."[57]

Such views were alarming to Whigs who considered the Constitution the only bar to the absolute tyranny of the majority. Whigs were not convinced that the majority was always on the side of order and right. A Whig warned in the Boston *Courier* that "the power of the many is as much to be dreaded as that of the few." Unlike many Jacksonians, he found nothing "more easy to imagine than that a majority might be corrupt; nothing is more easy, than to imagine the minds of the majority so swayed by the passionate desire to secure a real good, and at the same time so blinded in regard to the real character of the measures, by which they attempt to secure it, as to act in a manner inconsistent with the equality of Republicanism." Majorities were to be feared as much as any who held power because "majorities may abuse their power. They may ride rough-shod over the feelings of their opponents. They may treat with contempt and derision the wisdom of the ages, quoted against them, and stigmatize saint-like purity if it should venture to oppose them." Majorities ruled, according to Whigs, not because they were wiser or better than individuals, but "because we have no means of ascertaining who are the wise, and because if we were able to ascertain them, we would not agree with one consent to entrust them with power." Believing, then, that the power of the majority was based on convenience or necessity, rather than on any faith that wisdom lay in numbers, Whigs revered the Constitution for setting limits on that power.[58]

Whigs were inherently more willing to trust others and more convinced of the benefits which would accrue from that trust. However, their faith was less in individuals than it was in the law. It was the authority of the law which allowed them to believe in the beneficence and justice of government. As the law of the majority protected individuals from each other, the higher law of the Constitution protected individuals from the law of the majority.

In order for trust among men to flourish, there could be no arbitrary or capricious element in the exercise of authority. All power had to be limited and guided by fundamental principles of justice that all could know and on which all could agree. Even majorities must be so regulated. Whig Daniel D. Barnard could not agree with those who argued that "government has no legitimacy, and law no standard, no foundation, no sanction, except what is found in the absolute Will of the major number in the community, for the time being." Horace Greeley agreed with a fellow Whig who asserted that the essence of freedom lay in the supremacy of law over will, "whether the will, or wills, of the one, the few, or the many." Greeley went on to explain that "if the ruler—whether a monarchy or a majority—be above the Law, then the Government is a despotism; but if the ruler and the ruled are alike governed [by] well settled, clearly defined law, then that State is essentially a Free one."[59]

The Constitution was of central importance to Whigs because it provided a tangible higher law to which even ruling majorities were subject. It was not the vague and arguable law of nature, but a unique document to which all Americans implicitly gave their assent, and whose meaning, at least in Whig eyes, was made definitive by the authoritative decisions of the Supreme Court.

It was part of the special genius of their heritage that "the United States of America, having declared a system of government based upon the abstract rights of man, gave it an organized form by a Constitution that recognized no arbitrary element, either for the people or against them, (knowing by an instinctive wisdom that that which is arbitrary has no limits, and is the root of all tyranny), but built upon *principles* their whole structure." Law which claimed an authority above the Constitution could provide no basis for social order, since its meaning—like beauty—could lie only in the eyes of the beholder. The great advance which Americans had made over past civilizations in providing security for their liberty was, according to Daniel Webster, their creation of "a fixed, settled, definite, fundamental law, or constitution, imposing limitations and restraints equally on governors and governed."[60]

To remind individuals that the Constitution was the only higher law to which they might legitimately appeal in normal times, Whigs were prone to invoke the divine will in its support. Although God may have provided men with a notion of morality not yet realized, they argued that God would rather have them adhere to imperfect laws than to unsettle society with ideas of heavenly perfection. "Civil government," said Horace Greeley, "is a Divine institution, and ought to be obeyed for conscience sake." The Constitution, another Whig asserted, was manifestly *"the gift of that Supreme Director and the highest proof of that Superintending Providence."* Calvin Colton argued that "obedience to civil society results from Divine command; that political society, as it exists at any time, in any place is 'the ordinance of God.'" He believed that "no man can, with propriety or good reason, invoke Divine authority to justify a use of political power in upsetting political society, or reforming the State."[61]

Whigs sanctified the Constitution because they were convinced that the American nation could not exist without it. Its delicate compromises were the basis on which so many diverse individuals, interests, and regions were enabled to work together for their mutual benefit. Whatever unity America possessed was dependent on the maintenance of those compromises.

To Daniel Webster, the Constitution and the Union were "among the greatest political blessings ever bestowed by Providence on man." Webster called "The Constitution and the Union" the most important speech of his life. Like many of his greatest orations, it was devoted to demonstrating the importance of maintaining the Constitution as the only safeguard against the dissolution of the Union. He was convinced that "if they stand, they must stand together; if they fall they must fall together. They are the images which present to every American his surest reliance, and his brightest hopes."[62]

Webster believed that the Union which the Constitution "so happily cemented" was a miraculous achievement, not likely to be duplicated. "Where," he asked, "among all the political thinkers, the constitution-makers and the constitution-menders of the present day, could we find a man to make us another?" He was incensed that there were

> persons weak enough, to think and say that if the Constitution which holds these States together should be broken up, there would be found some other and some better chain of connection. This is rash! This is rash! . . . I no more believe it possible that this Union, should it once be dissolved, could ever again be re-formed, and all the States re-associated, than I believe it possible that, if, by the fiat of Almighty power, the law of gravitation should be abolished, and the orbs which compose the Universe should rush into illimitable space, jostling against each other, they could be brought back and re-adjusted into harmony by any new principle of attraction.

William Seward, too, could see only disorder beyond the Constitution. It was "the only form consistent with the preservation of our national existence. Here all innovation is usurpation, and all usurpation leads, either directly or indirectly, to revolution and anarchy."[63]

To the Jacksonian, the Constitution was neither so fragile nor so important to national existence. Perceiving a society held together by natural bonds, no artificial construction like the Constitution could be all-important to its survival. When the Democrat asked, "What is that bond of union that keeps together this wonderful *E pluribus Unum?*," he did not answer, the Constitution. It was not "the external forms of institutions and the organized machinery of government" that held Americans together. It was "a common sentiment of mutuality" that existed "in the bosom of every individual."[64] Because Democrats believed in natural affinities among Americans which were sufficient to maintain civilization and in the innate goodness and wisdom of "the people," the Constitution was not to them the bulwark against disunion and anarchy that it was to Whigs.

This contrast between Whig and Democratic views of the Constitution, however, like the contrast in their views on all law and order questions, was not always as obvious as it has been made to seem here. Jacksonians were not altogether blind to the role the Constitution played in protecting minorities and in maintaining the Union. Yet, given their outlook on the world, it could never have for them the significance it had for Whigs, nor could their respect for it equal the almost religious awe which many Whigs felt. On most occasions it would be difficult to separate Whig from Democratic statements on the Constitution in terms of pure political theory. The parties' differing attitudes were expressed only in their degree of passion and in the telling way they sometimes strayed into the kind of extreme statements quoted above. Few Whigs could express a faith in the innate goodness of unchecked majorities as the Jacksonian sometimes did. And few Jacksonians shared the Whig's propensity to see revolution and anarchy behind every breach of law and every attempt to modify the Constitution.

These different reactions to human events which shaped political controversy lay deeper than politics. They had their basis in the character of individuals. The problem of order in society brought these differences out because the shift in character which was taking place was actually a transformation of the source of order in an individual's life. Whereas the tradition-directed individual still looked to the external world for guidance in his life, the inner-directed individual had to find it within himself or he would find it nowhere.

Perceiving no necessary or obvious relations among inward-looking individuals, the Whig was intent with preserving those few mechanisms which allowed self-directing and self-interested men to work together. Freely given consent between equals was now the only basis for order and for the authority which could maintain it. Seeing in his contemporaries, especially in his Jacksonian opponent, a great reluctance to consent to any strengthening of the forces of order and authority, he clung desperately to those mechanisms to which Americans had already given their consent—the right of property, the sanctity of contracts, the rule of law, and, above all, the higher law of the Constitution.

The Jacksonian, on the other hand, still retained a frustrating tendency to look outward toward the society to order his life. But what he found there were men corrupted by self-interest and institutions which no longer cared about him. When he gave his allegiance to others they manipulated him and used him for their own purposes. His great need was to withdraw from society and to stand alone. The external sources of order in society had to be questioned because they had violated the trust he had put in them. They could be questioned without destroying the social order because he felt his ties to others so palpably that he was unable to fear the atomistic isolation which haunted the dreams of his Whig opponent.

Public conceptions of order, then, emerged from private conceptions of order. Perceptive public figures shaped their language and their arguments on great political questions to tap the concerns of common men seeking order within the modest circle of their own lives.

❧ 5 ❧

Economic Inequality: The Individual and the Social Hierarchy

> *If the inequalities of artificial condition bore any relation to those of nature; if they were determined by the comparative degrees of men's wisdom and strength, or of their providence and frugality, there would be no cause to complain. But the direct contrary is, to a very great extent, the truth.* WILLIAM LEGGETT[1]

> *Whatever objections may be made to the existing distribution of riches, and to the artificial processes by which it is regulated, . . . this at least must be conceded, that no mere redistribution of wealth could effectually answer the proposed purpose of elevating the people. Any such redistribution . . . would still leave everybody poor, at the same time that it would cut up by the roots a great mass of industrious occupations.* RICHARD HILDRETH[2]

"The American people may be mistaken as to men and measures," wrote Orestes Brownson, "but we are confident that in principle they will all assent to the doctrine of equality."[3] Both Whigs and Democrats believed that no man was born booted and spurred and ready to ride, while others came into the world merely to be ridden. The natural rights of all white men were equal, and it was the responsibility of society to protect those rights. Equality before God, equality before the law, and even political equality were generally accepted in the age of Jackson. Yet important inequalities remained.

186

The chief mark of distinction in society was wealth. Other distinctions existed—of power, of influence, of esteem—but the inequality of wealth had come to be seen as the central one from which the others were derived. Jacksonian America was rapidly becoming a "cash nexus" society; increasingly, individuals were bound together by their pecuniary interests. Power and influence were less personal than economic. As the Bangor (Maine) *Mechanic and Farmer* complained, the influence the American elite enjoyed was based on "nothing more or less than their money bags."[4] Esteem, as well as power, now seemed a function of wealth. Many resented being judged on the basis of the property they owned rather than on the desirable personal qualities they possessed.

In principle, few objected to the existence of economic inequality. "Distinctions in society will always exist under every just government," Andrew Jackson declared. "Equality of talents, of education, or of wealth can not be produced by human institutions." The *Democratic Review* went even further. It argued that *"it is . . . very desirable that an inequality should exist."* Whigs were no less emphatic. A correspondent of the Boston *Courier* asserted: "Nothing but the most wild imagination has ever tempted men to believe that a state of society could be made to exist, in which all men should possess an equal amount of property."[5]

In practice, however, Jacksonians often denied that existing economic inequalities were legitimate. They were willing to accept distinctions grounded in the natural differences among men, but they could detect no such foundation for those which characterized their age. "In some way," lamented the *Democratic Review*, "a principle of artificial inequality has crept in among us." It was not, said the *Globe*, "an inequality founded on the eternal basis of a difference in personal vigor, personal activity, superior talent, prudence or enterprise."[6]

Jacksonians were primarily concerned about the effect of these artificial inequalities on those who worked with their hands. The "Elevation of the Laboring Portion of the Community" they considered the highest earthly aim of America's democratic civilization. "In comparison with this," the *Democratic Review* averred, "every other question which the widest range and loftiest flight of human inquiry can present . . . sinks into an insignificance that seems unworthy of engaging the attention of a thinking man." For a time, America had offered bright hopes to the working man, but it was becoming apparent that his situation was deteriorating. He was slowly sinking back into the insignificance and subordination which had been his lot throughout human history. The power, the esteem and even the self-esteem of the individual worker were being undermined by an artificial economic system which robbed him of the fruits of his labor and made of him a pawn to be controlled by others.[7]

An inequality of wealth was not intrinsically evil, then, but an "artificial" inequality had dangerous moral and political implications. It threatened to destroy the independence of—and thereby degrade—a group which constituted perhaps a majority of the American people. This inequality had a dynamic character which, if not reversed, would eventually result in the permanent dependence of the majority on the favors of a wealthy few.

Whigs too were concerned about the inability of the working-man to attain independence. They knew that equality of rights was empty if Americans were unable to secure a competence by their industry. Democracy was a sham unless men could deliberate freely in the political arena. Morality and social order were precarious where men were degraded by poverty.

Yet Whigs seldom questioned the way in which wealth was distributed in their society. The system by which different kinds of labor were rewarded was in some sense "artificial," but it was not detrimental to the elevation of the laboring portion of the community. The chief hindrance to the economic advancement of the worker was, in the Whig mind, the low productivity of his labor, and no mere equalization of existing wealth could remedy this defect. In the words of Richard Hildreth, "in order to redeem the mass of the people from poverty and its incidents, a great increase in the amount of accumulated wealth and of annual products is absolutely essential."[8] Whigs did not question the "artificial" inequality which resulted from the operations of the market because they believed that it augmented the creation of new wealth. Capital had to accumulate where it would be most active. Bankers, manufacturers, merchants, and speculators had to control wealth if the economy were to grow. Equality of incomes was neither a proper definition of American equality nor an effective means for achieving true American equality: an equality of rights among men whose economic productivity freed them to exercise those rights.

In the rhetoric of each party, then, one finds different attitudes about the existing inequality of wealth and its consequences for American life. It is possible to trace these attitudes back to different conceptions of how wealth was created. Ideas about the proper distribution of national riches were powerfully affected by notions of who had been primarily responsible for producing them and, as a corollary, who should control future wealth so as best to ensure that it would continue to increase. Yet it would be superficial to ascribe the true origin of Jacksonian-Whig differences to this complex economic question. Both views of how wealth was created were plausible, and few men had more than their own experience of economic processes upon which to base their choice of one or the other. Since it appears that individuals with similar economic experiences put their faith in different explanations of inequality, the origin of their beliefs must be sought elsewhere. Once again, the concept of social character suggests what lay behind the conflicting views of reality held by individual Americans.

The Jacksonian was prone to take a more traditional view of economic processes. He was uncomfortable with the implications of a market economy. He was suspicious of entrepreneurial activities and of modern corporations which depersonalized economic relations. He denied that either of the two produced wealth more abundantly than did the patient industry of individuals. He saw great wealth as the product of exploitation and he feared its power to degrade and enslave him.

The Whig, on the other hand, was convinced that modern economic processes were the foundation of American progress. He defended the new ways and the new institutions against Jacksonian attacks. He viewed economic inequality as necessary to elevate the condition of all. He looked upon wealthy entrepreneurs as public benefactors. He identified freedom and well-being with economic development, and he sought to stimulate economic growth even if it widened the gap between rich and poor.

The Creation of Wealth

The Jacksonian-Whig debate regarding the proper distribution of wealth in America was an outgrowth of an even more fundamental division between the parties on how wealth was created. Few questioned that a man was entitled to enjoy the fruits of his labor, but in an increasingly complex economy it was no longer clear just whose labor had produced the fruits. Farmers, mechanics, laborers, merchants, manufacturers, bankers, and lawyers, among others, all laid claim to a share in the national wealth. In the mind of the individual, the legitimacy of the claims of each required an understanding of how the various occupations had contributed to the production of that wealth. On this point there was no agreement.

Of course wealth was not actually distributed on the basis of any individual or even party estimation of the contribution of each man to national production. Individuals were compensated for their labor via the impersonal mechanism of the market. Yet submitting men's claims of service performed or value created to the judgment of the marketplace constituted a revolutionary departure in the organization of society. In the age of Jackson there were many who were still suspicious of its workings. In light of earlier economic and moral understanding, the market often seemed to reward most profusely those who were least responsible for America's growing prosperity. This was certainly the Jacksonian position.[9]

In particular, Democrats objected to the way in which the whole corpus of Whiggish laws and institutions—banks and other corporations, tariffs, internal improvements—rewarded men far beyond the level of compensation their services justified. At the root of these objections was the Jacksonian belief that however effective the Whig program was in channeling prosperity, it was an ineffectual method of creating it. It was the farmers, mechanics, and laborers, the "real democracy of the country," who were chiefly responsible for America's prosperity.

There was nothing unusual in believing labor to be the source of all wealth; the labor theory of value dominated the economic thinking of the time. What was distinctive in Jacksonian thought was the narrowness of its definition of productive labor. There was a tendency in Democratic rhetoric to devalue all but physical labor. Others performed useful services by safeguarding and transferring money, by exchanging products and carrying them to distant markets, by adding capital to labor and by maintaining a legal system which protected life and property. But such services, though they were useful and deserved a certain compensation, did not contribute greatly to the production of wealth. Those who performed them were seen as subsidiary to and ultimately dependent upon those whose labor and skill produced the material products which supported life. As one Jacksonian farmer observed, "However complicated the economical relations of men may become in an artificial state of society, the great truth cannot be concealed, that he who does not raise his own bread, eats the fruits of another man's labor."[10]

Banks, for example, if properly constituted, could be beneficial institutions, but they did not produce wealth. Apart from the monopolistic character of special charters and the privilege of limited liability, what Democrats most objected to about banks was their ability to create money. To the Democrat, when a bank issued currency or extended credit beyond the amount of specie in its vaults it was engaging in fraud. The increase in the money supply did indeed cause prices to rise, encourage industry and stimulate enterprise. But in the Jacksonian mind the resulting prosperity was an illusion. The increased wealth was a fiction, an inflated bubble which would inevitably burst, revealing the fallacy of trying to make something out of nothing.

Only gold and silver had "intrinsic value," said William Gouge, chief Democratic theorist on banking. By supplementing the circulation of specie with factitious paper money, "the valuation or relative estimation of things, is thereby enhanced, but not an atom is added to the wealth of the country." A nation could not supplant its "*natural* money [gold and silver], by the use of paper money, without involving itself in distress and embarrassment." Bank credit extended beyond specie reserves had a similar effect. Any prosperity which resulted was tempo-rary and illusory. "No instance is on record," warned Gouge, "of a nation's having arrived at great wealth without the use of gold and silver money." If confined to their proper functions banks could prove useful, but, Gouge concluded, they "contribute little to the production of wealth."[11]

The corporate form itself came under Jacksonian attack, and not merely on the basis of its departure from equal rights. While some Democrats accepted the trend toward general incorpora-tion laws, others remained adamant against the proliferation of corporations. The latter were disturbed by their impersonality, their separation of ownership and control, and their lack of concern for the community. Moreover, as the Wetumpka (Ala.) *Argus* asserted, "Incorporated companies create no wealth, they fatten upon the labor and industry of the poor man who lives by the sweat of his brow." By taking business transactions out of the realm of face-to-face relations, where individual responsibility and the healthy restraint of prudent self-interest reigned, cor-porations might actually hinder progress. "Corporations," Gouge said in his *Journal of Banking*, "are unfavorable to the progress of national wealth. As the Argus eyes of private interest do not watch over their concerns, their actions are much more carelessly and much more expensively conducted than those of individuals." There were some objects attainable in no other way—particularly the building of canals and railroads—but whenever it was feasible, Jacksonians preferred individual partnerships with individual liability.[12]

An important reason for Democratic resistance to an elastic currency and the business corporation was that both tended to put money into the hands of "speculators." The line between an honest banker, merchant, or manufacturer and a speculator was a fine one. The speculator was the business man who, in Jacksonian eyes, had lost sight of the public and become consumed in the single-minded pursuit of money. Rather than pursue the steady gains of his occupation in the time-honored way, he sought instant wealth. Taking great risks was his way of life. By anticipating the rise of a stock, the rapid population growth along a railroad right of way, or a sudden increase in the demand for cotton, the speculator tried to get rich without labor. Such activities were nothing more than gambling to the Democrat, and they were immoral. "Though a depraved habit of opinion among a large portion of society recognizes it [speculation] as not *dishonorable*," said the *Democratic Review*, "it is yet essentially *dishonest* in its nature." Like gambling, it involved "the dishonesty of receiving from another money not fairly earned, by an equivalent of service rendered."[13]

Jacksonians denied that any "short rail-road cut to wealth had been invented." As one Mississippi Democrat remarked, "No plan that ever has, or ever will be devised, by the ingenuity of man, can succeed in changing the condition of our existence here upon earth; men must still eat their bread by the sweat of their face." Fictitious capital had augmented the number of speculators and stockjobbers, "men who wish to live by their wits, without labor," but they contributed nothing to the wealth of society. Democrats mourned the loss of "the sagacious merchant of the good olden time—content with moderate, sure and progressive profits, well acquainted with his particular line of business, and less ambitious of great wealth than jealous of the unquestioned purity of his commercial integrity." There was a "certain degree of hazard" inevitable in commerce, but the merchant in the days of republican simplicity and republican integrity "might on the whole calculate with all but absolute certainty on the reward which would accumulate upon his hands." It was to be lamented that "men still hope to find out some means of producing wealth without labor. All such schemes will, in the end, be found visionary, and we will all find it much to our advantage to settle down at once to an honest and industrious course of life."[14]

Some of the most frequent objects of speculation were programs of internal improvements. Jacksonians rarely denied the ability of railroads or canals to bring prosperity to the regions through which they passed. Bringing prosperity to one region, however, would not increase the wealth of the whole if another region was injured in the process. Public aid to internal improvements, said the *Globe,* was often nothing more than "robbing Peter to pay Paul." It was not general, but partial in its effect. "The sole and only objects for which those kinds of companies [railroads] were created," one citizen wrote to the Columbus (Mississippi) *Democrat,* "was to make fortunes for the stockholders, and to promote the prosperity of particular towns." "The system of Internal Improvement by the General Government," said a group of Mississippi Democrats, "is nothing more than taxing a whole country to aggrandize a particular section."[15]

Similarly, most Jacksonians believed that a protective tariff "builds up one interest and depresses all others." Its benefits were not general; it did not add to national wealth. Its effect was rather "to enhance the natural concentration of wealth into the hands of the few, and to leave the masses impoverished."

In the Democratic mind, then, the Whig plan for economic development and the entrepreneurial activities which it stimulated did not promote economic growth. Real wealth was increased only gradually by traditional patterns of industry and frugality. Some improvement in skill or technology could increase output, but any appearance of sudden gain was necessarily illusory. Whig economic programs might temporarily produce the appearance of prosperity or redistribute the real gains of economic activity, but they could not permanently increase American productivity.

Whigs, as we have seen, were more optimistic about the possibility of increasing the rate of America's material growth. They believed that their program did not simply create the appearance of prosperity; it produced prosperity itself. If it did have the effect of redistributing wealth, the result was beneficial to all. By channeling resources to the dynamic sectors and the active men in the economy, Whigs hoped to stimulate a general expansion of economic activity which would ultimately benefit everyone. The key to this Whig program was the bane of society to Democrats: the credit system.

The essence of the credit system was the expansion of the money supply by banking corporations. Since economic growth was promoted by the application of capital to labor, the way to increase that growth was by expanding the supply of capital. America already had a skilled labor force; she required only capital to develop her bountiful resources.

Whigs believed that the prosperity which resulted from expanding the money supply was not deceptive, but real. It was to the augmenting of the circulating medium by banks, said Calvin Colton, "that, as a nation, we owe our unrivalled march to prosperity and wealth. By the use of the *principle of credit . . . it has anticipated means,* and produced incalculable wealth out of resources which otherwise might have lain dormant." "To attain high prosperity," said the Boston *Courier,* "the whole dormant capital or fixed property must be rendered active by means of credit. . . . Credit . . . is to capital much like what steam is to water; and although water has weight and power, we should come short of much of the benefit to be derived from it, if limited to using it in its natural state." It was essential that the "artificial" banking system produce an elasticity in the money of the country so that it could expand to encompass the wants of society. If money were limited to specie, of which America was chronically short, "the grand enterprises of the country must be abandoned—and with them the spirit of improvement must cease." It seemed apparent to Whigs "that the present amount of activity of trade could not possibly be carried on by such a currency." "We must separate, divorce ourselves from the commercial world," Henry Clay concluded, "and throw ourselves back for centuries, if we restrict our business to the exclusive use of specie."[17]

Of course each party often distorted the views of the other. Jacksonians did not want to outlaw the use of all business paper, nor were they blind to the power of credit to help those without capital of their own to develop the nation's resources. Nor were Whigs unmindful of the dangers inherent in the credit system. While the Boston *Courier* appreciated the benefits of expanded facilities of credit, it also observed that the system had "overpowering seductive influences." "The tendency to these is so great," the *Courier* said, "that many wise and prudent men would greatly limit its use."[18] Yet the parties' differences remained sharp. To the Jacksonian, the artificial increase of the currency brought ruin, while to the Whig it was essential to increase the pace of America's growth.

Similarly, Whigs seldom questioned the value of corporations for creating wealth. Capital not only had to be increased, it had to be concentrated to realize its greatest potential. In America, the corporation seemed the most efficient way of accomplishing this task. Banking corporations, by drawing together capital which would otherwise be scattered and useless, made dormant resources active and productive. Whigs believed that in most fields "large capitalists can produce cheaper than small ones." Aggregated wealth was an agent of progress. Because there were few in America "of sufficient wealth to build and carry on an establishment by their own means," said Webster, "a union of capitals [was] necessary, and among us is conveniently effected by corporations which are but partnerships regulated by law." "Notwithstanding the prejudices which have been enlisted, in times of party excitement, against corporations, it is obvious," insisted the *New York Review*, "that the present advancement of America in her lines of communication, is due more to the spirit of association than to any other cause."[19]

The tendency of the credit system to increase speculation did not trouble Whigs. Speculators, men willing to take risks to realize quick profits, were some of the most valuable men in an active economy. Speculators gave dynamism to economic life and created wealth not only by their own efforts but by the stimulating effect they had on others. In his essay "Wealth," Ralph Waldo Emerson recognized the value of "the monomaniacs who talk up their project in marts and offices and entreat men to subscribe—how did our factories get built? How did North America get netted by iron rails, except by the importunity of these orators who dragged all the prudent men in?" The secret to the production of wealth lay not in the steady habits of merchants, farmers, and artisans: "Wealth is in applications of mind to nature; and the art of getting rich consists not in industry, much less in saving, but in a better order, in timeliness, in being at the right spot."[20]

The credit system ensured that capital would be available to the man with the new idea, the bold project to get rich quickly. "In a country like the United States, with such vast natural wealth, scattered over so vast an extent of territory, there is a peculiar field for the energy and activity of bold and prudent projectors," asserted the New York *Enquirer*. If all were to advance, "it must be by encouraging not by depressing enterprise; it must be by bringing the aid of Government to the Credit System, not by stimulating government to its overthrow; it must be by cherishing and sustaining legitimate and prudent speculation." Attempts to repress speculation, the *American Quarterly Review* argued, restricts "all that human ingenuity projects for the benefit of mankind."[21]

Whigs were more willing than their opponents to assert the superiority of mental over physical labor in the production of wealth. While they gave the conventional praise to the virtues of honest sweat, they also occasionally viewed manual labor as "corporeal drudgery" which degraded man. One Whig became so caught up in the idea of eliminating manual labor as to announce: "How grand would be the spectacle of a nation whose inhabitants were all abundantly supplied with every article of comfort, luxury, and taste, by machinery alone, and whose whole time should be occupied in the pursuit and enjoyment of that happiness which springs from the exercise and improvement of the mind, the enjoyment of social and domestic affections, and the refined pleasure of taste!" In producing such a world, mind, not strength or even physical skill, would be the chief factor. Here again, Emerson caught the spirit of the times. "Property is an intellectual production," he argued. "Cultivated labor drives out brute labor. An infinite number of shrewd men, in infinite years, have arrived at certain best and shortest ways of doing, and this accumulated skill in arts, cultures, harvestings, curings, manufactures, navigations, exchanges, constitutes the worth of our world to-day."[22]

Whigs, convinced of the centrality of the intellect in the creation of wealth, were strong advocates of education. "Intelligence is a primary ingredient in the wealth of nations," Horace Mann declared in 1846. "That political economy," he added in 1848, "which busies itself about capital and labor, supply and demand, interest and rents, favorable and unfavorable balances of trade, but leaves out of account the element of a widespread mental development, is nought but stupendous folly." The *New York Review* looked to Mann's common school system in Massachusetts to provide an example for the whole country: "We shall look there to see if all the productive energies of the state are not increased . . . at a rate that shall, in a tenfold degree, more than compensate for all the expenditures for popular education."[23]

Whigs saw a central role in the production of wealth for inventors, statesmen, lawyers, doctors, and clergymen—professions about whose productive capacities Jacksonians were skeptical. In the Whig mind such men were much more than "useful" auxiliaries to the truly "productive" men of the fields and factories. The *American Quarterly Review* sought a new definition of productivity so that the "man of science and the successful statesman, will no longer be degraded below the rank of the meanest individual who handles a pickaxe or a shovel, by being denominated an unproductive labourer." The journal thought it "very obvious, that some of the unproductive labourers, contribute in an eminent degree to the production of wealth, though this be done only *indirectly*."[24]

> Who would for an instant hesitate to acknowledge the vast accession made to the comforts and gratifications of society, in the shape of material products, that is to wealth, by the industry of such unproductive labourers as Whitney or Fulton? An able statesman, or skilful general, may add more to the wealth of his country, by the results of his exertions, than thousands of productive labourers. And there can be no comparison between the influence on the progress of national wealth of a common field-labourer, and the physician who is instrumental in saving the life of an Arkwright or a Watt.[25]

Jacksonians, Whigs knew, were aware that the services of such men were important to the community. But by stigmatizing them as "unproductive," highly undesirable social consequences could follow. It was only a word, admonished the *Review*, "but words are sometimes more important than things."[26]

Nor could Whigs agree with Jacksonians that the primary effect of internal improvements and the tariff was redistributive rather than productive. "The cause of internal improvement is the hinging question of our national prosperity," declared one Whig writer. Another argued: "A government need not fear to contract debt for works which are certain to be of public utility. . . . [W]hen the debt is contracted in order to be expended in creating a permanent and productive capital in public works, no loss can take place in any direction." This Whig thought that "of all sources of national wealth, internal commerce is not only the most secure, but the most productive." Railroads and canals, by bringing new productive resources into contact with markets, stimulated competition and cheapened the products of human industry. "Is there any other principle than this," asked the *New York Review*, "by which wealth has in any age accumulated, or society grown up to what it now is, or man has been converted from the savage to the citizen?" The railroad system, in particular, was "an instrument of unequalled power in advancing the prosperity of a country."[27]

The chief cause of the "unprecedented augmentation of general wealth" in the previous fifty years, Webster told the Society for the Diffusion of Useful Knowledge in 1836, was "the progress of scientific art." By that Webster principally meant the introduction of machinery. Though Democrats were aware of the enhanced productivity of highly capitalized labor, they were not convinced that the gains were so powerful and general that they offset losses suffered by much of society as a result of tariff protection. Whigs believed that the tariff, by encouraging the development of highly productive industries, would ultimately increase national wealth. Factories produced wealth by diminishing the cost of articles to consumers, which, in turn, resulted from the elimination of costly overseas transportation. Meanwhile, manufactures stimulated agricultural production by creating a home market and increased the average reward of labor by drawing excess agricultural workers into more productive industrial pursuits.[28]

It was essential that America build up manufactures as well as agriculture and commerce, because "nations that are merely agricultural, are proverbially poor." "The most prosperous state of society," declaimed Edward Everett, "is that, where all the great branches of industry are successfully carried on, side by side, feeding, clothing, supplying, and thus sustaining each other." "Neither agriculture, manufactures, nor commerce, taken separately, is the cause of national wealth," observed the *American Whig Review*, "it flows from the three combined, and cannot exist without each." In light of this fact, the *Review* saw the tariff as the key to American productivity. Of the three pillars of the social edifice, only manufactures could not, at least for the time being, prosper without government support:

The most important branch of public policy advocated by the Whig party, is doubtless that of the Protective System, or the encouragement of American Industry by the enactment of well-arranged revenue laws. Without protection we hold that it is impossible for a full development of the resources of the country to be made. The real wealth of a nation consists in its industry; in its availing itself of its capital, skill, and labor, to the full development of all its natural endowments, and its general moral and physical advantages, resulting as well from the genius of its people, as from its peculiar position and institutions.[29]

Whigs, then, justified their program by arguing that it increased the nation's wealth. They denied Jacksonian charges that it merely redistributed rewards and burdens in society. The credit system and entrepreneurial activity, the chief objects of Jacksonian vituperation, were central to the Whig notion of how wealth was created. Whigs envisaged an economy which, because it made sharp departures from the steady habits of the past, would grow at an unprecedented pace.

Everyone was aware that America's bounty had grown prodigiously in the nineteenth century, and that this bounty had not distributed itself evenly among the American people. But while Whigs rarely questioned the basis on which individual efforts were rewarded, Democrats were disturbed by what they considered to be injustices in the distribution of wealth. Given their different impressions of which groups in society were primarily responsible for cultivating the crop, it is understandable that they should have disagreed on who should reap the harvest.

The Distribution of Wealth

A great inequality of wealth existed in Jacksonian America. There were men who enjoyed fortunes comparable to the largest European fortunes of the day. At the other end of the scale, especially in the cities of the Northeast, a type of poverty almost unknown in previous generations had become noticeable. Though economists were already beginning to trace the progress of national wealth, contemporaries were aware that all were not sharing equally in that progress. Both the very rich and the very poor had become objects of political concern—and political controversy. What had caused the unequal distribution of American abundance? Was there any rational justification for the different conditions in which men lived?[30]

Jacksonians might have varied somewhat in their answers to the first question, but to the latter they were nearly unanimous: the answer was no. When Jacksonians looked at the world around them, wrote William Gouge, "they see wealth passing continually out of the hands of those whose labor produced it, or whose economy saved it, into the hands of those who neither work nor save. They do not clearly perceive *how* the transfer takes place: but they are certain of the fact." Gouge's statement is a concise summation of Democratic fears about the growing inequality of wealth in their society. His views were echoed endlessly by others. John Pickering, author of *The Working Man's Political Economy,* declared, "Whoever will but open his eyes, and take an unprejudiced view of society as it is now organized, cannot fail to observe that men do not accumulate property in proportion to their industry; but the reverse is the fact." "It may be laid down as a general rule, with but few exceptions," Orestes Brownson concluded, "that men are rewarded in an inverse ratio to the amount of actual service they perform."[31]

The contest of the age, Democrats contended, was that between the producers of wealth and the non-producers, those "hoards of loafers upon the body politic" who sought to live off the labor of others. The great question was: "Shall labor receive its just reward?" Because they believed that all wealth was the production of labor "and belongs of right to him who produces it," Jacksonians were incensed by the tendency of wealth to accumulate in the hands of bankers, speculators, and others whose services apparently contributed little to its original creation. "Who is it that rolls in his carriage with gilded harness; revels in all the luxuries of the earth; builds palaces and outdoes princes in his entertainments?" asked the New York *Evening Post.* "Is it the man who labours all day and every day? Is it the possessor of houses and lands or anything real? No—it is the minion of paper money." Those who labor for a living were the most virtuous and deserving portion of society, and yet, Samuel Clesson Allen lamented, "How small a part of the products of its labor falls to the laboring class!"[32]

How had this iniquitous distribution of the proceeds of labor come about? Though much of the process seemed veiled and mysterious to Jacksonians, most were certain that the central agency of corruption had been government. "Too much government," said the *Democratic Review,* "has a direct tendency to aid one man or set of men in the 'pursuit of happiness,' and in the 'acquiring, possessing, and protecting property,' if not at the expense of the rest, at least without rendering them the like assistance." Some men's industry, frugality, and skill would enable them to outpace the rest even if government restricted itself to its proper sphere, but differences in wealth would not be as extreme as those which obtained under the present system. "Four fifths of the action of all legislation is," declared the *Review,* "by law, to promote the accumulation of prosperity in a few hands."[33]

Of all legislation, that which contributed most heavily to the increasing inequality of wealth was legislation supporting the credit system. "It is a system of credit," argued the *Globe,* "whose very essence is inequality; not an inequality founded on the eternal basis of a difference in personal vigor, personal activity, superior talent, prudence or enterprise, . . . but an inequality created by legislative enactments, and sustained by the partiality of the law." The system would have collapsed if bank notes had not been given legitimacy by being made receivable in payments owed to government, if bankers had not been granted monopolistic powers by special charters, and if bank stockholders had not been allowed the privilege of limited liability. The banks "owe their credit to acts of Assembly," William Gouge asserted. "If their charters were taken from them, not even their own stockholders would trust them."[34]

The banking system was a means "by which the subtle and ambitious acquire wealth without toil and force the rest of mankind to labor for its support," the *Globe* declared. Its whole operation was "to enrich one class of men by impoverishing another." It was the working man who was impoverished by the credit system. Farmers and laborers and other men of small means could not advance by borrowing from banks: "The crediting class always grow richer, and the debtor class poorer, from year to year." Wage earners were affected adversely by bank operations even if they stayed out of debt. Fluctuations of the currency worked a special hardship on the laborer, asserted the *Democratic Review:* "The price of labor is always the last and least of all to be raised by the expansion of the currency." Thus the worker's buying power was eroded by the rapid price rises which accompanied the growth of the money supply. Meanwhile, the bankers and speculators, who had inside knowledge of the rise and fall of credit operations, were able to work the system to great advantage. "Is it, then, any wonder," asked the *Globe,* "that the laboring classes complain of the operation of a system which presses solely on them?"[35]

Because Jacksonians believed neither banks nor any other privileged corporations produced wealth more abundantly than individuals who enjoyed no special advantages, they saw only their redistributive effects. Privileges and exemptions enriched stockholders and directors by enabling them to monopolize the profits of labor: "Unequal political and commercial institutions *invert* the operation of the natural and just causes of wealth and poverty—take much of the capital of a country from those whose industry produced it, and give it to those who neither work nor save." So central were the banks to this process that the *Democratic Review* believed that, if their privileges were destroyed, "our republican institutions will, not immediately, but in the course of no very long period, begin to produce their proper and natural effects. The advantages that flow from discoveries in the sciences, and improvements in the arts, will not then be confined to the few, but be diffused among all."[36]

Democrats were also skeptical of Whig claims of the wide-spread benefits which would accrue from the artificial stimulation of American industry. Whatever the productive power of the factory and the machine, they did not distribute benefits equally among the population. Most obviously, farmers had to pay higher prices for manufactured items. Whole areas of the South and West, it seemed, were taxed for the benefit of the Northeast. But the tariff was not merely a question of regions; it was also a question of classes.

Even those laborers who found employment in the factories did not share in the productivity of the machine. One worker expressed his frustration in a letter to the *Bay State Democrat* in 1841:

> There have been numerous machines invented which save an immense expenditure of animal labor. And is the condition of the workingman ameliorated by this means? Do they find their toil the lighter, in consequence? No! they reap not the benefit of this; they have to work as many hours now, as ever. It is the *gentlemen* who monopolize all the benefits of science; they well know how to make each benefit and improvement add to their comfort, and minister to their ease;—but the honest producers must be kept down, and compelled to toil on, as their fathers did before them.[37]

Machines were not going to improve the life of laborers. "The introduction of manufactures in any country is the introduction of a very uncertain and precarious employment for workmen," observed the New York *Evening Post for the Country*. "The Manufacturing System," the *Bay State Democrat* argued, "if it works well, carries wealth to the pockets of the capitalists; if ill, it bears heaviest upon the laborer." It was a system designed "to extort from the human machine all the muscular exertion of which it is capable, in one unvaried task, for the emolument of the more opulent classes."[38]

The inevitable result of the introduction of manufactures was a great disparity of fortunes. Such had been the result wherever manufacturing had taken hold in Europe, and there was little

evidence that it would affect America differently. The factory
system created a gulf between the employer and the employed:
"Labor, the creative agent, becomes subordinate to the merely
secondary force of capital; the employer will, even with the usual
risks, reap large fortunes, while the employed is irretrievably
bound to the degrading condition to which the system hurries
him."[39]

The Whig system of government, then, was designed to
advance the interests of a single class. "The 'prosperity' for
which Whigism [sic] labours is not general but particular," said
the New York *Evening Post for the Country*. It was a system which
helped those who least needed—and least deserved—assistance.
Worse yet, it enabled these men to prey upon the rest of society,
to drain away the resources of the humble and industrious. "It
enables men 'to grow rich,'" the paper admitted, "but at the
expense of the people." Every day the gulf between the rich and
the poor grew wider.[40]

Though Democrats knew that an inequality of wealth was
inevitable, they were outraged by the extremes which now
existed. Because their thinking was shaped by more traditional
economic assumptions, they were unable to accept the idea that
the services of any individual could be worth much more than
those of another. "There is nothing in the actual difference of
the powers of individuals," wrote Orestes Brownson, "which
accounts for the striking inequalities we everywhere discover in
their condition." Jacksonians' tendency to see manual labor as
the source of wealth led them to deny that an extreme inequality
of wealth was possible in a just society. "As far as the conditions
of animal existence go there is very little difference in the ability
of all men to provide for themselves and families; and," reasoned the *Democratic Review*, "if all were left without any special
aid from government, both land and the products of industry
would be far more equally distributed than they are."[41]

Believing that there were no great differences in the productivity of labor, it was but a short step for Jacksonians to the idea
that great wealth could be achieved only by living off the

productivity of others. Such wealth was, by itself, almost conclusive evidence of injustice. "Riches," said a writer in the *Globe*, "consist in commanding other men's labor." "If a portion have too much," said the *Democratic Review*, "others of necessity have too little." Jacksonians had a kind of "zero-sum" conception of economic reality. They had less appreciation than the Whigs of the explosive growth potential of the modern economy. Since in their minds society could advance only by degrees, individuals could not make sudden gains without oppressing others. An article in the *Globe* lamented the development of "a state of society in which a few favored ones should possess so great a portion of the bounties of Providence, that the multitude should be destitute of the common necessaries of life." That the rich could become richer without further depressing the poor did not seem reasonable when one assumed an economy in which growth was limited.[42]

Concentrations of wealth, whether controlled by individuals or corporations, were dangerous to the rest of society. "Accumulated wealth is the dynasty of modern states," was a favorite Democratic aphorism. "In all ages and all countries," declared a letter to the Boston *Morning Post*, "wealth is to the body politic, what blood is to the human system; when diffused through the *whole system*, it produces the most genial and salutary influences, but forced by contusions or disease from its natural and healthy operations, it produces disorder, decay, and death." Great wealth was almost certain to be used to destroy the well-being of lesser men, not to advance their interests. Whig apologies for large accumulations of capital had blinded many to their disastrous effects. In the Springfield *Gazette*, William S. Waite mourned the ascendancy of Whig views: "'Security to property' no longer means security to the citizen in the possession of his moderate competency, . . . but security to a few, who may live in luxury and ease upon the blood and sweat of many."[43]

Jacksonians assessed their economic position by their relationship to others, not by their individual accomplishments. It was not enough to examine one's own progress. Too many ways had been devised by which the growing inequalities were concealed: "The only means for the people to detect (amid the deceptive arts and mysteries of government) the frauds which are practised on them, is to examine often, the relative condition of men and classes." Even when Democrats acknowledged that growth had advanced the standard of living for all, they maintained that absolute improvements were not sufficient. The *Democratic Review* was willing to admit that labor enjoyed comforts unknown to earlier ages, but insisted that there was more "relative poverty" in their age because there was greater distance between the poor and the rich.[44]

If legal privileges were eliminated, the *Democratic Review* argued,

> it would tend to equalize the distribution of wealth. Without wholly removing poverty, it would lessen dependence. The strange contrasts created by overgrown affluence and wretched poverty would give place to apportionments of property more equitably adjusted to the degrees of personal capacity and merit.[45]

Men were born equal, said the *Hampshire Republican,* and "it is the proper end of a just government to keep men so." There was no need for government to play an active role in accomplishing this equalization; if government would only learn to leave men alone, "nature's own levelling process" would bring it about. Without government privileges to the favored few, America would realize "that happy mediocrity of fortune which is so favorable to the practice of Christian and republican virtues."[46]

Whigs too wanted to see an America where the great mass of men enjoyed "that happy mediocrity of fortune" which led to independence and self-respect. They too looked forward to the elevation of the laboring classes by the elimination of poverty and dependence. They differed from the Jacksonians, however, in their strategy for achieving this result. Concentrated wealth was considered an ally, not an opponent in their battle against poverty. In the words of Edward Everett, one of the most eloquent of Whig spokesmen on the subject, "Instead of considering accumulated capital as fraught with danger to public liberty, observation will, I think, teach us to regard it . . . as an important instrument of public and private prosperity."[47]

Everett as well as other Whigs admitted that the power of concentrated wealth was sometimes abused, yet they insisted that the interests of capital and labor were not in conflict. "I see no reason in the nature of things to assume a necessary antagonism between labor and capital," Everett maintained, "on the contrary they seem to me the most faithful of allies and best of friends." Wealth, at least wealth collected in order to develop America's resources, added Webster, was misunderstood when viewed "as being hostile to the common good, or having an interest separate from that of the majority of the community." A war upon the rich, argued Calvin Colton, was "a war upon the most vital interests of society." Small masses of capital alone were "not sufficient for the highest degree of prosperity." Capital was "the mainspring of the business operations of civilized society" and to secure its greatest effects, must be collected and concentrated. Large accumulations were required "to keep the smaller capitals in steady movement, and to circulate their products."

If manufactures are to flourish, a very great outlay in buildings, fixtures, machinery, and power, is necessary. If internal intercourse is to diffuse its inestimable moral, social, and economical blessings through the land, canals, railroads, and steamboats, are to be constructed, at vast expense. To effect these objects, capital must go forth, like a mighty genius, bidding the mountains bow their heads, and the valleys to rise, the crooked places to be straight and the rough places plain. If agriculture is to be perfected, costly experiments in husbandry must be instituted, by those who are able to advance, and can afford to lose, the funds which are required for the purpose. Commerce, on a large scale, cannot flourish, without resources adequate to the construction of large vessels, and their outfit for long voyages, and the exchange of valuable cargoes.[48]

The accumulation of wealth in the hands of individuals or corporations, then, was not to be discouraged lest these projects not be carried out. In America, great wealth should not carry the stigma which more aristocratic and less progressive countries had given it. Here wealth "may be traced back to industry and frugality; the paths which lead to it are open to all; the laws which protect it are equal to all." It was not the product of oppression transmitted through generations in hereditary estates. Moreover, American wealth was not hoarded and concealed or used for lavish but useless displays of conspicuous consumption. It was active, it "walks boldly abroad; seeks investment; gives life to commerce, manufactures, and the arts; traverses the land side by side with her sister credit, scattering plenty by the way."[49]

Whigs looked on the rich as public benefactors whose successes did not diminish, but augmented the earnings of men in more humble walks of life. A writer in the Boston *Courier* felt no hostility toward the rich: "The envy, with which they are sometimes viewed and the accusations which are brought against them, as if they were fed by robbery of the poor, are unjust." There was no reason to resent the wealth they possessed:

> It is wealth which they have created; no man is poorer because they possess it. It has been taken from no man. The community, as well as the individual possessor is richer by its whole amount. It has been created, out of that which before was valueless.[50]

The active wealth of great capitalists, by the very nature of the economic system, had to serve the interests of all: "Great investments of capital, whatever selfish objects their proprietors may have, must, before that object can be attained, have been the means of supplying the demand of people for some great article of necessity, convenience, or indulgence." "In a free and just commonwealth," said Emerson, "property rushes from the idle and imbecile to the industrious, brave and persevering." It was important to all that it should. Wealth should be in the hands of those who could use it in ways which produced the greatest benefit to all:

Some men are born to own, and can animate all their possessions. Others cannot. . . . They should own who can administer, not they who, the greater proprietors they are, are only the greater beggars, but they whose work carves out work for more, opens a path for all.[51]

A more equal distribution of wealth was likely to retard improvement. The tendency of businessmen to amass large fortunes was a "public benefit." No clearer example of this was there than the application of aggregated capital to the development of America's resources. Speaking of millionaire merchant Stephen Girard's fortune, Edward Everett asked,

> What better use could have been made of it? Will it be said, divide it equally among the community; give each individual in the United States a share? It would have amounted to half a dollar each for man, woman, and child; and of course, might as well have been sunk in the middle of the sea. Such a distribution would have been another name for annihilation. How many ships would have furled their sails, how many warehouses would have closed their shutters, how many wheels, heavily laden with the products of industry, would have stood still, how many families would have been reduced to want, and without any advantage resulting from the distribution![52]

The only inequality which had to be redressed was that which resulted from the existence of poverty. And poverty had to be eradicated, "not by bringing down the rich, but by lifting up the poor." The concentration of wealth, not its wider distribution, was most likely to effect this result. The *New York Review* called upon the workingman "to behold in the advancement of society, his own advancing state of comfort and happiness; and to feel himself identified with all its varying interests—above all with the prosperity of the capitalist."[53]

There was no such thing as "relative poverty" for Whigs. Poverty was an absolute condition in which a man is unable to provide the basic necessities for himself and his family. It is this kind of absolute poverty which forces an individual to deliver himself into the hands of those who can secure him from want. Great wealth need not overawe and control the lives of those who are able, however modestly, to provide for their own needs. Thus, for Whigs, the ultimate test of an economic system was not its tendency to produce a relative equality of wealth, but its ability to lift the greatest number of individuals above the threshold of economic competence through the creation of abundance.

Whigs never doubted that their economic program was superior to the Democratic "natural system" in this respect. They attacked the Democratic economy not so much because it sought to help the poor at the expense of the rich, as because they did not believe it really helped the poor. The credit system had made America "the heaven of the poor man"; its destruction would make the country "comparatively a hell to him." The measure of prosperity in any country, said Henry Clay, was "the high price of manual labor." Whig stimulation of economic development would best ensure that those at the bottom of society would be appropriately rewarded for their labor.[54]

The credit system was not a system of privilege for the rich, but was, insisted the New York *Enquirer,* "emphatically, the friend of the poor." The Boston *Atlas* was convinced that it benefited the laborer more than the capitalist:

> Who then suffers from the system of CREDIT? Who runs all the risks, and sustains all the losses of the system? The CAPITALIST. Who derives all the benefit, in the stimulation of enterprise, the competition for labor, and the consequent advance of wages? The LABORER. Who can get along very well without credit? The capitalist. Who can do nothing without credit? The poor man.

Poverty, the kind of helpless and hopeless poverty which existed in Europe, would come about only if Jacksonian policy was pursued:

> This policy has already *made* some men poor; continue it, and they may remain poor. Pursue the distinction which the Globe draws between *capital* and *credit;* pursue the system which recognizes

nothing but gold, silver, and lands as property; and you at once give the monopoly of wealth to land holders and money holders, and cut adrift that numerous class who have hitherto found, under the benign protection of institutions truly republican, capital in their character, and in their enterprise and industry an efficient substitute for houses and lands.[55]

All the developments which the Whig system made possible—in trade, manufactures, agriculture, and transportation—were designed, so Whigs believed, to benefit the entire community. The increased demand for labor and the progressive cheapening of the products of labor raised wages and gave those wages a greater purchasing power. Those at the bottom of society had the most to gain. It was for the poor, Henry Clay argued, that the tariff was created: "It affords them profitable employment, and supplies the means of comfortable subsistence." Internal improvements, William Seward declared, visit "with peculiar beneficence citizens of humble circumstances and assiduous industry, indirectly augmenting and actively distributing capital, diminishing the necessity for its use, and reducing the cost of subsistence and exchange." Corporations, aside from the benefits which the entire community enjoyed as a result of their aid in prosecuting large works of public improvement, in expanding the supply of credit, and in making insurance readily available, provided special opportunities to men whose resources were limited: "They enable men . . . of the smallest means, by a concentration of their capitals and the credit created by that operation, to originate and to carry on undertakings which, without the power, credit and facilities derived from such acts, would either not be undertaken at all, or only by individuals of great wealth and for their sole benefit." Acts of incorporation, the Boston *Courier* maintained, do not "favor the rich at the expense of the poor," but "place those who are in pursuit of wealth on a level, as men of business, with those who are already in possession of it."[56]

"The truth is, and universal history will confirm the observation," said the Boston *Atlas*, "that trade and manufactures have

ever been the nursing mothers of liberty, equality, and civilization." Rapid development did not destroy equality, it created it.
It seemed to Whigs that the Democrats' vaunted principle of
equality consisted of a desire "to reduce all classes to a wretched
equality of poverty and degradation." "The Whig party, on the
other hand," the *American Whig Review* declared, "has ever been
guided by the principle of popular elevation." Its purpose was to
create equality "not by destroying national progress, but by
hastening and establishing it." This is what Webster meant by his
assertion that the effect of railroads would be "to equalize the
condition of men." The rich man might profit most economi-
cally from the railroad, but the poor man would not have been
able to travel at all without it.[57]

Whigs, then, were not critical of the distribution of wealth in
their society because they believed inequality necessary to create
a larger economic pie. Moreover, they were confident that the
means by which this larger pie was created inevitably allowed all
to benefit from its existence. Corporations and capitalists pros-
pered only by improving the lives of the many. Whigs were
relatively undisturbed by the type of man who attained wealth in
the mid-nineteenth century—bankers, speculators, and the
like—because they considered them prime movers in the process
by which the entire community advanced. Collective improvement, not economic equality was their aim; for in that improvement they saw the opportunity for every individual to attain the
independence and self-respect which alone could make them
the equals of other men. To the Whig it was no paradox that
capitalist accumulations of wealth would go far toward equaliz-
ing the conditions of men.

The Consequences of Economic Inequality

The distribution of wealth in Jacksonian America was a highly
emotional point of political controversy. Contemporaries differed violently on the direction in which society was being

carried, but they all agreed that the tendency of wealth to flow in new channels was reshaping America. Society, politics, and even morality were being affected by the way in which the economy bestowed its gifts among the population.

The Jacksonian conception of the consequences of material inequality was based on the idea that the interests of rich and poor, of lender and borrower, of capitalist and laborer tended to diverge. The progress of the former did not result in the progress of the latter; it tended rather to the deterioration of his condition. Jacksonians feared that this dynamic was creating a permanent aristocracy which would force the majority of Americans back into subordination and dependency.

This emergent American aristocracy was a direct result of the concentration of wealth in the hands of a few men by means of bank credit and corporations:

> To the evils of all other kinds of aristocracies, landed, feudal, military, and ecclesiastical, the American people were wide awake. But of the nature of moneyed corporations they knew but little. Here was a loop-hole for aristocracy to creep in at, and true to its own insidious character it soon took advantage of the only opening left to it for entrance and now occupies the length and breadth of the land.[58]

Jacksonians objected to this concentration of wealth and power in the first place because it was effected by violations of equal rights. Privileges and exemptions enabled the few to amass riches. But the corrupt manner in which wealth was gained was not the only threat to American society.

No matter how it was accomplished, the concentration of economic power in individuals or corporations was corrupting. The *Democratic Review* noted that "in our country, wealth has more power than in any other." It was capable of deceiving, corrupting, or coercing even those most dedicated to resisting its influence. Because great wealth was intrinsically dangerous, a writer in the New York *New Era* declared, American Democracy was opposed "to the incorporation of numbers with or without prerogatives or privileges." And the *Globe* was opposed even to individuals amassing too much wealth. It deplored the emergence within the mercantile community of "millionaires," men who, "by absolutely engrossing all credit, make men of real, substantial means, their mere jobbers and understrappers . . . mere saplings, overshadowed by an enormous tree." The *Globe* was concerned that "the moderate capitalist, hitherto safely and industriously, and usefully, to himself and others, employed in carrying on the sale and transfer of commodities, should be superseded by the mammoth merchant, and be converted into a sort of factor and dependent on another."[59]

Jacksonians complained that the rich and powerful in society exercised an undue influence in public life. Their wealth alone, because it "always had a powerful influence over those who feel themselves a little dependent" and because it can always inflict "oppression and distress" upon the poor, made the rich a mighty adversary. But the wealthy also had other advantages. They "always have the greatest opportunity of education, of leisure, and other means of carrying on their operations," said the *Ohio Statesman*. "They have time to work head-work and lay deep plans, while the poorer class are obliged to be at their daily labor." Moreover, America's elite formed a naturally unified class. Being set off from the rest of society by their places of residence, their occupations, and their associations, they came to know one another intimately and share their interests.[60]

Riches also enabled men to maintain a style of life which set them apart. Large homes, fashionable dress, and lavish entertainments all seemed, in Jacksonian eyes, to degrade those who had to live without them. The *Hampshire Republican* believed that a certain degree of equality in all things was necessary. If you once encourage men in "their equal hopes of self consequence," the paper maintained, a "conscious relative inferiority" would "paralyze the better feelings of our nature . . . and vice and degradation are sure to follow." The puritanical condemnation of luxury and ease which permeated Democratic writings was evidence that its readers were painfully envious of the trappings of wealth. A long piece in the *Globe* lamented the fate of the poor farmer when bank-created wealth entered his neighborhood. The bank minions had new houses, new furniture, and went to church "in fine coaches with gilded harnesses and foaming steeds." While the farmer "must still live in his old weather-beaten house; be content with his old homely furniture, go to church in his country wagon, and drink hard cider instead of old wine." It was impossible for him to miss the contrast since his wife too "puts him out of conceit of his homespun clothes by abundance of certain lectures about the finery of Mrs. Spriggins and Mrs. Higgins." No matter how fervently Jacksonians denied the validity of such "artificial" and frivolous tests of merit, their dismay at seeing others enjoy them reveals that they had accepted them, however reluctantly, as tests of their own worth."[61]

Although Jacksonians often attributed devilish motives to the aristocracy of wealth, they sometimes appeared to feel that the selfish and inconsiderate ways of the rich were but the regrettable consequences of their isolation from the people. Affluent circumstances, the New York *Evening Post* contended, were "apt to blunt their moral energies and sensibilities." Because the rich associated only with their own kind, they were "deprived of that general knowledge and enlarged philosophy only to be obtained by mixing with people of various classes, various fortunes and various habits." Instead, in their isolated position, they "imbibe the prejudices of a set, and are especially imbued with a distrust of the knowledge and virtue of the vast mass of the people who earn their bread by manual exertion." The rich were not inherently evil: "They possess among their number heads as sound and hearts as true as any party can boast, but taken as a mass they have not those habits nor that knowledge which would enable them on practical matters concerning the great body of the people to judge or act with wisdom."[62]

Wealth thus exercised far too much influence in America for the Jacksonian taste. It appeared to create a class set apart from the average American which was able to exert inordinate influ-

ence on both public and private life. This aristocracy, by its idle
and luxurious life style, made common men ashamed of their
honest labor and simplicity. It created a world in which men were
judged not by their industry or their talents, but by their purse.
Reinforcing the evil power of wealth to influence, corrupt, and
degrade was the motivation it provided the rich to seek to perpetuate and to increase the privileges that they already enjoyed.

Since great wealth was acquired by living off the proceeds of
others' labor, the rich naturally looked to the government for
the power to enable them to extract those proceeds from an
unwilling populace. Once they had attained their ascendant
position, the wealthy would necessarily have a powerful incentive to see that their ascendancy was not challenged. As the *Bay
State Democrat* observed, "It needs no open avowal and public
profession of party action with those who profit by these
corruptions, to ensure a concentrated and effective effort to
sustain the government in its unjust course; for their community
of interest in preserving the unequal privileges and favors which
they receive from the government, operates most effectually in
combining them into a powerful party in opposition to every
effort to reform these abuses." Nor were they likely to stop at
those privileges that they already enjoyed. Power was aggressive.
"Can you suppose for a moment," said one Democrat to his
listeners, "after past experience, that if such men had the power
to put still more burdens on you, that they would not use it?"[63]

One of the chief ways, Democrats believed, in which the rich
would seek to retain their hold on government was by disen-
franchising the poor. The rich man, said the *Globe,* "is naturally
inclined towards institutions which secure to him more than the
just and natural advantages derived from his wealth. He does
not like to see others, who have not the same worldly advantages, enjoying the same privileges with himself." Because they
measured men by their fortune, the aristocracy of wealth was
said to have no concern for "personal rights." The only rights
they knew were "rights of property." Those with no substantial
stake in the community were not entitled to have their say in

determining its course. The wealthy had "always endeavored to monopolize the right of suffrage, to the entire exclusion of the poor." They "cannot bear the idea that the poor shall have an equal voice in the state."[64]

The ultimate threat, then, which extremes of wealth posed to the Jacksonian was the loss of his equality and his freedom. He did not fear material inequality itself so much as he feared the incentive and the power which wealth provided its owner to subordinate others. Jacksonians believed that the rich would never be satisfied with mere high living. It was "the love of enslaving man to human influence, and human power which actuates them." It was their purpose "to keep in subjection to the several classes of the rulers of the day, the souls, and as far as possible, the bodies of men." A few Jacksonians held that this purpose was not malicious. Flowing from "sincere distrust" of most men's ability to manage their own lives, it involved "possibly an honest desire to govern them for their own good through the intelligence of the more cultivated and wealthy few."[65]

If artificial extremes of wealth were allowed to exist, Jacksonians believed, they "might soon expect to become the mere hewers of wood and drawers of water, for [their] masters." Associated wealth would crush its competitors and "the inevitable consequence will be . . . the complete monopoly of the profits of labor, in the hands of a comparatively few individuals, and the consequent degradation and serf-like dependence of the great body of the laboring classes, upon a few lordly employers and patrons." Political power was essential to resist the encroachment of wealth upon equal rights. If the poor allowed the rich to deprive them of their voice in government, they were told by Jacksonians, "You will be kicked away with arrogant contempt or supercilious disdain, for it will no longer be worth while for the exclusive men of merit [i.e. money] to disguise their feelings or their principles. You will sink into a degraded class—degraded morally and politically."[66]

So however vigorously Jacksonians condemned extremes of material inequality and the economic system which created them, their primary concern was actually the maintainance of self-direction and the self-respect which was the consequence of it. Ultimately it was a kind of social, not material equality which they sought. What set them apart from Whigs was that they did not believe that extreme material inequality could develop without oppression or that it could long exist without reducing the masses to a subservient role in society.

Whigs, needless to say, did not share Jacksonian fears that a new aristocracy of wealth was developing in America. To them, no opposition of interests existed between capital and labor. Capital and labor shared the same ultimate fate in that neither could progress without advancing the interest of the other. Thus no gulf need ever divide them. The greater wealth which accrued to those who possessed capital and used it productively would of course distinguish these men from those whose income was solely dependent upon their physical strength. "But because wealth distinguishes those who possess it from those who are without it," observed a correspondent of the Boston *Courier,* "it need not be a line of separation in society. It can distinguish without dividing."[67]

Whigs did not fear that the distinctions which existed in society would become permanent. The laws and institutions which elsewhere tended to perpetuate property in the same hands were absent in America: "Here are no laws of primogeniture—no privileged orders—no enormous salaries—no monopolies to favorites—no means of perpetuating property in the same families—as exist in other countries; by all of which the inequality of property is increased and maintained." In America, wealth was constantly circulating. "The wheel of fortune is in constant revolution," Edward Everett declared, "and the poor in one generation, furnish the rich of the next."[68]

Mobility was a central concept in Whig economic thinking. No man, they thought, should attack the rich, since he or his descendants might expect one day to attain wealth: "The poor man, who nourishes feelings of unkindness and bitterness against wealth, makes war with the prospects of his children."

Whigs were confident that the way was open for all to get rich and that every American was anxious to do so. "No man in America is contented to be poor," observed the *American Whig Review*, "or expects to continue so." There were "no rounds in the social ladder to which the humblest may not aspire." The genius of America was that it had brought "the facilities of independence and wealth . . . within the reach of every honest, industrious, and clever man."[69]

The Whig system, which appeared in Jacksonian eyes to close off opportunities for the humble, in Whig eyes actually increased those opportunities and afforded "incentives to universal activity and emulation." It diversified and increased the demand for labor while it augmented substantially the sum of national wealth. The intoxicating effect such growth had on individuals caused the *American Whig Review* to observe, "There are no bounds among us to the restless desire to be better off." The success of others in the relentless pursuit of wealth was no cause for alarm. Their prosperity represented no drain on the earnings of those who remained behind. Their attainment of high social station did not close off opportunities for the rest. It only increased desire and gave renewed vigor to their efforts to get ahead: "Many of those who are without property, seeing the field of competition open to all, and that a large proportion who have attained affluence or distinction, were once as poor as themselves, are encouraged to hope for similar favors of fortune."[70]

In any case, no permanent gulf could separate rich and poor because in a capitalist economy, Whigs believed, it was impossible for men to get rich without improving the lot of the poor. Factories, steamboats, railroads, and other improvements required the concentration of wealth and no doubt returned handsome dividends to the owners of that wealth. Yet, Webster insisted, "The unquestionable operation of all these things has been not only to increase property, but to equalize it, to diffuse it, to scatter its advantages among the many, and to give content, cheerfulness, and animation to all classes of the social system." Wealth, in a country like America, could not be an agent of mass oppression, for "it seeks of necessity those instruments which promote the public accommodation and benefit."[71]

Whigs saw no discrepancy between this rosy picture of economic development and the reality of economic conditions. They emphatically denied the accuracy of Jacksonian pronouncements on the decline of the laborer: "While the orators of the Union would persuade the work man that the encroachments of capital are constantly advancing, and that he is fast sinking to a condition of 'white slavery,' worse than that occupied by the bondmen of the cotton field or the sugar-plantation, facts prove that he is participating in the progress of the age." Labor, said Daniel Webster in 1836, "has been constantly rising, and is at this very moment, notwithstanding the present scarcity of money, and the constant pressure on capital, higher than it ever was before in the history of the country." The United States, the *American Whig Review* asserted, gives "to the laborer a much larger portion of his earnings than is yielded to him in any other country on the globe."[72]

As long as national wealth increased, Whigs remained undisturbed about its unequal distribution among the people. Collective advancement ensured that all groups in society would move forward together. As a consequence of economic advance, American civilization would also experience political, social, and moral benefits. Wealth was the key to all progress: "A people degraded by poverty and ignorance must ever be slaves or savages; and the history of the world shows that the mass have always risen, where they have risen at all, by industry to wealth, by wealth to knowledge, and by knowledge to power." As a result of the augmentation of general wealth, said Webster, "vastly increased comforts have come to be enjoyed by the industrious classes, and vastly more leisure and time are found for the cultivation of the mind." The Whig program for development, the *New York Review* contended, was "essentially interwoven with the morals of the nation, and with its civilization—with the development of all its resources, intellectual as well as physical—in short, with every scheme of good, whether educational, benevolent or religious, throughout our land." So powerful was America's credit system in uplifting a nation, thought Horace Greeley, that if "put in operation in Italy but for a single generation, it would transform two-thirds of the beggars and Lazzaroni who now swarm that fertile and favored but most wretched country into industrious, useful and respected citizens, and melt down its hundred petty and grinding despotisms into one essentially free, enlightened and happy commonwealth."[73]

The only threat to America's progress was the Democratic party. If Jacksonians had their way, Whigs believed, there would be little hope for improvement. Their "natural system," with its preference for hard money, its prejudice against speculation and enterprise, and its professed intention to equalize the distribution of wealth, would inhibit the growth of national prosperity. Their program would enervate the most dynamic elements in society. The sources of venture capital would dry up, and ambitious individuals would lose the incentives which stimulated their effort. The working classes would not benefit from the equalization of incomes. Lower levels of capital investment would limit the productivity of their labor. They would remain bound to a life of physical drudgery and have diminished prospects for intellectual and moral cultivation. Ignorance and poverty would remain the inevitable lot of many for the foreseeable future.

Such a state of society would have serious political implications. "To be free," Webster admonished a Buffalo audience, "the people must be intelligently free; to be substantially independent, they must be able to secure themselves against want, by sobriety and industry; to be safe depositories of political power they must be able to comprehend and understand the general interests of the community, and must themselves have a stake in the welfare of that community."[74] It was essential that all Americans be "levelled upwards" to the point at which they were able to maintain an enlightened independence. Only a highly prosperous community could support such a population.

The contradictions between the Whig and the Jacksonian impressions of the economic trends of the age could hardly have been more complete. While Whigs saw an ever-ascending spiral of growth showering benefits upon all and lifting even the lowest to an unprecedented position in the community, Jacksonians beheld a vast system of corruption draining the lifeblood of the most industrious classes, driving them into poverty and subjection, and robbing them of the dignity to which all were entitled. Each of these views was profoundly satisfying to a distinctive constituency in Jacksonian America. To understand the nature of these constituencies, it is necessary to return once again to the fundamental world views of the Democrat and the Whig.

The Appeal of Economic Argument

The parties' views on the sources and consequences of economic inequality did not rely on their rational merits for their political appeal. These views were rarely, if ever, developed fully, even by the most articulate party spokesmen. In any event, few voters had the time or the inclination to consider dispassionately the merits of conflicting economic arguments. But nearly all heard bits and pieces of both views—with each bit implying the more complete and coherent analysis described above. Each individual was receptive to some of these ideas and unreceptive to others. No doubt some individuals, by accepting certain arguments from each of the interpretations, subscribed to a rather inconsistent and contradictory view of the age. It is likely, however, that for most individuals the "persuasive" explanations for economic inequality clustered about the Democratic and Whig poles described above.

The appeal or the non-appeal of each perspective for any given individual appears not to have been a function of his economic position. Neither wealth nor occupation clearly distinguished those who put their faith in one view from those who believed the other. It has also been suggested that the dynamics of the individual's social position determined his outlook: the rising elements in society becoming Whigs, the injured and declining becoming Jacksonians.[75] But all individuals do not measure their future prospects by their past experience. Some feel ruin becomes more certain as their lot improves. Others remain hopelessly optimistic despite repeated blows from experience. Men's notions of how they fit into their world, not their outward circumstances—whether static or dynamic—govern which arguments they will find persuasive. Ideas seem compelling when they speak to deeply felt perceptions of self and to pressing psychological needs.

The Democratic perspective on economic inequality was especially convincing to the individual still drawn to a more traditional world. Its view of economic processes was that of an idealized American past. Growth was the steady and gradual result of individual industry and frugality. Differences of wealth were not substantial, and such as did exist, if not always justifiable, were at least understandable. It was a world of human scale and individual morality, where rewards were traceable to service to the community, not to self-interested manipulation of commodities or credit.

The Jacksonian found himself, however, in a society where time-honored patterns of industry and frugality brought only degradation and contempt, but where men who were too impatient to make their way legitimately, men who used fraud and coercion to live at the expense of others, grew rich and powerful. Worse yet, his Whig opponent declared that these "speculators" were public benefactors who were not only entitled to the lion's share of the nation's wealth but also to the homage of the rest of society. The Whig appeared to argue that the Jacksonian could not advance on his own and that his fate was dependent on the very institutions and men which robbed and degraded him. The Jacksonian could not accept the validity of Whig arguments without admitting his own dependency and suffering a terrible blow to his self-esteem. His only way out was to deny the legitimacy of his current "betters" and of the new economic and social bonds which they were creating. By condemning the inequality of his day the Jacksonian made peace with himself and his society.

The Whig view of economic inequality reveals a more complete adjustment to modern economic relations. It displays fewer fears of abstract corporate arrangements and impersonal monetary transactions. Whigs accepted more readily the workings of the market. They had a greater faith that it rewarded beneficial activities, even if the benefit was not immediately apparent. Their business morality was more concerned with effect than intention. Self-interested action could yet serve the public good. Whigs also demonstrated a greater appreciation for the explosive possibilities of economic growth and the critical importance of particular men, ideas, and processes in producing it. Whigs believed rightly that their age marked a sharp break with the past. Now, both men and societies, by the proper organization of their economic affairs, could advance at unprecedented rates. Whigs were also emphatic in their claim that prosperity would be the agent of collective advancement in social, political, and moral life.

The Whig view of economic inequality was, however, something more than evidence of an accommodation to individualism. It provided, as did the Jacksonian perspective, psychological comfort to individuals troubled by their position in society. But while the Jacksonian version relieved fears of failure, the Whig version relieved fears of success. It seems apparent from Whig rhetoric that, however fully Whigs accepted self-interested economic striving, many needed to feel that their achievements were not, as Jacksonians charged, made only at the expense of others. Economic theory might argue that the capitalist was a public benefactor, but economic theory cannot explain why Whigs had such a strong desire to hear the idea endlessly stated. Economic growth might promote equality for all in theory, but it was easy to doubt the fact when poverty and ignorance persisted in the face of rapid economic growth. Even Whig attempts to redefine the term "productive," so as not to leave out the learned professions and other non-laborers, can be viewed as something more than efforts to refine economic theory. They may also be seen as attempts to assuage the consciences of men who questioned their worthiness to receive lucrative rewards from their society.

Each view of inequality thus emerged from a view of economic processes—one essentially traditional, the other essentially modern. And each view provided comfort to men beset by special problems of adjustment as they and the world about them were transformed by modernity.

Conclusion

It is easy to see that a greater self-reliance must work a revolu-
tion in all the offices and relations of men.

RALPH WALDO EMERSON

Between the Revolution and the 1830s dramatic social change transformed America and Americans. Rapid modernization swept away the remnants of traditional society and left a social order dominated by an ethic of individualism. While the community no longer controlled the individual's life, neither was it responsible any longer for his success or failure. Cut adrift from society, the American was expected to think, act, and provide for himself. He had to make his way alone in a world of strangers.

Americans of the Jacksonian generation responded to this new world with varying degrees of success. Some navigated these uncharted seas well, for they had early internalized values and habits of behavior that guided their passage through life. Others, because they lacked this inner guidance, found their voyage rough going. Relying too much on social ties and a social order that no longer existed, they expressed frustration and anger with the impersonal and aggressive world they actually encountered. When these two types of individuals confronted public life, they were bound to see the issues of their day differently.

In the Jacksonian era two great political parties arose to represent these divergent reactions to the emergence of individualism. The Whig party championed the cause of those whose adjustment was relatively untroubled, while the Jacksonian Democrats spoke for Americans whose accommodation was reluctant and painful. Each party developed a world view, expressed in their political rhetoric, which spoke to the needs and understandings of those who rallied under its banner. When public issues were discussed in the context of these world views, they held private meaning for individuals whose everyday lives were dominated by the problem of adjustment to a new form of human relations.

In fact, the politics of the Jacksonian era was actually "the politics of individualism," a dialogue over the proper nature of the individual's relations with his fellow men in an individualistic social order. The public arena became a forum for a generation-long debate on questions that still have meaning today. In a society where individuals are ends and not means, what are one's obligations to the state and to one's fellows? In a nation devoted to the rule of law, does legislation enlarge or constrict the realm of personal freedom? In a society dedicated to equality, how may men be allowed to rise above the mass or to remain below?

Notes

Preface

1. John Murrin and Rowland Berthoff, "Feudalism, Communalism, and the Yeoman Freeholder: The American Revolution Considered as a Social Accident," in Stephen G. Kurtz and James H. Hutson, eds., *Essays on the American Revolution* (Chapel Hill: Univ. of North Carolina Press, 1973), 287.

2. Arthur Schlesinger, Jr., *The Age of Jackson* (Boston: Little, Brown 1945), 279; Bray Hammond, *Banks and Politics in America, from the Revolution to the Civil War* (Princeton: Princeton Univ. Press, 1957), 361, 345.

3. Lee Benson, *The Concept of Jacksonian Democracy: New York as a Test Case* (Princeton: Princeton Univ. Press, 1961). The best analysis of Benson's and subsequent ethnocultural interpretations of politics is Richard L. McCormick, "Ethno-Cultural Interpretations of Nineteenth-Century American Voting Behavior," *Political Science Quarterly* 89 (June 1974): 351–77.

Introduction

1. Alexis de Tocqueville, *Democracy in America,* ed. Phillips Bradley (New York: Random House, 1945), 2: v.

2. J. Hector St. John de Crevecoeur, *Letters from an American Farmer* (New York: E.P. Dutton, 1957), 39.

3. Washington Irving, "Rip Van Winkle," in *Washington Irving* (New York: Library of America, 1983) 778–81.

4. Chilton Williamson, *American Suffrage from Property to Democracy, 1760–1860* (Princeton: Princeton Univ. Press, 1960).

5. Richard P. McCormick, "New Perspectives on Jacksonian Politics," *American Historical Review* 65 (Jan. 1960): 288–301.

6. Quoted in William J. Cooper, *The South and the Politics of Slavery, 1828–1856* (Baton Rouge: Louisiana State Univ. Press, 1978), 36.

7. For discussions of Jacksonian historiography, see: Charles G. Sellers, Jr., "Andrew Jackson versus the Historians," *Mississippi Valley Historical Review* 44 (March 1958): 615–34; Alfred A. Cave, *Jacksonian Democracy and the Historians,* University of Florida Monographs: Social Sciences, no. 22 (Gainesville: Univ. of Florida Press, 1964); and Ronald P. Formisano, "Toward a Reorientation of Jacksonian Politics: A Review of the Literature, 1959–1975," *Journal of American History* 63 (June 1976): 42–65.

8. "'Social character' is that part of 'character' which is shared among significant social groups and is the product of the experience of these groups." The concept permits one to speak of the character of classes, groups, regions, or nations. These common elements of character occur because every society, in conscious or unconscious ways, attempts to ensure its continued existence by shaping its members to "fit in." In the words of Erich Fromm: "In order that any society may function well, its members must acquire the kind of character which makes them *want* to act in the way they *have* to act as members of the society or of a special class within it. They have to *desire* what objectively is *necessary* for them to do. *Outer force* is replaced by *inner compulsion,* and by the particular kind of human energy which is channeled into character traits." Building upon this insight, Riesman delineates three types of social character—tradition-directed, inner-directed, and other-directed—which are based on "the way in which society ensures some degree of conformity from the individuals who make it up." To Riesman, "mode of conformity" may be considered a synonym for social character. David Riesman, *The Lonely Crowd* (New Haven: Yale Univ. Press, 1970), 3–6.

9. Riesman defines inner-direction in *Lonely Crowd,* 13–17.

10. Riesman defines tradition-direction in *Lonely Crowd,* 9–13.

11. *Ibid.,* 4.

12. Alex Inkeles, "Making Men Modern: On the Causes and Consequences of Individual Change in Six Developing Countries," *American Journal of Sociology* 75 (Sep. 1969): 224.

13. Some of the effects on women and the family of the emergence of individualism are suggestively outlined in a perceptive article by William E. Bridges, "Family Patterns and Social Values in America,

1825–1875," *American Quarterly* 17(Spring 1965): 3–11; the subsequent literature on this subject is voluminous, but the works of Nancy Cott, Barbara Welter, Gerda Lerner, and Mary Ryan will give the reader a good introduction to the subject.

14. Tocqueville's explanation of individualism can be found in *Democracy*, 2:104–6.

15. Riesman, *Lonely Crowd*, 9–13.

16. The works which elaborate the many facets of the social transformation of America from settlement to the age of Jackson are much too numerous to list. The best overviews for understanding the nature of the changes I emphasize here, however, are Rowland Berthoff, *An Unsettled People: Social Order and Disorder in American History* (New York: Harper and Row, 1971), and Richard D. Brown, *Modernization: The Transformation of American Life, 1600–1865* (New York: Hill and Wang, 1976).

17. Riesman, *Lonely Crowd*, 13–17.

18. Many others have seen the general period 1776–1830 as encompassing the greatest changes in the American character and American society. Among them are: Rowland Berthoff, *An Unsettled People* (New York: Harper and Row, 1971); Brown, *Modernization*; and Robert Wiebe, *The Segmented Society: An Introduction to the Meaning of America* (New York: Oxford Univ. Press, 1975).

19. Tocqueville, *Democracy*, 2:104–5. I have taken the liberty of modifying the Phillips Bradley edition's translation of the line "its members become undifferentiated and lose their class identity for each other" (p. 105) to read "its members become indifferent, and as strangers to one another," as it is translated in the abridged edition edited by Richard D. Heffner (New York: New American Library, 1956), 194.

20. "Privatism" is the term preferred by Sam Bass Warner, Jr., *The Private City: Philadelphia in Three Periods of Its Growth* (Philadelpha: Univ. of Pennsylvania Press, 1968). "Modern man" is used by Alex Inkeles and David H. Smith, *Becoming Modern: Individual Change in Six Developing Countries* (Cambridge, Mass.: Harvard Univ. Press, 1974).

21. Tocqueville, *Democracy*, 2:104.

22. *Ibid.*, 104–5.

23. *Ibid.*, 114–28.

24. *Ibid.*, 104.

25. This interpretation, by seeing an underlying social meaning in political rhetoric, provides an explanation for the similarity of rhetoric used to discuss a wide range of issues. And the ability of the era's political rhetoric to touch psychological conflicts within individuals

helps explain why it elicited such a deep emotional response in Americans.

26. This interpretation finds a greater unity within each political party than many recent scholars have found. First, it sees more congruence between party elites and rank and file voters. The charge that public policy interested only elites or that elites had one political agenda and the rank and file had another is false. Some issues may have *seemed* to benefit only one group or the other, but within the comprehensive world view that all members of the party shared, these issues took on meaning for everyone. Second, this interpretation finds common bonds uniting some internal party divisions that fractured even elites. Daniel Walker Howe, for example, sees Whigs as split into "Modernizers," "Conservatives," and "Evangelicals." *Political Culture of the American Whigs* (Chicago: Univ. of Chicago Press, 1979), 150–237. Here, however, these dispositions are considered only varied responses to a common problem: the inner-directed man coping with the world of individualism. Moreover, these responses were often found within the same individual. Finally, this interpretation finds a greater unity between the northern and southern party systems. When the ethno-cultural interpretation of voting behavior began to dominate political history, it inhibited the formulation of national frameworks for understanding Jacksonian politics because ethno-cultural issues were so obviously less important in the South. Here, however, since both economic issues and ethno-cultural ones are viewed within a common framework—the transition to an individualistic society—the way is once again open to viewing Jacksonian era politics as the national system it was.

27. Although this work does not attempt to analyze the social composition of the parties, it does suggest a way of understanding the findings of historians who have attempted to do so. The ethno-religious basis for parties which Benson, Formisano, and Holt have seen in antebellum politics (Whigs = "pietistic" Protestants, Democrats = "ritualistic" Protestants and Catholic immigrants), can be explained within the framework of modernization employed here. Eric Foner's insights on the 1850s in his essay, "The Causes of the American Civil War: Recent Interpretations and New Directions," provide a concise, suggestive example of this line of argument: "If we do expand our notion of culture beyond a relatively narrow definition of ethnicity and religious belief, we may find that 'pietists' were much more hospitable to the Protestant work ethic and the economic demands of a modernizing society than were "ritualists" and Catholic immigrants. Is it possible that the resistance of the Irish to 'Americanization,' rather than

simply a desire to maintain cultural identity, was the attempt of a
pre-industrial people to resist the hegemony of a modernizing culture,
with all that that implied for character structure, work patterns, and
life styles? May we view the Democratic party as the representative of
the great pre-modern cultures within American society—the white
South and the Irish immigrants—and perhaps then better understand
why the nativist image of the Irish and the anti-slavery critique of the
southern slaveholder stressed the same 'undesirable' traits of lack of
economic enterprise and self-discipline . . . ? Was the northern
Democratic machine at the local level attuned to the communal,
traditionalist behavior of the peasant immigrants, while the intense
individualism of the Republicans had little to offer them?" The
ethno-cultural interpretation is elaborated in Lee Benson, *The Concept
of Jacksonian Democracy: New York as a Test Case* (Princeton: Princeton
Univ. Press, 1961); Michael F. Holt, *Forging a Majority: The Formation of
the Republican Party in Pittsburgh, 1848–1860* (New Haven: Yale Univ.
Press, 1969); and Ronald P. Formisano, *The Birth of Mass Political
Parties: Michigan, 1827–1861* (Princeton: Princeton Univ. Press, 1971).
Foner's essay appears in *Politics and Ideology in the Age of the Civil War*
(New York: Oxford Univ. Press, 1980), 15–33. The quotation is from
page 26.

28. There is much dispute about the similarity of southern politics to
the other regions under the second party system. William J. Cooper, in
particular, argues that southern politics had a distinctive problem, the
defense of slavery, which overrode all other considerations (Cooper,
South and the Politics of Slavery). Of course when slavery was attacked,
southerners closed ranks behind it. But Whigs and Democrats fiercely
contested each other in the Jacksonian South, and they did so on the
same bases as their northern counterparts. For excellent analyses of
party differences in the Jacksonian South, see J. Mills Thornton III,
Politics and Power in a Slave Society: Alabama, 1800–1860 (Baton Rouge:
Louisiana State Univ. Press, 1978), Marc W. Kruman, *Parties and Politics
in North Carolina, 1836–1865* (Baton Rouge: Louisiana State Univ.
Press, 1983), and Harry L. Watson, *Jacksonian Politics and Community
Conflict: The Emergence of the Second American Party System in Cumberland
County North Carolina* (Baton Rouge: Louisiana State Univ. Press, 1981).

29. Tocqueville, *Democracy*, 2:239–40.

30. Walter Dean Burnham, "Theory and Voting Research: Some
Reflections on Converse's 'Change in the American Electorate,'" *American Political Science Review* 68 (Sep. 1974): 1002–23. John Michael
Rozett found that in Green County, Illinois, individual Whigs and
Democrats cast less than 10 percent of their votes for candidates from

the opposing party in 20 elections during the period 1840–1848. "The Social Bases of Party Conflict in the Age of Jackson: Individual Voting Behavior in Green County, Illinois, 1838–1848" (Ph.D. dissertation, Univ. of Michigan, 1974), 33. Similarly, Paul Goodman's study of 2,200 New England voters from 1832–52 concluded that "New England voters were highly partisan, rarely independent or doubtful, and little inclined to split their ticket." "The Social Basis of New England Politics," *Journal of the Early Republic* 6 (Spring 1986): 31.

31. This work makes much use (though not explicitly) of the psychological concept of projection. Projection is a "psychological phenomenon involving the unconscious attribution to other people of attitudes or characteristics that are in fact properties of the individual who projects them" (*Encyclopedia of Sociology* (Guilford, Connecticut: Dushkin Publishing, 1974), 225). Projection was one of the defense mechanisms, first proposed by Freud, which protect the ego from impulses which are "incompatible either with other impulses or with one's moral standards." By attributing one's own unacceptable impulses to others, one is relieved of guilt and anxiety. Although projection was originally associated with neurosis, today many feel "that projection is an inherent part of all perception" (Daniel R. Miller, "Defense Mechanisms," in *International Encyclopedia of the Social Sciences,* 1968 ed.). In the context of this work, projection is used in an attempt to reveal the inner life of normal men. We cannot know directly the inner concerns of Whigs, for example, but we can discover in their perceptions of Democrats certain distortions and exaggerations. We may surmise, for instance, that their exaggerated concern for the passionate and violent nature of Jacksonians was, to some degree, a projection of their own unacceptable impulses to reject self-control. It is important to remember that Whigs could have no direct knowledge of the motives and intentions of a Jacksonian; they could only project what *they* would feel if they were in his place in order to guess what the Jacksonian intended. And, of course, the same would be true of Jacksonians seeking to understand Whigs. Many of these attempts could be quite accurate and would reveal little more than that each party was a sensitive and perceptive observer of the other. But when fears seem out of proportion, when intentions appear distorted, we may suspect that inner turmoil is affecting perception. One need not recur to depth psychology to accept what should be a commonsense conclusion, what the theologian Dietrich Bonhoeffer put quite simply: "It is precisely when a man descerns his own foible in another man that he is impelled to condemn him with particular severity" (Bonhoeffer, *Ethics* (New York: MacMillan, 1965), 32).

Chapter 1. The Jacksonian World

1. Boston *Weekly Reformer, or Herald of Union and Progress,* Jan. 20, 1837.

2. Robert Remini, *The Election of Andrew Jackson* (Philadelphia: J.B. Lippincott, 1963), 28–29.

3. "Legislative Embodiment of Public Opinion," *The United States Magazine and Democratic Review* (hereafter *Democratic Review*) 19 (Aug. 1846): 83.

4. Jackson *Mississippian,* July 6, 1838; *Argus of Western America* (Frankfort, Ky.), Aug. 6, 1828; *Hampshire Republican* (Northampton, Mass.), Oct. 12, 1836.

5. "The Banks and the Currency," *Democratic Review* 2 (April, 1838): 3; New York *Evening Post for the Country,* Jan. 22, July 27, 1844; Boston *Weekly Reformer,* June 2, 1837; *Globe* (Washington, D.C.), Jan. 24, 1844.

6. Boston *Morning Post* reprinted in *Globe,* April 10, 1835.

7. *Globe,* Jan. 18, 1839.

8. Richmond *Enquirer,* Nov. 1, 1839; William Allen, "Speech of Mr. Allen of Ohio, on the Bill to Separate the Government from the Banks," (Washington: Globe Office, 1838), 5.

9. Winchester *Virginian* reprinted in *Globe,* Sep. 10, 1833; *Bay State Democrat* (Boston), March 9, 1842; *Globe,* Nov. 5, 1842.

10. Andrew Jackson, "Veto Message," July 10, 1832, *Compilation of the Messages and Papers of the Presidents, 1789–1907,* J.D. Richardson, ed. (Washington D.C.: Bureau of National Literature and Art, 1908), 2:590.

11. *Globe,* April 22, 1841.

12. James K. Polk, "Fourth Annual Message," Dec. 5, 1848, *Messages and Papers,* 4:655; *Plaindealer,* Dec. 24, 1836; "The Moral of the Crisis," *Democratic Review* 1 (Oct. 1837): 119; *Argus of Western America,* June 30, 1830.

13. *Globe,* Jan. 10, 1844; Nov. 7, 1839.

14. "Public Currency," *Democratic Review* 5 (March 1839): 323.

15. "Ultraism," *Boston Quarterly Review* 1 (July 1838): 379.

16. "Introduction," *Democratic Review,* 1 (Oct. 1837): 11; Boston *Morning Post,* May 11, 1839.

17. "National Costume," *American Monthly Magazine,* n.s., 5 (June 1838): 510, 511.

18. *Log Cabin* (New York and Albany), Sep. 12, 1840.

19. *Hampshire Republican,* (Northampton, Mass.) Dec. 7, 1836; William Allen, "Speech," 4.

20. (Ann Arbor) *Michigan Argus,* Aug. 30, Sep. 20, 1838.

21. *Globe,* April 22, 1841; Richmond *Enquirer,* April 10, 1840; Little Rock *Arkansas Gazette,* Feb. 5, 1840.

22. *Globe,* April 13, 1835; April 18, 1840; April 21, 1835.

23. *Globe,* Feb. 17, 1841; New York *Evening Post,* Aug. 28, 1834; April 23, 1836; June 3, 1834.

24. *Globe,* July 23, 1840; Merrill D. Peterson, *The Jefferson Image in the American Mind* (New York: Oxford Univ. Press, 1962), 72–73; *Globe,* July 12, 1832; "The Independent Treasury Reform," *Democratic Review* 8 (Aug. 1840): 99; "The Tariff—Its History and Influence," *Democratic Review* 19 (Sep. 1846): 163.

25. *Globe,* Feb. 10, 1841.

26. "Introduction," *Democratic Review* 1 (Oct. 1837), 12–13.

27. *Hampshire Republican,* Oct. 26, 1836; "Introduction," *Democratic Review* 1 (Oct. 1837): 11–12.

28. New York *Evening Post,* Oct. 18, 1836; New York *New Era* reprinted in Columbus (Miss.) *Democrat,* June 13, 1840.

29. Milledgeville *Federal Union,* April 28, 1840; *Globe,* July 13, 1837; New York *Times* reprinted in *Hampshire Republican,* Oct. 12, 1836.

30. *Globe,* Aug. 11, 1837.

31. Milledgeville *Federal Union,* Dec. 10, 1839.

32. "Address to the Journeymen Cordwainers of all Branches throughout the United States," Boston *Weekly Reformer,* May 5, 1837.

33. Fall River *Patriot* reprinted in Columbus (Miss.) *Democrat,* Dec. 21, 1839; "Introduction," *Democratic Review* 1 (Oct. 1837): 11; Richmond *Enquirer,* Feb. 27, 1840.

34. New York *Evening Post for the Country,* March 20, 1844.

35. New York *Evening Post for the Country,* March 18, 1837; *Globe,* Feb. 1, 1834.

36. *Globe,* Oct. 9, 1834.

37. *United States Telegraph* (Washington, D.C.), May 7, 1829; Jackson *Mississippian,* March 6, 1835.

38. *Globe,* April 3, 1834.

39. William Allen, "Speech," 6; Jackson *Mississippian,* May 1, 1835.

40. *Argus of Western America,* June 30, 1830.

41. *Globe,* Feb. 1, 1834; *United States Telegraph,* Aug. 2, 1828; New York *Evening Post for the Country,* March 18, 1837.

42. James C. Curtis, *Andrew Jackson and the Search for Vindication* (Boston: Little, Brown, 1976), 94–101, 103.

43. Boston *Morning Post,* May 23, 1838; New York *Evening Post,* April 7, 1834; Jackson *Mississippian,* Nov. 28, 1834.

44. Nativism, especially antipathy to Irish Catholics, was more common among Whig voters than among Democratic ones, though most

Whig leaders condemned the practice. Edward Pessen, *Jacksonian America: Society, Personality, and Politics*, rev. ed. (Homewood, Ill.: Dorsey Press, 1978), 279–83; In his "First Annual Message," Jackson himself asserted, "The duties of all public officers are, or at least admit of being made, so plain and simple that men of intelligence may readily qualify themselves for their performance." Dec. 8, 1829, *Messages and Papers*, 2: 449; "The Tariff—Its History and Influence," *Democratic Review* 19(Sep. 1846): 163.

45. "Democracy," *Democratic Review* 7(March 1840): 219.

46. "New York City vs. New York State," *Democratic Review* 6 (Dec. 1839): 502; *Hampshire Republican*, July 6, 1836; *Ohio Statesman* (Columbus), July 28, 1840; Albany *Rough-hewer*, March 5, 1840.

47. Boston *Weekly Reformer*, Jan. 20, 1837; March 31, 1837; New York *New Era* reprinted in Columbus *Democrat*, June 13, 1840.

48. "The Sober Second-Thought of the People," *Democratic Review* 3 (Nov. 1838): 282; *Globe*, March 30, 1840; "Democracy," *Democratic Review* 7(March 1840): 223; *Globe*, April 7, 1835.

49. New York *Evening Post*, April 4, 1834; Jackson *Mississippian*, Oct. 19, 1838.

50. *Ohio Statesman*, Aug. 30, 1837; New York *Weekly Herald* reprinted in Columbus *Democrat*, March 16, 1839.

51. "Democracy," *Democratic Review* 7 (March 1840): 228–9.

52. *Ibid.*

53. *Bay State Democrat*, July 21, 1841; Gallatin *Democrat* reprinted in Jackson *Mississippian*, March 27, 1835.

54. Milledgeville *Federal Union*, Jan. 18, 1842; New York *Evening Post*, Feb. 13, 1836.

55. "Democracy," *Democratic Review* 7(March 1840): 224.

56. James K. Polk, "Fourth Annual Message," Dec. 5, 1848, *Messages and Papers*, 4: 654–655.

57. *Ibid.*, 655–56.

58. *Ibid.*, 657–58.

59. Boston *Morning Post*, Nov. 20, 1837.

60. *Globe*, June 3, 1837; Boston *Morning Post*, Nov. 20, 1837.

61. Jackson *Mississippian*, Nov. 21, 1834; Montgomery *Advertiser* quoted in J. Mills Thornton III, *Politics and Power in a Slave Society: Alabama, 1800–1860* (Baton Rouge: Louisiana State Univ. Press, 1978), 51; Milledgeville *Federal Union*, Aug. 8, 1843; Huntsville (Ala.) *Democrat*, Aug. 17, 1839.

62. "The History of Uncle Sam's Patriarchal System of Government," *Democratic Review* 9 (Dec. 1841): 586.

63. "Democracy," *Democratic Review* 7 (March 1840): 221, 219.

64. These generalizations are drawn from: Joel Silbey, *The Shrine of Party: Congressional Voting Behavior, 1841–1852* (Pittsburgh: Univ. of Pittsburgh Press, 1967), 28–29, 31–32, 52–54, 56–58, 63, 73, 88; Herbert Ershkowitz and William G. Shade, "Consensus or Conflict?: Political Behavior in the State Legislatures during the Jacksonian Era," *Journal of American History* 58 (Dec. 1971): 598–604. Detailed analysis of congressional voting on these issues can be found in Thomas B. Alexander, *Sectional Stress and Party Strength: A Computer Analysis of Roll-Call Voting Patterns in the United States House of Representatives, 1836–1860* (Nashville: Vanderbilt Univ. Press, 1967).

65. Silbey, *Shrine of Party*, 30–31, 54–55, 63; Ershkowitz and Shade, "Consensus or Conflict?," 606–11.

66. Free banking was advocated by Jacksonians only where banks were too entrenched to be destroyed. In states where banks were vulnerable, Jacksonians sought to do away entirely with them. See James Roger Sharp, *The Jacksonians versus the Banks: Politics in the States after the Panic of 1837* (New York: Columbia Univ. Press, 1970), 321–25; "The Political Crisis," *Democratic Review* 2 (June 1838): 318.

67. *Plaindealer*, Aug. 19, 1837.

68. Richmond *Enquirer*, Aug. 14, 1840.

69. John William Ward, *Andrew Jackson: Symbol for an Age* (New York: Oxford Univ. Press, 1955), 53; "Jacksonian Democratic Thought: 'A Natural Charter of Privilege,'" in Stanley Coben and Lorman Ratner. eds., *The Development of an American Culture*, 2nd ed. (New York: St. Martin's, 1983), 69–73; Boston *Weekly Reformer*, Dec. 9, 1836.

70. James Buchanan, "Speech, January 22, 1840, in Reply to Mr. Clay on the Independent Treasury Bill," *The Works of James Buchanan*, 4: 148–49.

71. Although it is ironic that the Democratic party as a whole supported policies that accelerated the pace of modernization, there were, of course, individual Democrats who actually intended this result. As noted below, Democratic anti-monopoly rhetoric sometimes attracted men who simply wanted to eliminate any regulation of or obstacles to their own rush to get rich. Jacksonians frequently noted that there were men in the party who were not of it.

72. Vermont *Statesman* quoted in John Ashworth, "The Jacksonian as Leveller," *Journal of American Studies* 14 (Dec. 1980): 415.

73. See especially Richard Hofstadter's argument in "Andrew Jackson and the Rise of Liberal Capitalism," which appears in his *The American Political Tradition* (New York: Random House, 1948); and, of course, the argument of Bray Hammond in his *Banks and Politics in*

America from the Revolution to the Civil War (Princeton: Princeton Univ. Press, 1957).

74. Bray Hammond, *Banks and Politics.*

75. Sharp, *Jacksonians versus the Banks,* 321–25; See, for example, the running war which Isaac Hill carried on with radical Democrats in his *Hill's New Hampshire Patriot* (Concord) in 1843–44. The New York *Plebian* and the *Bay State Democrat* in particular accused him of selling out to corporate interests.

Chapter 2. The Whig World

1. Ralph Waldo Emerson, "Society and Solitude," *Selected Writings of Emerson* (New York: Random House, 1950), 745.

2. Webster, "Lecture before the Society for the Diffusion of Useful Knowledge," Nov. 11, 1836, *Writings and Speeches,* 13: 72, 74.

3. Troy *Morning Mail* quoted in Albany *Evening Journal,* Aug. 27, 1839; *Morning Courier and New-York Enquirer* (New York) (hereafter New York *Enquirer*), April 30, 1835; Springfield (Mass.) *Republican,* May 20, 1837; Calvin Colton, *Manual for Emigrants to America* (London: F. Westley and A. H. Davis, 1832), 171–72.

4. Boston *Courier,* Feb. 22, 1836.

5. Clay, "On the Plan of the Sub-Treasury," Feb. 19, 1838, *Works,* 8: 127; Webster, "The Continuance of the Bank Charter," March 18, 1834, *Writings and Speeches,* 7: 94; Calvin Colton in his introduction to Henry Clay's speech "On President Jackson's Veto of the Bank Bill," July 10, 1832, Clay, *Works,* 7: 523–24.

6. Albany *Jeffersonian,* May 12, 1838; Calvin Colton [Junius], "The Currency," *The Junius Tracts* (New York: Greeley and McElrath, 1844), 21; Albany *Jeffersonian,* May 12, 1838.

7. Washington *National Intelligencer* quoted in the Fayetteville (N.C.) *Observer,* Aug. 11, 1846; Webster, "Speech at Boston," Sep. 19, 1844, *Writings and Speeches,* 13: 264; Fayetteville *Observer,* Aug. 11, 1846; Augusta (Ga.) *Chronicle and Sentinel,* Sep. 29, 1843.

8. William R. Taylor, *Cavalier and Yankee: The Old South and American National Character* (New York: Harper and Row, 1969), 127.

9. Edward Everett, "Conditions of a Good School," Aug. 2, 1851, *Orations and Speeches on Various Occasions,* 4 vols. (Boston: Little, Brown, 1870–72), 3: 76; Everett, "Superior and Popular Education," Aug. 16, 1837, *Orations and Speeches,* 2: 225.

10. New York *Evening Post for the Country,* Oct. 22, 1838; "First and Second Rate Men," *Democratic Review* 15 (Aug. 1844): 116; Washington

Globe, July 2, 1839; Boston *Morning Post* quoted in Washington *Globe,* April 16, 1835.

11. Aaron N. Skinner, *An Oration at the Whig Celebration, New Haven, July 4, 1834* (New Haven: James F. Babcock, 1834), 8; New York *Weekly Tribune* (hereafter New York *Tribune*), Nov. 1, 1845; Skinner, *Oration,* 3.

12. Seward, "Daniel Webster," Dec. 14, 1852, *Works,* 3: 113; Lincoln, "Eulogy on Henry Clay," July 6, 1852, *Collected Works,* 2: 125; Colton (Junius), "Life of Henry Clay," *The Junius Tracts,* 64.

13. Clay, "On Our Relations with the Cherokee Indians," Feb. 4, 1835, *Works,* 7: 651; Fayetteville *Observer,* Feb. 15, 1, 1848.

14. Daniel D. Barnard, *The Social System: An Address Pronounced before the House of Convocation, of Trinity College, Hartford, August 2, 1848* (Hartford: Calendar Press, 1848), 29; *An Address Delivered before the Connecticut Alpha of the Phi Beta Kappa at Yale College, August 19, 1846* (New Haven: B. L. Hamlen, 1846), 19–20.

15. Catherine Beecher, *A Treatise on Domestic Economy,* reprint ed. (New York: Schocken, 1977), viii, 13, 225; Taylor, *Cavalier and Yankee,* 115, 124, 141.

16. Daniel Walker Howe, *The Political Culture of the American Whigs* (Chicago: Univ. of Chicago Press, 1979), 156; Albany *Jeffersonian,* Dec. 1, 1838; Marshall *Western Statesman,* July 8, 1841; New Orleans *Picayune,* Jan. 19, 1840; Skinner, *Oration,* 18.

17. Charles Haddock, "Circular, to the Teachers of Common Schools in New-Hampshire," in Edward Pessen, ed., *Jacksonian Panorama* (Indianapolis: Bobbs-Merrill, 1976), 413; Carl F. Kaestle, *Pillars of the Republic: Common Schools and American Society, 1780–1860* (New York: Hill and Wang, 1983), 96.

18. Ronald G. Walters, *American Reformers, 1815–1860* (New York: Hill and Wang, 1978), 123; Howe, *American Whigs,* 159; Walters, *American Reformers,* 128; Lincoln, "Temperance Address," Feb. 22, 1842, *Collected Works,* 1: 278–79.

19. David J. Rothman, *The Discovery of the Asylum: Social Order and Disorder in the New Republic* (Boston: Little, Brown, 1971), 144–45, 212, 213.

20. *Ibid.,* 133.

21. *Ibid.,* 122, 78, 212.

22. The term "social control" was first used by Clifford Griffin in "Religious Benevolence as Social Control, 1815–1860," *Mississippi Valley Historical Review* 44 (Dec. 1957): 423–44. The concept dominates much of the writing on religious and humanitarian reform in the Middle Period. See especially: John R. Bodo, *The Protestant Clergy and Public Issues, 1812–1848* (Princeton: Princeton Univ. Press, 1954);

Charles C. Cole, Jr., *The Social Ideas of the Northern Evangelists,
1820–1860,* Columbia Studies in the Social Sciences, no. 580 (New
York: Columbia Univ. Press, 1954); Charles I. Foster, *An Errand of
Mercy: The Evangelical United Front, 1790–1837* (Chapel Hill: Univ.
of North Carolina Press, 1960); Clifford S. Griffin, *Their Brothers'
Keepers: Moral Stewardship in the United States, 1800–1865* (New
Brunswick: Rutgers Univ. Press, 1960); Rothman, *Discovery of the
Asylum.* For my own criticisms of the concept of social control, see,
Lawrence Frederick Kohl, "The Concept of Social Control and the
History of Jacksonian America," *Journal of the Early Republic* 5 (Spring
1985): 21–34.

23. Rothman, *Discovery of the Asylum,* 127–29.

24. *Ibid.,* 155, 144.

25. Webster, "Mass Meeting at Saratoga," Aug. 19, 1840, *Writings and
Speeches,* 3: 34; Clay, "On the Reduction of Duties on Imports," Jan. 11,
1832, *Works,* 7: 420–21; Seward, "Improvement of Farms and Farmers," Sep. 2, 1852, *Works,* 3: 190.

26. Webster, "Mass Meeting at Albany," Aug. 27, 1844, *Writings and
Speeches,* 3: 223; Webster to the Rev. Ebenezer Price and Others,
Neighbors of Mr. Webster in New Hampshire," Sep. 21, 1850, *Writings
and Speeches,* 12: 249–50; Webster to Mark A. Cooper, Esq., Macon,
Georgia, Oct. 6, 1851, *Writings and Speeches,* 274.

27. Colton [Junius], "Labor and Capital," *The Junius Tracts,* 109; John
Quincy Adams, "Fourth Annual Message," Dec. 2, 1828, *Messages and
Papers,* 2: 413; Clay, "On the Cumberland Road Bill," Feb. 11, 1835,
Works, 8: 9; Webster, "Address Delivered to the Citizens of Pittsburgh,"
July 8, 1833, *Writings and Speeches,* 2: 147.

28. Seward, "Address on Internal Improvements," Sep. 5, 1839,
Works, 3: 216.

29. Webster, "Reception at Madison," June 1, 1837, *Writings and
Speeches,* 2: 255.

30. Seward, "Annual Message to the Legislature," Jan. 5, 1841,
Works, 2: 258; "The Administration: The Party," *American Whig Review*
15 (April 1852): 293; New York *Tribune,* Nov. 16, 1844; Montgomery
Alabama Journal, Jan. 15, 1840.

31. New York *Tribune,* June 7, 1845; Petersburg *Intelligencer* and
Albany *Daily Advertiser* quoted in Washington *National Intelligencer,* Oct.
16, 1839.

32. Seward, "Annual Message to the Legislature," Jan. 5, 1841,
Works, 2: 258; Boston *Atlas,* Jan. 19, 1837.

33. New York *Tribune,* June 7, 1845; Daniel D. Barnard, *A Plea for
Social and Popular Repose; Being an Address Delivered before the Philoma-*

thean and Eucleian Societies of the University of the City of New York, July 1, 1845* (New York: Tribune Job Printing, 1845), 17; Clay, "On the Sub-Treasury Bill," Sep. 25, 1837, *Works*, 8: 75.

34. Clay, "Outline of a National Bank," May 21, 1838, *Life and Speeches of Henry Clay*, 2 vols. (New York: Greeley and McElrath, 1844), 2: 393–94; "On the Compromise Tariff," Feb. 12, 1833, *Works*, 7: 546; "On the Admission of Arkansas as a State," April 11, 1836, *Works*, 8: 37.

35. Clay, "A Speech at Buffalo, New York," July 17, 1839, *Works*, 8: 162; Webster, "The Constitution Not a Compact between Sovereign States," Feb. 16, 1833, *Writings and Speeches*, 6: 211.

36. Meyers, *Jacksonian Persuasion*, 14.

37. Boston *Courier*, Sep. 9, 1839; New York *Tribune*, Sep. 16, 1843.

38. "Morals of Trade," *Hunt's Merchants' Magazine* 7 (Oct. 1842): 352; "On the Moral End of Business," *ibid.* 1 (Nov. 1839): 390. See also 1 (Oct. 1839): 295–306; 1 (Nov. 1839): 369–90; 2 (Jan. 1840): 9–24; 3 (July 1840): 9–22, 76–80; 4 (May 1841): 415–25; 5 (Dec. 1841): 526–30; 6 (Jan. 1842): 23–27; 6 (Feb. 1842): 151–55; 6 (March 1842): 252–56; 6 (May 1842): 450–54; 7 (Aug. 1842): 179–84; 7 (Oct. 1842): 348–52.

39. *American Monthly Magazine* 3 (March 1834): 21; New York *Tribune*, Nov. 1, 1845; *American Monthly Magazine*, n.s. 2 (Nov. 1836): 516.

40. Boston *Bay State Democrat*, July 15, 1841; Boston *Courier*, Dec. 5, 1839; "Political Responsibilities," *American Whig Review* 14 (Nov. 1851): 365.

41. Edward Everett, "Accumulation, Property, Capital, Credit," *Orations and Speeches*, 2: 300, 296–97.

42. Riesman, *Lonely Crowd*, 123.

43. "Political Responsibilities," *American Whig Review* 14 (Nov. 1851): 366; Albany *Evening Journal*, Aug. 28, 1838.

44. Milledgeville *Southern Recorder*, June 16, 1840; Colton [Junius], "Labor and Capital," *The Junius Tracts*, 109; Albany *Evening Journal*, June 25, 1838; New York *Log Cabin*, Nov. 13, 1841; Milledgeville *Southern Recorder*, June 16, 1840; "Whig Principle and Its Development," *American Whig Review* 15 (Feb. 1852): 135.

45. Seward, "Improvement of Farms and Farmers," Sep. 2, 1852, *Works*, 3:182.

46. Colton [Junius], "Political Abolition," *The Junius Tracts*, 76.

47. Albany *Evening Journal*, July 25, 1840; Philadelphia *World* quoted in Washington *National Intelligencer*, May 6, 1839; Mobile *Advertiser and Chronicle* quoted in Fayetteville *Observer*, Sep. 16, 1840; Albany *Evening Journal*, July 29, 1840.

48. "Whig Principle and Its Development," *American Whig Review* 15 (Feb. 1852): 129; Boston, *Atlas*, July 31, 1834; Colton, *Crisis of the Country*, 6.

49. Colton [Junius], "The Currency," *The Junius Tracts*, 37; Milledgeville *Southern Recorder*, Aug. 25, 1840; Detroit *Daily Advertiser*, Jan. 22, 1840.

50. New York *Enquirer*, Jan. 19, 1835.

51. Boston *Atlas*, Dec. 11, 1840; Colton, *Manual for Emigrants*, 63; Springfield *Republican*, Aug. 22, 1835.

52. New York *Log Cabin*, Nov. 13, 1841; Lincoln et al., "Campaign Circular from Whig Committee," *Collected Works*, 1: 201; Skinner, *Oration*, 15; Springfield *Republican*, Feb. 27, 1841.

53. Silbey, *Shrine of Party*, 28–32.

54. Ershkowitz and Shade, "Consensus or Conflict," 598–604.

55. Skinner, *Oration*, 18, 14; "The Age of Cotton," *American Monthly Magazine*, Jan. 1838, n.s. 5:11.

56. Fayetteville *Observer*, Feb. 26, 1840.

57. Sydney G. Fisher, "The Science of Government," *American Monthly Magazine* n.s. 6 (Sep. 1838): 202.

58. Edwin C. Rozwenc, ed., *Ideology and Power in the Age of Jackson* (Garden City, N.Y.: Doubleday, 1964), xx.

Chapter 3. Private and Public: The Individual and Society

1. "Introduction," *Democratic Review* 1 (Oct. 1837): 6.

2. Lincoln, "Fragment on Government," July 1, 1854, *Collected Works*, 2: 220.

3. Tocqueville, *Democracy*, 2: 104.

4. Sam Bass Warner, Jr., *The Private City: Philadelphia in Three Periods of Its Growth* (Philadelphia: Univ. of Pennsylvania Press, 1968), 3–4.

5. *Globe*, July 27, 1831; Columbus *Democrat*, June 29, 1839.

6. "Democracy," *Democratic Review* 7 (March 1840): 225; "Introduction," *ibid.*, 1 (Oct. 1837): 6.

7. Seward, "Address," Aug. 15, 1839, *Works*, 3: 213; "Whig Principle and Its Development," *American Whig Review* 15 (Feb. 1852): 134; John P. Kennedy, "Letter of J. P. Kennedy to His Constituents; Citizens of the Fourth Congressional District in the State of Maryland, on the Principles and Values of the Protective System," (Baltimore, Md., 1842), 26.

8. New York *Tribune*, Aug. 30, 1845; Jan. 27, 1844; *Log Cabin*, Sep. 4, March 27, 1841; New York *Tribune*, Oct. 14, 1843.

9. Sidney G. Fisher, "The Science of Government," *American Monthly Magazine*, n.s. 6 (Sep. 1838): 213–14.

10. "Democracy," *Boston Quarterly Review* 1 (Jan. 1838): 60; "The American Democrat," *ibid.*, 375.

11. "Whittier's Poems," *Boston Quarterly Review* 1 (Jan. 1838): 24; "The American Democrat," *ibid.* 1 (July 1838): 377; "Democracy," *ibid.* 1 (Jan. 1838): 59; "The American Democrat," *ibid.* 1 (July 1838): 377.

12. "The American Democrat," *ibid.* 1 (July 1838): 376–77; "Democracy," *ibid.* 1 (Jan. 1838): 57.

13. "The American Democrat," *ibid.* 1 (July 1838): 375; [Review of] "An Oration Delivered before the Inhabitants of the Town of Newburyport, at Their Request, on the Sixty-first Anniversary of the Declaration of Independence, July 4, 1837 by John Quincy Adams," *ibid.* 1 (April 1838): 159.

14. Jackson, "Veto Message," July 10, 1832, *Messages and Papers*, 2: 585–86; *Hampshire Republican*, Sep. 28, 1836.

15. Andrew Jackson quoted in Schlesinger, *Age of Jackson*, 354.

16. *Plaindealer*, Aug. 12, 1837; "The Moral of the Crisis," *Democratic Review* 1 (Oct. 1837): 121.

17. "The Duty of the Democratic Party," *Democratic Review* 6 (Nov. 1839): 440–41; "Introduction," *Democratic Review* 1 (Oct. 1837): 6.

18. *Bay State Democrat*, Sep. 8, 1841; Aug. 30, 1841; July 26, 1842.

19. New York *Tribune*, Oct. 7, 1843; Webster to Mr. Coffin, June 11, 1840, *Writings and Speeches*, 18: 84; *Jeffersonian*, Sep. 29, 1838.

20. Thomas Paine had anticipated a concept of the public good which both Whigs and Jacksonians would share: "Public good is not a term opposed to the good of individuals; on the contrary, it is the good of every individual collected. It is the good of all, because it is the good of every one: for as the public body is every individual collected, so the public good is the collected good of those individuals." Quoted in Stephen Lukes, *Individualism* (Oxford: Basil Blackwell, 1973), 49; New York *Enquirer*, Jan. 30, 1840; Ralph Waldo Emerson, *Heart of Emerson's Journals*, Bliss Perry, ed. (Boston: Houghton Mifflin, 1926), 211.

21. Tocqueville, *Democracy*, 2: 111; Webster, "Remarks Made to the Citizens of Bangor, Maine," Aug. 25, 1835, *Writings and Speeches*, 2: 160;

22. Webster, "The Presidential Veto of the United States Bank Bill," July 11, 1832, *Writings and Speeches*, 6: 157; Clay, "On the Sub-Treasury Bill," Sep. 25, 1837, *Works*, 8: 74; "On the Sub-Treasury Bill," Jan. 20, 1840, *Works*, 8: 174.

23. Tocqueville, *Democracy*, 2: 119.

24. Lawrence M. Friedman, *A History of American Law* (New York: Simon and Schuster, 1973), 157.

25. New York *Evening Post*, Nov. 21, 1834; Columbus *Democrat*, June 29, 1839; *Globe*, Sep. 28, 1837.

26. "Union and Progress," *Boston Quarterly Review* 1 (April 1838): 194; Boston *Morning Post*, March 14, 1837.

27. *Globe*, Dec. 8, 1837; "Democracy," *Democratic Review* 7(March 1840): 225; *Globe*, Dec. 8, 1837; *Plaindealer*, Dec. 10, 1836.

28. *Globe*, June 24, 1836; New York *Evening Post*, Nov. 28, 1834.

29. New York *Evening Post for the Country*, March 8, 1843; "Introduction," *Democratic Review* 1 (Oct. 1837): 7–8.

30. *Ibid.*, 6; New York *Journal of Commerce* reprinted in *Hill's New Hampshire Patriot*, Dec. 5, 1844; *Globe*, Nov. 24, 1836; Dugald Stewart quoted in *Plaindealer*, Dec. 17, 1836.

31. "Whig Principle and Its Development," *American Whig Review* 15 (Feb. 1852): 124.

32. Boston *Atlas*, Oct. 8, 1839; "Unity of the Whigs: Their Principles and Measures," *American Whig Review* 14 (Sep. 1851): 184; Webster, "Mass Meeting at Albany," Aug. 27, 1844, *Writings and Speeches*, 3: 246.

33. Webster, "Address Delivered to the Citizens of Pittsburgh," July 8, 1833, *Writings and Speeches*, 2: 154; Seward, "Annual Message to the Legislature," Jan. 4, 1842, *Works*, 2: 318; New York *Enquirer*, Nov. 16, 1839.

34. Clay, "On American Industry," March 30–31, 1824, *Works*, 6: 278–79, 292.

35. Colton [Junius], "The Tariff," *The Junius Tracts*, 42.

36. "Unity of the Whigs: Their Principles and Measures," *American Whig Review* 14 (Sep. 1851): 183; Clay, "On American Industry," March 30–31, 1824, *Works*, 6: 278–79.

37. Seward, "Annual Message to the Legislature," Jan. 1, 1839, *Works*, 2: 205.

38. Clay, "On American Industry," March 30–31, 1824, *Works*, 6: 263–64; "On the American System," Feb. 2, 3, 6, 1832, *Works*, 7: 474; *Globe*, July 27, 1831; Albany *Jeffersonian*, March 17, 1838.

39. *Log Cabin*, Jan. 30, 1841; *Jeffersonian*, Sep. 8, 1838.

40. "True Theory and Philosophy of Our System of Government," *Democratic Review* 15 (Sep. 1844): 231; "Democracy," *Boston Quarterly Review* 1 (Jan. 1838): 46; Winchester *Virginian* quoted in the *Globe*, Sep. 10, 1833; *United States Telegraph*, Dec. 5, 1828.

41. New York *Evening Post for the Country*, March 8, 1837; New York *Evening Post*, Sep. 9, 1836.

42. Jackson, "First Annual Message," Dec. 8, 1829, *Messages and Papers*, 2: 449.

43. "The Duty of the Democratic Party," *Democratic Review* 6 (Nov. 1839): 437; *Bay State Democrat*, March 1, 1842; *Ohio Monitor* (Columbus), Nov. 23, 1835.

44. *Argus of Western America*, Sep. 24, 1828; Sep. 17, 1828.

45. *Hampshire Republican*, Feb. 3, 1836; George Sidney Camp quoted in John Ashworth, "The Jacksonian as Leveller," *Journal of American Studies*, 14 (Dec. 1980): 410.

46. *Hampshire Republican*, Feb. 3, 1836.

47. *Globe*, July 14, 1831.

48. *Globe*, Oct. 7, 1831.

49. "Political Patronage," *Democratic Review* 17 (Sep. 1845): 167.

50. *Globe*, Oct. 10, 1840; "Free Trade," *Democratic Review* 9 (Oct. 1841): 332; *Bay State Democrat*, Feb. 10, 1841; New York *Evening Post for the Country*, March 10, 1841; "A Letter to Farmer Issachar," *Democratic Review* 15 (Oct. 1844): 387.

51. *Globe*, Jan. 30, 1838; New York *Evening Post for the Country*, March 25, 1843.

52. Webster, "Mass Meeting at Saratoga," Aug. 19, 1840, *Writings and Speeches*, 3: 19–20.

53. Boston *Atlas*, Oct. 6, 1834.

54. Detroit *Daily Advertiser*, Dec. 2, 1839; Albany *Evening Journal*, Jan. 22, 1840; "The Progress of the Ultra-Democratic Principle," *American Monthly Magazine*, n.s. 6 (Aug. 1838): 110; Hammond to Henry Clay, Jan. 21, 1840, *Works*, 5: 443.

55. Albany *Evening Journal*, May 30, 1838; Daniel D. Barnard, *An Address Delivered before the Philoclean and Peithessophian Societies of Rutgers College, at the Request of the Philoclean Society, July 18, 1837* (Albany: Hoffman and White, 1837), 19.

56. Webster, "A Speech Delivered at the National Republican Convention Held at Worchester, Massachusetts," Oct. 12, 1832, *Writings and Speeches*, 2: 112; "Whig Principles and Purposes," Sep. 10, 1840, *ibid.*, 3: 48–49; "Unity of the Whigs: Their Principles and Measures," *American Whig Review* 14 (Sep. 1851): 181; Webster, "A Speech Delivered at the National Republican Convention Held at Worchester, Massachusetts," Oct. 12, 1832, *Writings and Speeches*, 2: 112; Clay, "On the Sub-Treasury Bill," Sep. 25, 1837, *Works*, 8: 70.

57. *The Federalist,* no. 51, p. 536. For a discussion of the Whigs' opposition to the veto and presidential power, see the section of Chapter Four entitled "Personal Will and the Rule of Law."

58. New York *Enquirer,* Feb. 9, 1836.

59. "Glances at Congress," *Democratic Review* 1 (Oct. 1837): 70; Major L. Wilson, "The Concept of Time and the Political Dialogue in the United States, 1828–1848," *American Quarterly* 19 (Winter 1967): 623. See also Wilson's *Space, Time, and Freedom: The Quest for Nationality and the Irrepressible Conflict, 1815–1861,* Contributions in American History, no. 35 (Westport, Conn.: Greenwood Press, 1974).

60. Here the *Democratic Review* employs a conception of individualism different from the conception of Alexis de Tocqueville which I have used throughout this work. Tocqueville's individualism involved only an intellectual or psychological separation of Americans, and, unlike the *Democratic Review*'s individualism, it had little to do with their physical separation from each other. "The Course of Civilization," *Democratic Review* 6 (Sep. 1839): 209.

61. In his autobiography, Martin Van Buren warned Democrats about letting down their guard and allowing the opposition to gain power. He reminded them that Monroe's attempt to abolish party differences during the "Era of Good Feelings" only resulted in the election to the presidency of John Quincy Adams, a man who did not share their political views. Van Buren argued that the Whig party was merely a reincarnation of the forces of Federalism and that because the "cohesive influences and innate qualities which originally united them remain," they would always "spring up and return to vigour with the return of propitious skies." Friends of the Democracy, then, had always to remain united to battle this foe. Martin Van Buren, *The Autobiography of Martin Van Buren,* ed. John C. Fitzpatrick (Washington: Government Printing Office, 1920), 124–25.

62. Henry C. Carey quoted in Wilson, "The Concept of Time," 625.

63. Webster, "Convention at Andover," Nov. 9, 1843, *Writings and Speeches,* 3: 179; Clay, "On the Plan of the Sub-Treasury," Feb. 19, 1838, *Works,* 8: 121; Seward, "Henry Clay," June 30, 1852, *Works,* 3: 107.

64. "Whig Principle and Its Development," *American Whig Review* 15 (Feb. 1852): 130; Webster, "Objects of the Mexican War," March 23, 1848, *Writings and Speeches,* 10: 32.

65. Clay, "On the Plan of the Sub-Treasury," Feb. 19, 1838, *Works* 8: 102; Webster, "Remarks on Different Occasions, on the Removal of the Deposits, and on the Subject of a National Bank, Delivered in the Senate of the United States, in the Course of the Session of 1833–34," *Writings and Speeches,* 6: 242.

66. Colton [Junius], "Political Abolition," *The Junius Tracts*, 71, 69.

67. Wilson, *Space, Time, and Freedom*, 12.

68. Boston, *Courier*, Dec. 19, 1836.

69. Abbott Lawrence to Henry Clay, March 26, 1833, Clay, *Works*, 358; Richmond *Compiler* quoted in Fayetteville (N.C.) *Observer*, Nov. 7, 1838.

70. Webster, "Remarks, on Different Occasions . . . ," *Writings and Speeches*, 6: 261; "On the Removal of the Deposits of the Public Money, and on the Subject of a National Bank, Delivered in the Senate of the United States on Several Occasions in the Course of the Session of 1833–34," *ibid.*, 7: 21; "Mass Meeting at Saratoga," Aug. 19, 1840, *ibid.*, 3: 7.

71. Webster to Fletcher Webster, March 11, 1845, *ibid.*, 18: 204; Webster to Citizens of Worchester County, Massachusetts, Jan. 23,1844, *Writings and Speeches*, 16: 423.

72. *Ohio Statesman*, July 17, 1839.

73. Milledgeville (Ga.) *Federal Union*, May 28, April 30, 1844; *Hampshire Republican* July 6, 1836.

74. "White Slavery," *Democratic Review* 11 (Sep. 1842): 269; *Globe*, July 12, 1833; Boston *Weekly Reformer*, Jan. 20, 1837; "White Slavery," *Democratic Review* 11 (Sep. 1842): 270; "Poverty and Misery, versus Reform and Progress," *Democratic Review* 23 (July 1848): 30; Wilson, "The Concept of Time," 639.

75. "European Views of American Democracy—No. II," *Democratic Review* 2 (July 1838): 354; James K. Polk, "Inaugural Address," March 4, 1845, *Messages and Papers*, 4: 380; "Glances at Congress," *Democratic Review* 1 (Oct. 1837): 70–71.

76. Webster to Citizens of Worchester County, Massachusetts, Jan. 23, 1844, *Writings and Speeches*, 16: 423.

77. *Ibid.*, 423–24.

78. Clay, "On Retiring to Private Life," June 9, 1842, *Works*, 9: 377; Wilson, *Space, Time, and Freedom*, 88.

79. Jackson, "Veto Message," July 10, 1832, *Messages and Papers*, 2: 590.

Chapter 4. Public Order:
The Individual and the Rule of Law

1. *Globe*, Aug. 24, 1840.

2. Seward, "The True Greatness of Our Country," Dec. 22, 1848, *Works*, 3: 18.

3. On the transformation of American law after the Revolution, see: William E. Nelson, *The Americanization of the Common Law: The Impact of Legal Change on Massachusetts Society, 1760–1830* (Cambridge, Mass.: Harvard Univ. Press, 1975), and Morton J. Horwitz, *The Transformation of American Law, 1780–1860* (Cambridge, Mass.: Harvard Univ. Press, 1977). On the transformation of American ideology and constitutions, see: Bernard Bailyn, *The Ideological Origins of the American Revolution* (Cambridge, Mass.: Harvard Univ. Press, 1967); Gordon S. Wood, *The Creation of the American Republic, 1776–1787* (Chapel Hill: Univ. of North Carolina Press, 1969); and Bernard Bailyn et al., *The Great Republic: A History of the American People* (Boston: D.C. Heath, 1977).

4. John Michael Rozett concluded that law and order was "the paramount issue of the Jacksonian period." "The Social Bases of Party Conflict in the Age of Jackson," 212.

5. H.L.A. Hart, *The Concept of Law* (New York: Oxford Univ. Press, 1961), 16, 88, 196–97.

6. Tocqueville, *Democracy*, explains his concept "self-interest rightly understood" in 2:129–32.

7. Tocqueville, *Democracy*, 2:132.

8. William B. Shepard quoted in Fayetteville (N.C.) *Observer*, Oct. 31, 1838.

9. Seward, "Education," July 26, 1837, *Works*, 3:140; 146; Webster, "Reception at Madison," June 1, 1837, *Writings and Speeches*, 2:253.

10. Detroit *Daily Advertiser*, May 4, 1840; Webster, "Remarks to the Ladies of Richmond," Oct. 5, 1840, *Writings and Speeches*, 3:107–8.

11. *Jeffersonian*, Dec. 1, 1838.

12. Tocqueville, *Democracy*, 2: 24.

13. Webster to Professor Pease, June 15, 1852, *Writings and Speeches*, 16:655; Tocqueville, *Democracy*, 2:29.

14. Lincoln, "Address before the Young Men's Lyceum of Springfield Illinois," Jan. 27, 1838, *Collected Works*, 1:108, 109, 110, 111.

15. *Ibid.*, 111.

16. *Log Cabin*, Nov., 20, 1841; Clay, "On the Sub-Treasury Bill," Jan. 20, 1840, *Works*, 8:172.

17. Rush Welter, *The Mind of America, 1820–1860* (New York: Columbia Univ. Press, 1975), 266, 267.

18. *Ibid.*, 269, 292.

19. John William Ward, *Andrew Jackson: Symbol for an Age* (London: Oxford Univ. Press, 1955), 151–204, 200, 185.

20. George Lippard quoted in *ibid.*, 161, 186–87.

21. Lincoln, "Address before the Young Men's Lyceum of Springfield, Illinois," Jan. 27, 1838, *Collected Works*, 1:114.

22. Montgomery *Alabama Journal,* Jan. 15, 1840; New York *Tribune,* June 28, 1845; Alexandria *Gazette* quoted in Boston *Courier,* Oct. 11, 1838.

23. U.S. Constitution, art. I, sec. 7, par. 2.

24. Clay, "On President Jackson's Veto of the Bank Bill," July 10, 1832, *Works,* 7:533; Jackson, Veto Message, July 10, 1832, *Messages and Papers,* 2:582; Webster, "National Convention at Worcester," Oct. 12, 1832, *Writings and Speeches,* 2:120.

25. *Ibid.,* 122.

26. *Ibid.,* 120–21; Webster, "The Presidential Veto of the Bank Bill," July 11, 1832, *Writings and Speeches, 6:165; Clay, "On President Jackson's Veto of the Bank Bill," July 10, 1832, Works,* 7:534; Webster, "The Presidential Veto of the Bank Bill," July 11, 1832, *Writings and Speeches,* 6:172.

27. Lincoln, "Address before the Young Men's Lyceum of Springfield, Illinois," Jan. 27, 1838, *Collected Works,* 1:115.

28. *Ibid.,* 1:112.

29. Alexis de Tocqueville, *Journey to America,* George Lawrence, trans., J. P. Mayer, ed. (Garden City, N.Y.: Doubleday, 1971), 44.

30. "Influence of Penal Laws," *Democratic Review* 22 (March 1848): 237.

31. "Law Reform," *Democratic Review* 21 (Dec. 1847): 477.

32. "The Abuses of Law Courts," *Democratic Review* 21 (Oct. 1847): 305, 309.

33. "The Supreme Court of the United States," *Democratic Review* 1 (Jan. 1838): 143; "Elective Judiciary," *ibid.,* 22 (March 1848): 201; quoted in Columbus *Democrat,* Dec. 19, 1840.

34. "The Duty of the Democratic Party," *Democratic Review* 6 (Nov. 1839): 441; Lincoln, "Address before the Young Men's Lyceum of Springfield, Illinois," Jan. 27, 1838, *Collected Works,* 1:114.

35. "Prospects of the Legal Profession in America," *Democratic Review* 18 (Jan. 1846): 29; quoted in *National Intelligencer,* May 28, 1834; New York *Tribune,* Nov. 25, 1843.

36. *Bay State Democrat,* June 22, 1841.

37. *Ibid.;* "The Specie Clause," *Democratic Review* 5 (Feb. 1839): 237.

38. "Democracy," *Boston Quarterly Review* 1 (Jan. 1838): 67; "An Inquiry into the Moral and Religious Character of the American Government," *ibid.* 1 (July 1838): 329; "Democracy," *Democratic Review* 7 (March 1840): 220, 222.

39. "The American Democrat," *Boston Quarterly Review* 1 (July 1838): 365; "Political Patronage," *Democratic Review* 17 (Sep. 1845): 165.

40. Colton [Junius], "Political Abolition," *The Junius Tracts,* 76; Daniel D. Barnard, *An Address Delivered before the Connecticut Alpha of the*

Phi Beta Kappa at Yale College, August 19, 1846 (New Haven: B.L. Hamlen, 1846), 15.

41. Barnard, *Address, August 19, 1846,* pp. 40–41; Thomas S. Grimke, *Oration on the Principle Duties of Americans Delivered before the Washington Society and Other Citizens of Charleston in the Second Presbyterian Church, July 4, 1833* (Charleston: William Estill, 1833), 30.

42. "The Mississippi Bond Question," *Democratic Review* 10 (April 1842): 382–83.

43. *Ibid.*

44. Schlesinger, *Age of Jackson,* 416; "Rhode Island—Its Rightful Governor and Unrighteous Government," *Democratic Review* 15 (Aug. 1844): 122; Clay, "On Retiring to Private Life," June 9 1842, *Works,* 9:383.

45. "Rhode Island—Its Rightful Governor and Unrighteous Government," *Democratic Review* 15 (Aug. 1844): 123, 122, 123–24.

46. Clay, "On Retiring to Private Life," June 9, 1842, *Works,* 9:382–83.

47. "The Rhode Island Question," *Democratic Review* 11 (July 1842): 79–80.

48. The issue of slavery deserves greater treatment than I am able to give it here. Although the issue was never one that defined the differences between the parties—my central concern in this work—Democrats and Whigs did approach the subject in distinctive and characteristic ways. I hope in a subsequent volume to explore these and carry my analysis of partisan rhetoric up to the Civil War.

49. Ralph Waldo Emerson, "Politics," *Selected Writings,* 427.

50. Clay, "Reply to Mr. Mendenhall," Oct. 1, 1842, *Works,* 9:387.

51. Seward, *Works,* 1: lxxxv–vi; 74; Glyndon G. Van Deusen, *William Henry Seward* (New York: Oxford Univ. Press, 1967), 125.

52. Colton [Junius], "Political Abolition," *The Junius Tracts,* 70–71.

53. Clay, "On Abolition," Feb. 7, 1839, *Works,* 8:158; Colton [Junius], "Political Abolition," *The Junius Tracts,* 79, 72; New York *Tribune,* Dec. 9, 1843.

54. Seward, "Daniel Webster," Dec. 14, 1852, *Works,* 3:116.

55. "Introduction," *Democratic Review* 1 (Oct. 1837): 3; "Executive Usurpation," *ibid.* 1 (Feb. 1838): 291; "Democracy," *ibid.* 7 (March 1840): 223; "Introduction," *ibid.* 1 (Oct. 1837): 4; "Democracy," *ibid.* 7 (March 1840): 224.

56. "Introduction," *ibid.* 1 (Oct. 1837): 6, 9.

57. "Introduction," *ibid.* 1 (Oct. 1837): 4; "Executive Usurpation," *ibid.* 1 (Feb. 1838): 282.

58. Boston *Courier,* Oct. 14, 17, 1839.

59. Barnard, *Address*, August 19, 1846, p. 7; New York *Tribune*, Nov. 25, 1843.

60. "Political Responsibilities," *American Whig Review* 14 (Nov. 1851): 366; Webster, "The Dignity and Importance of History," Feb. 23, 1852, *Writings and Speeches*, 13:469.

61. New York *Tribune*, Sep. 23, 1843; Grimke, *Oration, July 4, 1833*, 15–16; Colton [Junius], "Political Abolition," *The Junius Tracts*, 78.

62. Webster to Messrs. Richards and Others, March 21, 1851, *Writings and Speeches*, 18:424; Webster to Mr. Everett, September 27, 1851, *ibid.*, 18:473.

63. Webster, "Whig Principles and Purposes," Sept. 10, 1840, *ibid.*, 3:41; "Reception at Madison," June 1, 1837, *ibid.*, 2:254; "The Dignity and Importance of History," Feb. 23, 1852, *ibid.*, 13:495–96; Seward, "Education," July 26, 1837, *Works*, 3:138.

64. "Glances at Congress," *Democratic Review* 1 (Oct. 1837): 70.

Chapter 5. Economic Inequality: The Individual and the Social Hierarchy

1. *Plaindealer*, Dec. 31, 1836.

2. Richard Hildreth, *Theory of Politics* (New York: Harper and Brothers, 1853), 270.

3. "The Laboring Classes," *Boston Quarterly Review* 3 (Oct. 1840): 478.

4. Bangor (Maine) *Mechanic and Farmer* quoted in Boston *Weekly Reformer*, March 31, 1837.

5. Andrew Jackson, "Veto Message," July 10, 1832, *Messages and Papers*, 2: 590; "Thoughts on the Times," *Democratic Review* 6 (Dec. 1839): 461; Boston *Courier*, Sep. 9, 1839.

6. "Thoughts on the Times," *Democratic Review* 6 (Dec. 1839): 452; *Globe*, June 13, 1839.

7. "On the Elevation of the Laboring Portion of the Community," *Democratic Review* 7 (June 1840): 529.

8. Hildreth, *Theory of Politics*, 270.

9. Much recent work in social history has emphasized the reluctance of American farmers and laborers to involve themselves in the world of the market and capitalist production. See, for example: Christopher Clark, "Household Economy, Market Exchange and the Rise of Capitalism in the Connecticut Valley, 1800–1860," *Journal of*

Social History 13 (Winter 1979): 169–189; James A. Henretta, "Families and Farms: *Mentalite* in Pre-Industrial America," *William and Mary Quarterly* 35 (Jan. 1978): 3–32; Michael Merrill, "Cash Is Good to Eat: Self-Sufficiency and Exchange in the Rural Economy of the United States," *Radical History Review* 3 (Winter 1977): 42–71.

10. Samuel Clesson Allen, quoted in Schlesinger, *The Age of Jackson*, 153.

11. William M. Gouge, *Journal of Banking*, 243, 94, 45, 14.

12. Schlesinger, *Age of Jackson*, 335–36; Wetumpka (Ala.) *Argus* quoted in Thornton, *Politics and Power*, 109; Gouge, *Journal of Banking*, 80.

13. "The Independent Treasury Reform," *Democratic Review* 8 (Aug. 1840): 101–2.

14. "The Banks and the Currency," *Democratic Review* 2 (April 1838): 15; Columbus *Democrat*, Sep. 14, 1839; *Globe*, July 13, 1837; "The Independent Treasury Reform," *Democratic Review* 8 (Aug. 1840): 102; Columbus *Democrat*, Sep. 14, 1839.

15. *Globe*, Dec. 5, 1840; Columbus *Democrat*, Oct. 26, 1839; Jackson *Mississippian*, Aug. 10, 1838.

16. *Hill's New Hampshire Patriot*, July 4, 1844; "Free Trade," *Democratic Review* 14 (March 1844): 291.

17. Colton [Junius], "The Currency," *The Junius Tracts*, 21; Boston *Courier*, March 26, 1838; Boston *Atlas*, July 31, 1834; Colton [Junius], "The Currency," *The Junius Tracts*, 20; Clay, "On the Sub-Treasury Bill," Sep. 25, 1837, *Works*, 8:72.

18. Boston *Courier*, March 26, 1838.

19. "Wayland's Political Economy," *New York Review* 1 (Oct. 1837): 392; Webster, "Lecture before the Society for the Diffusion of Useful Knowledge," Nov. 11, 1836, *Writings and Speeches*, 13: 73; "Internal Improvements," *New York Review* 6 (April 1840): 302.

20. Emerson, "Wealth," *Selected Writings*, 698, 694.

21. New York *Enquirer*, April 1, 1840; "The Usury Laws," *American Quarterly Review* 21 (March 1837): 149.

22. "Results of Machinery," *American Quarterly Review* 12 (Dec. 1832): 310; Emerson, "Wealth," *Selected Writings*, 701–2.

23. Horace Mann, "Annual Report for 1846," in Carter Goodrich, ed., *The Government and the Economy: 1783–1861* (Indianapolis: Bobbs-Merrill, 1967), 436; "Annual Report for 1848," *ibid.*, 438; "On the Distribution of the Public Lands for the Purposes of Education," *New York Review* 10 (Jan. 1842): 176.

24. "McCulloch's Political Economy," *American Quarterly Review* 2 (Sep. 1827): 65, 56.

25. *Ibid.*, 56–57.

26. *Ibid.*, 65–66.

27. "American Finances and Credit," *New York Review* 7 (July 1840): 205; "Internal Improvement," *American Quarterly Review* 8 (Dec. 1830): 310–11, 283; "Carey on the Population and Condition of Mankind," *New York Review* 7(Oct. 1840): 317; "Internal Improvement," *New York Review* 6 (April 1840): 322.

28. Webster, "Lecture before the Society for the Diffusion of Useful Knowledge," Nov. 11, 1836, *Writings and Speeches*, 13:67; "The Infancy of American Manufactures," *American Whig Review* 1 (Jan. 1845): 58; "Mr. Secretary Walker's Agricultural Project," *American Whig Review* 4 (Oct. 1846): 410.

29. "Internal Improvements," *American Quarterly Review* 8 (Dec. 1830): 284; Edward Everett, "Progress of Agriculture," Oct. 7, 1852, *Orations and Speeches*, 3: 154; "Sketch of the Rise, Progress, and Influence of the Useful Arts," *American Whig Review* 5 (Jan. 1847): 95; "The Influence of Manufactures and the Protective System," *American Whig Review* 14 (Oct. 1851): 269.

30. On the inequality of wealth in Jacksonian America, see: Edward Pessen, *Jacksonian America*, 77–100; Pessen, "The Egalitarian Myth and the American Social Reality: Wealth, Mobility, and Equality in the 'Era of the Common Man,'" *American Historical Review* 76 (Oct. 1971): 989–1034. For an early attempt to plot the growth of national wealth, see George Tucker, *Progress of the United States in Population and Wealth* (reprint ed., New York: Burt Franklin, 1970).

31. Gouge, *Journal of Banking*, 169; John Pickering, *The Working Man's Political Economy* (1847; reprint ed., New York: Arno, 1971), 3; "The Laboring Classes," *Boston Quarterly Review* 3 (July 1840): 367.

32. *Ohio Statesman*, Feb. 22, 1840; *Bay State Democrat*, Oct. 15, 1841; Schlesinger, *Age of Jackson*, 153; New York *Evening Post*, Oct. 21, 1834; Schlesinger, *Age of Jackson*, 153.

33. "Constitutional Governments," *Democratic Review* 20 (March 1847): 202–3.

34. *Globe*, June 13, 1839; Gouge, *Journal of Banking*, 156–57, 95.

35. *Globe*, October 31, 1832; "Thoughts on the Times," *Democratic Review* 6 (Dec. 1839): 457; *Globe*, March 10, 1841; Gouge, *Journal of Banking*, 61–62; "Causes of Poverty," *Democratic Review* 5 (May 1839): 455; Gouge, *Journal of Banking*, 63–64; *Globe*, April 1, 1839.

36. Gouge, *Journal of Banking*, 160; "Thoughts on the Times," *Democratic Review* 6 (Dec. 1839): 462.

37. *Bay State Democrat*, Oct. 26, 1841.

38. New York *Evening Post for the Country*, March 20, 1844; *Bay State Democrat*, April 19, 1842; New York *Evening Post for the Country*, May 5, 1840.

39. *Globe*, June 14, 1843.

40. New York *Evening Post for the Country*, July 6, 1844.

41. "The Laboring Classes," *Boston Quarterly Review* 3 (July 1840): 377; "Constitutional Governments," *Democratic Review* 20 (March 1847): 202.

42. *Globe*, April 16, 1835; "Constitutional Governments," *Democratic Review* 20 (March 1847): 203; *Globe*, April 21, 1835

43. *Bay State Democrat*, March 23, 1842; *Boston Morning Post*, March 16, 1837; Schlesinger, *Age of Jackson*, 312.

44. *Globe*, April 21, 1835; "White Slavery," *Democratic Review* 11 (Sep. 1842): 260.

45. "The Course of Civilization," *Democratic Review* 6 (Sep. 1839): 215.

46. *Hampshire Republican*, Sep. 28, 1836; "Thoughts on the Times," *Democratic Review* 6 (Dec. 1839): 457.

47. Everett, "Dinner to Thomas Baring, Esq.," Sep. 16, 1852, *Orations and Speeches*, 3: 135.

48. Boston *Courier*, Sep. 9, 1839; Everett, "Dinner to Thomas Baring, Esq.," Sep. 16, 1852, *Orations and Speeches*, 3: 135; Webster, "Lecture before the Society for the Diffusion of Useful Knowledge," Nov. 11, 1836, *Writings and Speeches*, 13: 73; Colton [Junius], "Labor and Capital," *The Junius Tracts*, 109; Everett, "Accumulation, Property, Capital, Credit," Sep. 13, 1838, *Orations and Speeches*, 2: 295, 293, 295.

49. *Ibid.*, 2: 294, 302–3; "Dinner to Thomas Baring, Esq.," *Orations and Speeches*, 3: 136.

50. Boston *Courier*, Sep. 9, 1839.

51. Everett, "Accumulation, Property, Capital, Credit," *Orations and Speeches*, 2: 296–97; Emerson, "Wealth," *Selected Writings*, 705, 700.

52. Everett, "Accumulation, Property, Capital, Credit," *Orations and Speeches*, 2: 301–2.

53. "Trades' Unions," *New York Review* 2 (Jan. 1838): 17; "Carey's Principles of Political Economy," *New York Review* 3 (July 1838): 3.

54. Calvin Colton [Junius], *The Crisis of the Country* (Philadelphia: T. K. and P. G. Collins, 1840), 10; Clay, "On the Sub-Treasury Bill," *Works*, 8: 176.

55. New York *Enquirer*, July 13, 1836; Boston *Atlas* quoted in Springfield *Republican*, June 3, 1837; New York *Enquirer*, June 27, 1839.

56. Clay, "On the American System," Feb. 2, 3, 6, 1833, *Works,* 7: 482; Seward, "Annual Message to the Legislature," Jan. 4, 1842, *Works,* 2: 312; Boston, *Courier,* Feb. 22, 1836.

57. Boston *Atlas,* Oct. 8, 1839; "Whig Principle and Its Development," *American Whig Review* 15 (Feb. 1852): 135, 124; Webster, "Opening of the Western Railroad to Grafton, N. H.," Aug. 28, 1847, *Writings and Speeches,* 4: 109.

58. "Thoughts on the Times," *Democratic Review,* 6 (Dec. 1839): 458–59.

59. *Ibid.,* 454; New York *New Era* quoted in *Ohio Statesman,* Feb. 8, 1840; *Globe,* May 26, 1837.

60. *Ohio Statesman,* Oct. 13, 1840.

61. New York *Evening Post,* Oct. 21, 1834; *Globe,* March 19, 1841, Jan. 31, 1842; *Hampshire Republican,* Sept. 28, 1836; *Globe,* Oct. 29, 1834.

62. New York *Evening Post,* Sep. 16, 1834.

63. *Bay State Democrat,* April 5, 1842; *Globe,* April 7, 1835.

64. *Globe,* March 19, 1841; June 12, 1839; New York *Evening Post,* Oct,. 27, 1834.

65. *Hampshire Republican,* Sep. 21, 1836; "The Sober Second-Thought of the People," *Democratic Review* 3(Nov. 1838): 282.

66. *Globe,* April 7, 1835; *Bay State Democrat,* July 28, 1841; New York *Evening Post for the Country,* June 6, 1837.

67. Boston *Courier,* Sep. 9, 1839.

68. "Dangers to Be Guarded against in the Progress of the United States," *American Whig Review* 5 (June 1847): 625; Everett, "Accumulation, Property, Capital, Credit," *Orations and Speeches,* 2: 294.

69. *Ibid.*; "Influence of the Trading Spirit upon the Social and Moral Life of America," *American Whig Review* 1 (Jan. 1845): 95; Colton, *Manual for Emigrants,* 171.

70. Seward, "The True Basis of American Independence," Oct. 20, 1853, *Works,* 4: 149; "Influence of the Trading Spirit upon the Social and Moral Life of America," *American Whig Review* 1 (Jan. 1845): 95; "Dangers to Be Guarded against in the Progress of the United States," *American Whig Review* 5 (June 1847): 625.

71. Webster, "Lecture before the Society for the Diffusion of Useful Knowledge," *Writings and Speeches,* 13: 74; Everett, "Dinner to Thomas Baring, Esq.," *Orations and Speeches,* 3: 137.

72. "Trades' Unions," *New York Review* 2 (Jan. 1838): 28; Webster, "Lecture before the Society for the Diffusion of Useful Knowledge," *Writings and Speeches,* 13: 75; "The Creation of Values," *American Whig Review* 4: 643. Note the tendency, even in a Whig extolling the

advantages of American labor, to imply that the accumulations of others are drawn from the earnings of the workingman.

73. "The Science of Government," *American Monthly Magazine,* n.s. 6 (Sep. 1838): 202; Webster, "Lecture before the Society for the Diffusion of Useful Knowledge," *Writings and Speeches,* 13: 66; "Money and Banks," *New York Review* 5 (Oct. 1839): 334; Albany *Jeffersonian,* May 12, 1838.

74. Webster, "Reception at Buffalo," June 1833, *Writings and Speeches,* 2: 134.

75. Michael A. Lebowitz, "The Jacksonians: Paradox Lost?," in Barton J. Bernstein, ed., *Towards a New Past: Dissenting Essays in American History* (New York: Pantheon, 1968), 65–89.

Index

259